The Theory of Revolution in the Young Marx

Historical Materialism Book Series

Haymarket Books is proud to be working with Brill Academic Publishers (http://www.brill.nl/) and the journal Historical Materialism on the new Historical Materialism Book Series. We will be publishing paperback editions of a number of the titles initiated in hardcover by Brill.

Forthcoming titles in the series from Haymarket Books include:

Between Equal Rights: A Marxist Theory of International Law
China Miéville

The German Revolution, 1917–1923
Pierre Broué, Translated by John Archer. Edited by Ian Birchall and Brian Pearce. With an Introduction by Eric D. Weitz.

About the series

More than ten years after the collapse of the Berlin Wall and the disappearance of Marxism as a (supposed) state ideology, a need for a serious and long-term Marxist book publishing program has risen. Subjected to the whims of fashion, most contemporary publishers have abandoned any of the systematic production of Marxist theoretical work that they may have indulged in during the 1970s and early 1980s. The Historical Materialism book series addresses this great gap with original monographs, translated texts and reprints of "classics." At least three titles will be published every year. So far, eight titles have appeared in the series (for more details, see http://www.brill.nl/download/HiMaBookseries.pdf).

Editorial board: Paul Blackledge, Leeds; Sebastian Budgen, Paris; Jim Kincaid, Leeds; Stathis Kouvelakis, Paris; Marcel van der Linden, Amsterdam; China Miéville, London; Paul Reynolds, Lancashire; Peter Thomas, Amsterdam.

THE THEORY OF REVOLUTION IN THE YOUNG MARX

Michael Löwy

Haymarket Books
Chicago

© 2003, 2005 Michael Löwy
First published in 2003 by Brill Academic Publishers, Netherlands

Published in paperback in 2005 by Haymarket Books
P.O. Box 180165
Chicago, IL 60618
773-583-7884
www.haymarketbooks.org

ISBN: 978-1-93185-919-6

Cover design by Ragina Johnson.
Printed in the United States.

Entered into digital printing January 2019.

Library of Congress Cataloging-in-Publication data

Löwy, Michael, 1938-
  [Théorie de la révolution chez le jeune Marx. English]
  The theory of revolution in the young Marx / Michael Löwy.
     p. cm.
  Translation of: La Théorie de la révolution chez le jeune Marx.
  "First published in 2003 by Brill Academic Publishers, Netherlands"--Verso t.p.
  Includes bibliographical references and index.
  ISBN 1-931859-19-1 (pbk. : alk. paper)
  1. Marx, Karl, 1818-1883. 2. Revolutions. I. Title.
  HX39.5.L6513 2005
  335.4'11--dc22
                                        2004021411

Contents

vii	Preface
1	Introduction
23	CHAPTER ONE The Transition to Communism (1842–1844)
63	CHAPTER TWO The Theory of Communist Revolution (1844–1846)
119	CHAPTER THREE The Theory of the Party (1846–1848)
149	CHAPTER FOUR Party, Masses, and Revolution, from Marx's Time to Ours
201	Index

Preface

This book was first published in France in 1970, and later translated into Italian, Japanese, and Spanish. Its ideas were taken up by other Marxist committed scholars, also in the English speaking world, such as Hal Draper, in his well known *Karl Marx's Theory of Revolution* (Monthly Review Press, 1977), or Norman Geras, in his outstanding collection of essays *Literature of Revolution* (Verso, 1986).

It is basically an attempt at a Marxist interpretation of Marx, that is, a study of his philosophical and political evolution in the historical context of social struggles in Europe during the decisive years of 1840–48, and in particular of his relationship with the experiences of the emerging working class and the early socialist labor movement. It was through an active exchange with this social environment (as well as with the left-Hegelian currents) that the young Marx formulated the seminal kernel of a new worldview, the *philosophy of praxis*, which provides the theoretical foundation for his conception of revolution as proletarian self-emancipation.

During the twenty-five years since my book appeared, many things have changed in the world: is Marx's theory still relevant? Does it still offer a significant answer to the social contradictions at this strange end of century? With the demise of the so-called "really existing socialism" in Eastern Europe, there has been no lack of scholars, philosophers, economists, politicians, journalists, bankers, managers, theologians, members of parliament, ministers, social scientists, and experts of all kinds to proclaim, *urbi et orbi*, in the name of God, or of the Market – or both – that "Marx is dead." Neither has there been a shortage of former leftists, ex-communists, ex-socialists, ex-radicals, ex-revolutionaries, ex-anything-and-everything to join the chorus.

This is not a new idea. Already in 1907, the eminent liberal philosopher Benedetto Croce claimed that "Marxism is definitively dead for humanity." It was not a very accurate prophesy, as the Russian followers of liberalism would find out only ten years later.

In fact, now that Marxism has ceased to be used as an official state-ideology by parasitical bureaucratic regimes, there is an historical opportunity for re-discovering the original Marxian message, and developing it in a creative way.

As far as I am concerned, I still believe, as much as in 1970, that the young

Marx's theory of revolution – the *philosophy of praxis*, and, dialectically linked to it, the idea of *workers' self-emancipation* – remains the best compass to find one's way in the present confused historical panorama. Not only has it not been made obsolete by the crumbling of the Berlin Wall, but, on the contrary, it provides us with a decisive key to understand why the attempt to "build socialism" without the people (or against the people), to "emancipate" labor from above, by an authoritarian bureaucratic power, was inevitably doomed to failure. For Marx, revolutionary democracy – the political equivalent of self-emancipation – was not an optional dimension but rather the intrinsic nature of socialism itself, as the free association of individuals who take into their hands the production of their common life. The historical experience of the Stalinist USSR (and of the other Eastern European countries), far from "falsifying" the Marxian theory of revolution, is its most astonishing confirmation.

This does *not* mean that one can find in Marx the answers to all our problems, or that there is nothing to be reconsidered or criticized in the complex body of his economical or political views. Many decisive issues, such as the destruction of the environment by the "growth of productive forces," non-class forms of oppression (for example, of women and ethnic minorities), the importance of universal ethical rules and human rights, the struggle of the non-European nations and cultures against Western domination, are either absent or inadequately treated in his writings.

This is why Marx's legacy has to be completed with the contributions of modern Marxists, from Rosa Luxemburg and Trotsky to Walter Benjamin and Herbert Marcuse, from Lenin and Gramsci to José Carlos Mariategui and Ernst Bloch. It should also to be enriched with the experience of twentieth-century revolutions – both in their positive and their negative lessons – from October 1917 to the great social upheavals in Asia or Latin America: China, Indochina, Cuba, Nicaragua. And last but not least, it must be reviewed and corrected with the contributions of other socialist traditions (utopian, anarchist, communitarian) as well as of the new social movements that have developed during the last decades, such as feminism and ecology. It is precisely because it is not a dogmatic and closed system, but an open *and* critical tradition of revolutionary theory and praxis, that Marxism is able to grow and develop itself, constantly confronting new issues and new challenges, and learning from other experiences and other emancipatory movements.

* * *

One of the things that I have discovered during the twenty-five years that separate me from the first edition of this book is the importance of the romantic critique of bourgeois civilization, both as a neglected dimension of Marx's own thought, and as a powerful source for the renewal of socialist imagination.

By Romanticism I do not mean just a literary current of the nineteenth century, but a vast cultural movement of protest against modern industrial/capitalist society in the name of pre-modern (or pre-capitalist) values. It is a movement that began at the end of the eighteenth century but lives on in the present, in open rebellion against the disenchantment of the world, the quantification of all values, the mechanization of life and the destruction of community.

There exists a specific tradition of romantic socialism in England, which owes very much to Marx, but also takes its inspiration from Blake, Carlyle, and Ruskin. It has its origin in the writings of William Morris and achieved a significant influence after World War II, thanks to the works of E. P. Thompson and Raymond Williams. Rejecting utilitarianism, productivism, and bourgeois "modernization," and rescuing the rebellious potential of romantic poets and radical artisans, all three helped to "re-enchant" socialist culture. At the same time, by their active commitment to the self-emancipation of the working class, they were true inheritors of that radical wing of the Chartist movement that so strongly inspired the young Marx's theory of revolution.

Michael Löwy

Introduction

I. Notes on Method

The following observations do not aspire to solve the problems of Marxist epistemology, or of historical materialism in general, but are intended merely to make clear certain methodological presuppositions behind this work.

a) Premises of a Marxist study of Marxism

The general purpose of the book is to study in an historical materialist way the work of the young Marx. In other words, it aims to make a contribution – a very partial and limited one, of course – to a Marxist analysis of the origins of Marxism itself.

What are the methodological implications of such a program? Is this approach not inherently contradictory? Putting it another way, does not the application of Marxism to itself inevitably mean transcending it?

That seems, at any rate, to be the view taken by Karl Mannheim, who, in his *Ideology and Utopia*, criticizes socialist thought for never having applied to itself the procedures of "ideological unmasking" that it applies to its adversaries, and for never having raised the question of the social determination of its own position. Mannheim suggests that such a "self-unmasking" would show that Marxism constitutes, as the ideology of the proletariat, a standpoint which is just as partial and fragmentary as the ideologies of the other classes – and would therefore lead to the transcending of Marxism.[1]

---

[1] K. Mannheim, *Ideology and Utopia* (London: 1936), pp. 225, 232. For Mannheim, the transcending of Marxism would be achieved by a "dynamic synthesis" of the opposed standpoints, effected by "socially-unattached intellectuals" (*freischwebende*

The truth is, however, that by showing the socially conditioned nature of Marxism one does not in least, "settle its hash." On the contrary, it is upon its nature as the theory of the proletariat that Marxism bases its validity. Indeed, Marx did not merely admit, he even insisted on the connections between his political doctrine and the historical interests of a certain class of society. If, despite this "situational determinism" (to use Mannheim's terminology), Marxism lays claim to universal validity, this is because the proletariat is the only class whose historical interests require the unmasking of society's essential structure. As for the bourgeoisie, this unmasking, which exposes the springs of capitalist exploitation and challenges the "natural" character of the established order, goes directly against its interests as the ruling class. As for other social strata, such as the petty bourgeoisie or the small peasants, full awareness of the historical process would show them that their particular endeavors have no future.[2]

The above considerations do not seek to "prove" the validity of Marxism, or its non-transcendability, but merely to show that it is not enough to "unmask" the class nature of Marxism, its social and historical foundations, in order either automatically to transcend it (as Mannheim seems to suppose) or to topple over into the dark night of relativism, wherein all cats are gray.

It appears to me that a Marxist study of the political and philosophical evolution of the young Marx implies two essential approaches:

> (a) This evolution must be placed within the historical and social totality to which it belongs, within the social frameworks that conditioned it, namely, 19th-century capitalist society, the working-class movement before 1848, the Neo-Hegelian intelligentsia, etc. This does not mean that the thinking of the young Marx was a mere "reflection" of these economic, social, and political conditions, but that it cannot be "explained," as regards its origins, and "understood," as regards its content, without this socio-historical analysis.[3]

Intelligenz). But are not those intellectuals who consider themselves "unattached" precisely the ones who are attached to the petty bourgeoisie? And can their "synthesis" be anything more than an eclectic midway-position between the major conceptions of the world that are in conflict, something structurally identical with the "intermediate" position of their social group? These questions are left unanswered by Mannheim, and his Marxist critics throw back at him the reproaches he levels at socialism. Cf. G. Lukács, *The Destruction of Reason* (London: 1980), p. 637; cf. also L. Goldmann, *The Human Sciences and Philosophy*, (London: 1969) pp. 51–52.

[2] Lukács, *History and Class Consciousness* (London: 1971), pp. 61, 70. However, while affirming the "untranscendable" character of Marxism in our epoch, Lukács raises the question of its future transcendence in a classless society. Cf. *op. cit.*, p. 228. We find this theme also in Gramsci, for whom Marxism, being consciousness of the contradictions of the "realm of necessity" cannot but be transcended in the "realm of freedom." Cf. *Il Materialismo storico e la filosofia de Benedetto Croce* (Turin: 1948), p. 94.

[3] Nor does this mean that Marx's thought "belongs to the 19th century." Marx dis-

(b) In analyzing the content of Marx's work, one must not artificially separate "judgments of fact" from "value-judgments," "science" from "ethics." The Marxist category of praxis is, precisely, the dialectical transcending of these contradictions. Similarly, one must not separate Marx's theoretical work from his practical activity, the "scientist" from the "politician": for him, science had to be revolutionary and the revolution to be "scientific"...

b) *The social settings of Marxism: the proletariat*

It is indispensable to study the socio-historical settings of a work not only in order to explain this work, but also in order to understand it – these two proceedings being only two inseparable factors in any human science. In other words, seeking the economic, social, etc., foundations is not a sort of complementary activity, external to the task of the historian of ideas, but an indispensable condition for understanding the very content, the internal structure, and precise significance of what is being studied.[4] In the course of the present work, I have found that knowledge, in general outline at least, of the historical and social settings, was absolutely indispensable for:

1) Understanding the evolution of Marx's thought, its transformations, crises, qualitative leaps, "breaks," "political conversions," reorientations,[5] and so on.
2) Separating the essential from the secondary or accidental and revealing important elements which otherwise might have remained unobserved.
3) Disclosing the true meaning – concrete and historical – of vague categories, ambiguous terms, "enigmatic" formulas,[6] etc.
4) Situating each element in the whole and establishing the internal connections of this whole.

Applying this method to the history of Marxist ideas does not, of course, mean trying to grasp the *entire* reality (which is obviously not possible) but grasping this reality through the *methodological category* of totality, for which infrastructure and superstructure, thought and social settings, theory and practice, "consciousness" and "being" are not separated into watertight compartments congealed in abstract oppositions, but (while recognizing their relative autonomy) are dialectically linked together and integrated in the historical process.

---

covered, by way of the social reality of his century, the essential characteristics of capitalism, the proletariat, and the socialist revolution *as such*.

[4] Goldmann, *Recherches dialectiques*, 3rd edition (Paris: 1959), p. 42.
[5] The transition to communism in 1843–1844; the new theory of revolution adopted in 1845–1846, etc.
[6] For example, the concept of "party" in 1846–1848 (see Chapter III).

What, then, are the specific settings of the Marxist theory of revolution – which are not necessarily the same (especially at the superstructural level) as for other theoretical entities in Marx's work? In my view, we have to use the concept of "settings" in its broadest sense, which implies:

(a) the economic and social structure; the level of the productive forces; the general situation of the social classes; the situations of certain occupational categories (craftsmen, etc.) and social groups (intellectuals, etc.);
(b) the political superstructure: situation of the workers' movement and of the democratic, liberal, and socialist organizations, groups, parties, and newspapers;
(c) the ideological superstructure: collective attitudes and values; conceptions of the world; economic, social, and philosophical doctrines; conservative, liberal, socialist, and communist political theories;
(d) the precise historical "conjuncture"; economic, social, political, and military events (crises, revolutions, wars, etc.).[7] It is necessary to note, however, that infrastructure and superstructure, "conjuncture" and "structure" must not be treated as reified categories; in concrete reality, ideas can become material forces and structures can be reduced to a succession of conjunctures. If we proceed differently, we risk falling into the world of metaphysical contrasts between "matter" and "mind," "static" and "dynamic," etc.

The relations between settings, thus defined, and ideas can, in my view, be grasped only through the concept of *conditioning*, used not as a vague formula but in its strict and rigorous sense. Settings constitute the *conditions*, sometimes necessary but never sufficient (if taken in isolation), for the emergence of a doctrine. Each setting defines a certain ideological sphere, establishes certain limits for the development of ideas, creates or eliminates certain possibilities; and, of course, the more general limits are those imposed by the fundamental setting, namely, the economico-social infrastructure. Marx's doctrine could not have appeared during the peasant wars of the 16th century, nor could Münzer's doctrine have developed after the 1848 revolution. With that said, the social setting constituted by "the 19th century European proletariat" offered many "possibilities" besides Marxism: Weitling, Blanqui, utopian socialism, etc. To explain how the possibility called "Marx" was

---

[7] The social structure conditions the significant structure of a work; but, in order to grasp the evolution of the work, its development, changes, and reorientations, we need to take into account the historical *events* in the overall society, the group to which the thinker belongs, or the class with which he identifies himself. The historico-social conjuncture, and not merely the abstract structure, is the setting of thought. In order to understand Marx's political trajectory, it is not enough to place it in relation to "the proletariat" as a position in the production process – we have to relate it to the concrete development of the labor movement: strikes, uprisings, the evolution of trade unions, parties, and so on.

realized, we have to take into account a large number of other variables (the situation of the neo-Hegelian intelligentsia, the evolution of British political economy, the political level of the organizations of German emigrant craftsmen, etc.). It is this accumulation of conditions, structured as a group of concentric circles ("over-determination") that enables a possibility to become a necessity. In the last analysis, we can state that a fundamental setting, the proletariat, necessarily demands the formation of scientific socialism; but to explain why that doctrine made its appearance where and when it did, we need to bring in the other historical conditions as well.

However, analysis in terms of conditioning is still too schematic unless we bring in another factor, the *partial autonomy* of the sphere of ideas.[8] While it is true that the fundamental categories of a work can be socially conditioned, it is nevertheless necessary to observe that the development of thought is subject to a number of internal requirements of systematization, coherence, rationality, etc. Very often it is quite fruitless to look for the "economic bases" of the entire content of a work: the origin of this content has to be sought also in the specific rules of continuity and development of the history of ideas, in the demands imposed by the inner logic of the work, or even in the specific features of the given thinker as an individual. This concept of partial autonomy enables us to transcend the eternal polemic between the idealist history of thought, in which systems of ideas are completely detached from historical "contingencies" and float freely in the clear sky of the absolute, and the mechanical "economism" which reduces the entire world of thought to a direct reflection of the economic and social base.[9]

This concept of partial autonomy also enables us to deepen our analysis of the *dialectical* character of the relation between settings and ideas. This relationship is dialectical because ideologies react upon social conditions, creating a reciprocal relation in which, as Engels remarked, the notions of "cause" and "effect" are no longer meaningful. (For example, the relation between Marx's theory and the League of Communists during 1846–1847.) But it also appears dialectical because, in a certain way, the doctrinal system "selects" and interprets the settings, events, and ideas which are to condition its development. The importance of an event for the evolution of a theory does not depend only on its objective importance, but also on its significance *in relation to* the theory (to its themes, its significant structure). For example, the revolt of the Silesian weavers in 1844 was completely ignored by most of the German neo-Hegelians. It was taken notice of by a few doctrinaires without its causing any change in their positions (A. Ruge, Weitling, etc.). But it had a decisive influence on Marx's revolutionary conceptions. We thus

---

[8] Cf. Goldmann, *The Human Sciences*, pp. 95–96.
[9] The extent of this autonomy varies, of course, from the total (or almost total) independence of the natural sciences to the closer dependence of political doctrines.

perceive that, very often, it is not an historical event or a philosophical or political theory "in itself" that influences the development of a doctrine, but the event and the theory as these are grasped and interpreted by that doctrine.

The role of the economic basis (which is *decisive*) is played, as a rule, through a great number of mediations: social classes, organizations, parties and movements, conceptions of the world, economic, philosophical, and juridical doctrines, etc. It is the economic basis that decides, *in the last analysis*, which will be the mediation, which the level, that plays the principal role at a particular moment.[10] At different stages in Marx's intellectual development, the dominant role could be played by factors at the political or the ideological level, this role being assigned to them, in the last analysis, by the infrastructure. Thus, for example, the economic underdevelopment of Germany conditioned its philosophical "overdevelopment," and this accounts for the crucial role of neo-Hegelianism in Marx's political evolution between 1841 and 1844, the relative absence of economic considerations in his thinking before his arrival in France, and so on.

I have several times suggested that the proletariat was (from 1844) the chief social setting of Marx's political thought. It is obvious that Marx himself was not a worker (nor, moreover, were Lenin, Rosa Luxemburg, Gramsci, Lukacs, etc.), and this brings us to the general problem of imputation: by what criterion are we to attribute a set of ideas to a certain class or social grouping?

The "vulgar" theory of imputation answers this question very simply: the doctrine is that of the group to which its author belongs. While acknowledging that the class to which a thinker belongs often conditions, wholly or partly, his ideas, we must reject this sort of explanation, since it is clearly contradicted by the most elementary facts in the history of ideas. Concretely, we constantly see appearing ideologists of the bourgeoisie who are not bourgeois and theoreticians of the proletariat who are not proletarians. The truth is that most of the theoreticians of all the classes in industrial society are recruited from a specific group, the petty-bourgeois intellectuals. The reason for this is very simple: in the setting of capitalist division of labor, the professional activity assigned to this social group is "spiritual production." This does not mean that the intellectuals are "unattached," as Mannheim suggests. On the contrary, they are attached to the social classes in conflict. Those who imagine that they float "above" the class struggles are precisely the ones who become the ideologists of the class which is closest to their social condition, namely, the petty bourgeoisie. The others, affected by the greater economic, social, and political importance of the two principal classes of society and

---

[10] Cf. Louis Althusser, *Reading "Capital"* (London: 1970) and *For Marx* (London: 1969).

faced with the absence of any historical prospect for their own social status become theoreticians either of the bourgeoisie or of the proletariat.

To conclude: while not ignoring the social origin of a thinker, we have to ask ourselves, above all, not to what class he *belongs* (what his social condition is as a person) but what class he *represents* by his ideas. This is what Marx suggests in *The Eighteenth Brumaire*:

> Just as little must one imagine that the democratic representatives are indeed all shopkeepers or enthusiastic supporters of shopkeepers. In their education and individual position they may be as far apart from them as heaven from earth. What makes them representatives of the petty-bourgeoisie is the fact that in their minds they do not get beyond the limits which the latter do not get beyond in life, that they are consequently driven, theoretically, to the same problems and solutions to which material interest and social position drive the latter in practice. This is, in general, the relationship between the *political* and *literary* representatives of a class and the class they represent.[11]

These considerations apply, to a certain extent, to Marxism as well (Marx himself seems to suggest as much in the last sentence), and they lead us, in the last analysis, to the problem of imputed consciousness.

The concept of "representation" involves two essential questions which I shall examine successively:

(1) How does a thinker who belongs to a certain class become the political and theoretical representative of another class?
(2) How are we to identify, by its content, the class that a body of thought represents?

1. The most diverse reasons, objective and subjective, which need to be examined concretely in each specific case, may impel an intellectual to break with his class, or with the class he identifies himself with at first. This break creates a state of "intellectual availability" which can lead, in certain circumstances, to "intellectual adhesion" to another class. Through this "adhesion" an active relation is established between the thinker and the class. The intellectual identifies himself with the interests, aims, and aspirations of this class. He participates, within himself, in its problems, looks upon society and history from its standpoint and, if he is a "democratic philosopher" (cf. Gramsci) – that is to say, if he wants to change the class's cultural ambience, to win it for his ideas – he has to take account of the opinions and attitudes of his "public," subject his work to continual self-criticism, and direct it in accordance with the responses of his "audience."[12] It is by this active,

---

[11] *CW*, XI, 130–131.
[12] Cf. Gramsci, *Il Materialismo storico*, pp. 24–27; A. Child, "The problem of imputation

reciprocal, dialectical relation that the class becomes increasingly a setting for the intellectual's work, and that he becomes its *theoretical representative*. This schema seems to me valid not only for understanding the relations between Marxist thinkers and the proletariat, but also for understanding the links between ideologists of noble origin and the bourgeoisie (Saint-Simon) or *vice versa* (Burke).

The structuring of this dialectical process has two decisive consequences. On the one hand, the intellectual constructs his theory by using the "ideological fragments" that are spontaneously produced by the social class, while the latter, in its turn, despite all the differences of cultural level and degree of knowledge, accepts this doctrine, in broad outline, as its own. It must be emphasized, however, that the intellectual introduces into his political theory elements which are quite remote from the habitual concerns of the class, and the absorption of his doctrine by this class is neither immediate, nor unanimous, nor complete.

2. The social relation between intellectual and class becomes, at the level of content, the relation between imputed consciousness and psychological consciousness. Lukács defined "possible" or imputed consciousness (*Zugerechnetes Bewusstsein*) as:

> the thoughts and feelings which men *would have* in a particular situation if they were able to assess both it and the interests arising from it in their impact on immediate action and on the whole structure of society. That is to say, it would be possible to infer the thoughts and feelings appropriate to their objective situation.

Or, in other words,

> the appropriate and rational reactions "*imputed*" to a particular typical position in the process of production.[13]

In my view, this category of Lukács's, inspired at once by some remarks in *The Holy Family*, by procedures in Marxist economics, and, partly, by Max Weber's "ideal typology," should not be regarded as a purely operational concept (like Weber's ideal type), nor as a transcendental absolute truth, but as an *objective possibility* which at certain historical moments becomes real, in the form of a theory or of an organized theoretico-practical movement which is very close, relatively to others, to complete rationality and adequateness. It is in this sense and in this sense only that we can consider Marx's work to be the *Zugerechnetes Bewusstsein* of the proletariat, and the Marxist theory of revolution as one of the constituent features of this imputed consciousness.

---

resolved," *Ethics*, Vol. 54, 1944, p. 107; C. W. Mills, "Language, Logic and Culture," *American Sociological Review*, IV, No. 5, 1939, p. 675.

[13] Lukács, *History and Class Consciousness*, p. 51.

The "consciousness of the proletariat" thus defined is a coherent unity, in which recognitions of facts and value judgments, historical analyses, and projects for transformation are *strictly inseparable*.

This "possible class consciousness" obviously should not be confused with the *psychological consciousness* of the class, meaning "the empirically given" and "psychologically describable and explicable ideas which men form about their situation in life,"[14] an irregular collection of more or less confused conceptions (frequently mixed up with ideological elements from other classes), vague aspirations and desires, and projects for social transformation. However, one needs, once again, to be careful not to separate abstractly these two poles of a dialectical relation: "psychological consciousness" can come substantially close (especially in periods of crisis) to Zugerechnetes Bewusstsein; but, also, the latter is formed *on the basis of* the former.

In the light of these categories, the historical origin of the imputed consciousness of the proletariat can be presented, schematically, in the form of three moments:

(a) emergence of the psychological consciousness in the form of a certain community of feelings, thoughts, and actions (empirically observable) which is characteristic of the proletariat in formation and which opposes it to the other classes;

(b) an intellectual from the middle classes works out, on the basis of these aspirations and projects, which are more or less shapeless, *and on the basis of a scientific study of the socio-economic structures and of the historical processes under way*, a Weltanschauung which is rigorous and coherent and issues in a revolutionary praxis;

(c) the imputed consciousness thus created exerts an enormous influence on the proletariat's psychological consciousness, which draws near to or draws away from this model in the course of a contradictory and eventful historical evolution.

Starting from these considerations, we can establish simultaneously *the coherence and the gap between the two levels*, "imputed" and "psychological," of consciousness: coherence, without which one cannot grasp either the birth of Marxism or its diffusion among the proletariat; the inevitable gap in the working-out of the theoretical expression of the "possible consciousness," on the basis of a scientific analysis of historical and social reality, using all the existing theoretical material, including that created by the other classes (a gap which is due, in the last analysis, to the specific nature of the theoretical level, its internal logic and the rules of its immanent development).

A concrete study of the historical origin of Marxism reveals the existence of a series of mediations between the two extreme levels:

---

[14] *Ibid.*

1. The mass: "psychological consciousness," made up of aspirations and desires, a generalized state of revolt and dissatisfaction, which finds expression in rudimentary conceptual form (songs, poems, popular pamphlets) or in episodical revolutionary outbursts.
2. The "organic" intellectuals who emerge from the ranks of the mass and work out a first systematization, as yet confused and limited, of these popular aspirations (Weitling).
3. The leaders and ideologists of the conspiratorial or utopian sects, limited owing to their marginal relation to the mass labor movement (Cabet, Dézamy, etc.).
4. The "traditional" intellectuals, sprung from the middle strata and whose "socialist" ideology is limited by their class origins (Moses Hess, the German "True Socialists," etc.).
5. The "traditional" intellectual who transcends these limitations and succeeds in laying the foundations of a new conception of the world, rigorous, coherent, and rationally adequate to the proletariat's social situation (Marx).

The final stage is the dialectical synthesis, the *Aufhebung*, of the partial moments, the conclusion of a process of totalization, negation, and transcendence of the limitations, incoherences, and "inadequacies" of the previous levels.

c) *The revolutionary science of the young Marx*

Some modern sociologists (or "Marxologists"), taking up a theme dear to Austro-Marxism, try to establish a methodological distinction in Marx's work between his "objective sociology" and his "ethical postulates," his "positive science," and his "communist eschatology." However, at every step of this highly problematical approach, these writers stumble over insoluble difficulties when they seek to insert a peg between the socialism and the science in Marx's work. This trouble shows through in their terminology: M. Gurvitch speaks of "insufficient distinction," "ambiguity," "obvious mixture," or even of "struggle waged within his thought,"[15] while M. Rubel wavers between "complementarity," "implicit confusion," "voluntary confusion," and "harmonious mixture"[16] of these elements.

As I see it, what we find is not an "insufficient distinction," but, precisely, the touchstone of Marxist dialectics: the category of praxis as an effort to transcend the abstract opposition between facts and values, thought and action, theory and practice. Marx's work is not based on a "duality" of which the author, through lack of rigor or unconscious confusion, was unaware. It tends, on the contrary, towards a rigorous monism, in which facts and val-

---

[15] G. Gurvitch, *La Sociologie de Karl Marx* (Paris: 1960), pp. 39, 56, 28.
[16] M. Rubel, *Essai de Biographie Intellectuelle de Karl Marx* (Paris: 1957), pp. 216, 218, 220.

ues are not "mixed" but are organically linked within a single movement of thought, of "critical science" in which explanation and criticism of reality are dialectically integrated.[17] Of course, the political theory and, in particular, the theory of revolution which we are studying here is a specially favorable sphere for grasping this internal coherence, but I think that it is an essential dimension of Marxism, implicitly present even when appearances seem to contradict it, even when the thought is operating with a rigor comparable to that of the natural sciences.

But how are we to go over from interpretation of reality to criticism and transformation of it? Poincaré emphasized rightly that from premises in the indicative one cannot draw any conclusion in the imperative: there cannot be any necessary *logical* link there between "facts" and "values."

Indeed, the link between judgments of "fact" and value-choices in the human sciences is not a relation of formal logic. It is a *social* link which follows from the necessarily "committed" character of these sciences, regardless of the "goodwill" and desire for objectivity on the part of the thinkers.[18] It follows also from their unavoidable inclusion in an overall perspective, their connection, whether conscious or not, direct or indirect, total or partial, with the "visions of the world" held by the various classes or social strata in conflict.

It is within this "class perspective" that the connection is effected between judgments of "fact" and judgments of "value," between the indicative and the imperative. Thus, with Marx, the continuity between the "description" of capitalism and its "condemnation," the coherence between analysis and criticism of reality, can be perceived only if one takes up *the standpoint of the proletariat*. From an abstract, formal standpoint, even if I prove that the proletariat is exploited and oppressed under capitalism, nothing allows me

---

[17] Goldmann, *Recherches Dialectiques*, p. 300: "He [Marx] does not 'mix' a value-judgement with an objective analysis but, as everywhere else in his work makes a dialectical analysis in which understanding, explanation and valorization are strictly inseparable." J. Hyppolite, *Etudes sur Marx et Hegel* (Paris: 1955), p. 154: "His [Marx's] science is not only a science of social reality: it contributes, by becoming conscious of it, to the creation of this very reality, or at least to its profound modification ... We see how much any purely *objectivistic* interpretation of Marxism needs to be avoided. To be sure, reality supplies the foundations for the emancipating class, but this class has to become conscious of itself and of its universal role in the actual course of its struggle. Without this *creative* awareness, the historical liberation of humanity would not be possible." C. Lefort, "Reflexions Sociologiques sur Machiavel et Marx: la politique et le réel," *Cahiers internationaux de sociologie* Vol. XXVIII (Paris: 1960), p. 123: "For reality to be praxis means, at this level, that the present is apprehended as being what has come about through men's actions and calls for a task to be carried out: that knowledge of our world cannot be separated from the project of transforming it."

[18] Cf. the analysis of Durkheim's "Objectivism" by Goldmann, in *The Human Sciences*, pp. 37–41.

to say that capitalism is "good" or "bad," and that it should either be preserved or overthrown. Socially, concretely, however, most proletarians (or most of those who adopt their standpoint), when they come to the conclusion that capitalism exploits and oppresses them, are impelled to condemn it and take action against it.

In short, Marx's science is critical and revolutionary because it places itself in the class perspective of the proletariat and is the coherent form of the revolutionary consciousness of the proletarian class.

After trying to separate "science" and "ethics" in Marx's work, these same "Marxologists" separate the "sociologist" from the "politician," that is to say, Marx's writings from his activity, his theory from his practice. Maximilien Rubel leaves aside Marx's "strictly political" career in his "intellectual biography," having "deliberately avoided everything which did not directly concern the subject of this work,"[19] while Georges Gurvitch stresses the difference and even the contradiction between Marx, "the man of action," and Marx, "the man of science."[20]

In the first place, Marx's militant activity is not a biographical detail but the necessary complement of his writing, since both the one and the other had the same purpose, namely, not just to interpret the world but to *change* it, and to interpret it *in order to* change it.

Furthermore, separation of Marx's "theory" from his "practice" is arbitrary because:

(a) *all* of his theoretical work – and not merely the political doctrine – contains practical implications: by explaining reality, it establishes the conditions that make possible changing this reality, and so becomes an indispensable instrument of revolutionary action;
(b) his practical political activity, expressed in his letters, circulars, speeches, and, above all, political *decisions*, is filled with theoretical significance.

The theory of the communist revolution is obviously the moment in which the critico-practical nature of Marx's work appears most clearly. Within this particular structure, every theoretical element can at the same time have a practical dimension, every paragraph can become an instrument for acquiring consciousness and organizing revolutionary action. Moreover, the action prescribed by this theory – and practiced by Marx as a communist leader – is not voluntarist, like that of the Utopian Socialists or the Blanquists, it is a *realistic* policy, in the broad sense of the term, that is, it is based on the structure, the contradictions, and the movement of reality itself, and, because it is realistic, it presupposes a rigorous *science*, a science which establishes the

---

[19] Rubel, *Biographie intellectuelle*, p. 14.
[20] Gurvitch, *La Sociologie De K. Marx*, pp. 1, 50, 56.

conditions for revolutionary action at each moment of history. The synthesis between thought and "subversive praxis," which is present as a tendency in all of Marx's work, attains concrete form in the theory and practice of "the communism of the masses": revolution becomes "scientific" and science "revolutionary."[21]

II. The Communist Revolution and the Self-Emancipation of the Proletariat

a) *The myth of the savior from on high*

"Myth: a fabulous story . . . in which impersonal agents, usually forces of nature, are represented in the form of personified beings whose actions and adventures bear symbolic meanings." This rather broad definition from the *Vocabulaire technique et critique de la philosophie*,[22] if completed with the observation that the bourgeois social myth transforms history into nature,[23] enables us to grasp clearly the mythological character of the idea of the savior from on high, in its bourgeois form. In this conception, the "natural" laws of society – meaning by "natural" eternal, unchangeable, independent of human will and action – and the movement of history (also conceived in "naturalistic" terms) are represented in the form of a "transcendental" symbolic personage: the socio-historical world becomes nature, and the "forces of nature" are incarnated in a Hero.

This myth has a long history and goes back to times well before the appearance of the modern bourgeoisie. But, just as the "return" of Greco-Roman culture in the Renaissance must be explained by the conditions prevailing in the 14th, 15th, and 16th centuries, and the "reappearance" of medieval corporatism in Fascist ideology by the situation in the 20th century, so the development of the obsession with a transcendental Liberator in the political theory of the revolutionary bourgeoisie has to be studied in relation with the structure of the bourgeois world. At bottom, behind the apparent "resurrection" of an old theme, what we see here is, rather, a new form, with specific features, because it is bound up with a new historical totality.

---

[21] My book is based on a doctoral thesis presented at the Sorbonne in 1964, and so before the appearance of Althusser's principal writings, apart from his excellent article on the young Marx (1960). I share his general view of Marx's youthful writings as a theoretical "long march." I share also with Althusser the hypothesis of an "epistemological break" (a *political* break, too, in my opinion) which is observable in the *Theses on Feuerbach* and *The German Ideology*. Having said that, it will be quite plain that my "reading" of Marx is not at all the same as that of the author of *Reading "Capital."*
[22] Lalande, *Vocabulaire technique et critique de la philosophie* (Paris: 1951), p. 647.
[23] Cf. R. Barthes, *Mythologies* (London: 1972), p. 141.

The social basis of the bourgeois myth of the savior from on high is to be found in the constituent elements of "civil society" – private property and free competition, which turn this society into a grouping of "egoistic" atoms struggling against each other in a veritable *bellum omnium contra omnes* in which the "social," the "general interest," the "collective" has necessarily to be projected, hypostasized, eventually *alienated* as a being or an institution "outside" and "above" civil society.[24] From another angle, economic alienation, the separation of the producer from the production process as a whole, so that this looks to the isolated individual like a set of "natural" economic laws alien to his will, leads the bourgeois thinker into mechanistic materialism. In this way he arrives at the theory that "men are products of circumstances and upbringing," a theory which, as Marx noted in the third thesis on Feuerbach, "is bound to divide society into two parts, one of which is superior to society."[25] In fact, shut up in the vicious circle of "men/circumstances," the ideology of the revolutionary bourgeoisie cannot escape from mechanical materialism otherwise than by appealing to a "higher" being who is capable of breaking, from without, the irresistible social mechanism.

Upon the infrastructure of private property and the laws of the capitalist market there is thus built up the myth of the savior from on high, an incarnation of public virtue contrasted with the competition and particularism of individuals; a demiurge of history to break the chain of fatalism; a superhuman hero who liberates mankind and "constitutes" the new state. This myth appears, implicitly or explicitly, in most of the political doctrines of the bourgeoisie in its ascent. For Machiavelli, he is "the Prince," for Hobbes, "the Absolute Sovereign," for Voltaire, "the Enlightened Despot," for Rousseau, "the Lawgiver," for Carlyle, "the Hero." The 17th-century English Puritans thought they had found him in the person of "the Lord Protector" (Cromwell), the Jacobins in "the Incorruptible," the Bonapartists in the Emperor. "The world-soul on horseback," wrote Hegel about Napoleon, so summing up in a brilliant phrase the entire structure of the bourgeois mythology of the "savior." The Word is made flesh, the immense and uncontrollable forces of history are incarnate in a personified Higher Being.

---

[24] Lefort, *op. cit.*, p. 133: "Thus, the bourgeoisie usually finds the image of its own unity situated outside of itself, and it presents itself as an historical subject only through the mediation of a power which transcends the realm of the activities in which the bourgeoisie constitutes itself as an economic class." Marx, in "The Jewish Question," CW, III, 154:

> Where the political state has attained its true development, man – not only in thought, in consciousness, but in *reality*, in *life* – leads a twofold life, a heavenly and an earthly life: life in the *political community*, in which he considers himself a *communal being*, and life in civil society, in which he acts as a *private individual*, regards other men as a means, degrades himself into a means, and becomes the plaything of alien powers. The relation of the political state to civil society is just as spiritual as the relation of heaven to earth.

[25] Marx, *Theses on Feuerbach* (1845), CW, V, 7.

Liberation having been accomplished in this alienated fashion, the new state established by the "Liberator" cannot but be itself alienated. Constituted by the separation between "private" and "public," "man" and "citizen," "civil society" and "political state," it inherits from the Savior the role of protector of the "social" from the particularism of individuals. Whereas, under feudalism, the *Bürgerliche Gesellschaft* was directly political in character, the estates, corporations, etc., being elements in the life of the state, bourgeois political emancipation projects political life into a sphere that is above and outside society.²⁶ In conclusion, to the economic alienation of the capitalist market corresponds a political alienation which is expressed in the myth of the savior from on high and in the constitution of the liberal state. We can find traces of it in the political ideologies of the bourgeoisie on its way up between the 16th and the 19th centuries.

b) *Workers' self-emancipation*

The period 1789–1830, in the history of the modern labor movement and of modern socialism, is a transitional phase between "bourgeois messianism" and the idea of workers' self-emancipation, which finds expression in two characteristic forms: utopian socialism and secret societies (not to mention, of course, the adhesion of sections of the working people to Jacobinism and Bonapartism, more or less direct prolongations in the working class of the bourgeois myth). The historical bases of these forms must be sought in the still embryonic state of the labor movement and of the proletariat in the modern sense of the term. Analyzing the conditions of this epoch, Engels observed that

> the proletariat, which then for the first time evolved itself from these propertyless masses as the nucleus of a new class, as yet quite incapable of independent political action, appeared as an oppressed, suffering estate, to whom, in its incapacity to help itself, help could, at best, be brought in from without or down from above.²⁷

It was precisely this help "from above" that the utopian socialists sought to bring, presenting themselves as bearers of the Truth, Messiahs come to free humanity (Fourier), "New Christs" (Saint-Simon), or appealing to the Princes to grant emancipation to the peoples. Saint-Simon writes to Tsar Alexander I, to Louis XVIII, and to the Holy Alliance; Fourier addresses himself to Napoleon, to Louis XVIII, and to Louis-Philippe; Owen publishes a manifesto to the Congress of the Holy Alliance at Aachen. This ideological structure differs from bourgeois messianism only by the content of its program of emancipation, and it is precisely the clash between the communist content and the bourgeois form that makes these moves appear utopian and naïve.

---

²⁶ Marx, "The Jewish Question," *CW*, III, 166.
²⁷ Engels, *Anti-Dühring*, *CW*, X, 246.

The bourgeoisie might, with reason, entrust to a Napoleon the defense of its interests, but it seems curious to expect the liberation of the proletariat to come from Tsar Alexander I. The bourgeois myth was "realistic," that of the first socialists "utopian."

It was also a solution "from above" that was advocated by the group of neo-Babouvist conspirators whose program of action replaced the individual hero by the secret society of the initiated, and the dictatorship of the man sent by Providence by that of a "revolutionary directory" emerging from the conspiracy. This conception of the emancipation process, the immediate basis of which was the confusion between communists, Jacobins, and Republicans during the Restoration, constitutes a step forward from the messianism of the bourgeoisie and of the utopians. It is revolutionary and relatively "de-mystified" in character; however, the radical change is seen as being the work of an "enlightened" minority, the broad masses having no role but that of "supporting force." We shall examine later the origins and evolution of this intermediate form between the action of the "savior from on high" and Marx's "task of the workers themselves."

Utopian socialism and the secret societies had their *raison d'être* in the weakness of the independent labor movement, which until 1830 amounted to no more than the heritage of the *compagnonnages* together with a few movements of resistance and combination.[28] This weakness allowed the utopians practically to ignore the labor movement and the conspirators to regard the masses as "too immature" to carry out a revolution by themselves. Both sought for "socialist," "egalitarian," "industrial," "communist," etc., society a path that did not run through the masses – neither through their coming to consciousness nor through conscious revolutionary action. The new world would be established by the miraculous intervention of a "new Christ," if not of a monarch, or by a putsch effected by a handful of conspirators.

The conditions for the idea of self-emancipation to emerge can be either conjunctural – a revolutionary situation – or structural – the proletarian condition. It is the historical coincidence of these two orders that transforms it into an idea-force of the broad masses of the people.

The attitude of the workers during revolutionary conjunctures reflects the eminently practical character of their coming to consciousness: the experience of armed action by the people, the accentuation of social conflicts, the de-bunking of the "great men" of the ruling strata; in short, *revolutionary praxis* is reflected at the level of the consciousness of the vanguard and of the masses by the radicalization of aspirations for equality and the blossoming of the project of self-liberation.

---

[28] Cf. E. Labrousse, *Le Mouvement ouvrier et les théories socialistes en France de 1813 à 1848* (Paris: n.d.), pp. 70–89.

And so we see appearing the first modern manifestations of communism, the first outlines of the idea that the workers should free themselves by their own efforts, during the great bourgeois revolutionary upheavals, even before the modern proletariat has appeared. Engels notes these "revolutionary armed uprisings," these "independent outbursts of that class which was the forerunner, more or less developed, of the modern proletariat," during the Reformation and the great English and French revolutions (Münzer, the Levellers, Babeuf).[29]

Thomas Münzer's movement was millenarist but not messianic. The bands of armed peasants and plebeians whom he led or inspired did not look for their salvation to anyone sent from Heaven but to their own revolutionary action, aimed at establishing the Kingdom of God on Earth. Whereas Luther linked himself with the princes (the Elector of Saxony, etc.) and incited them to massacre the rebels, Münzer wrote that "the people would free themselves . . . and it would go with Dr. Luther as with a captive fox."[30]

The struggle of Münzer's plebeians against the "bourgeois" further becomes, during the great English revolution, the struggle between the Levellers and Cromwell. The political program of the Levellers was "self-government" for the broad masses, which they opposed to Cromwell's military dictatorship. In a pamphlet composed in March 1649, *The Hunting of the Foxes*, their leader, Richard Overton, wrote: "We were before ruled by King, Lords and Commons; now by a General, a Court Martial and House of Commons; and we pray you what is the difference?" Unlike Cromwell, who saw himself as having been sent by Providence to impose his conception of God's will upon a corrupted humanity, the Leveller leaders (Lilburne, Overton, etc.) gave expression to the inarticulate passions, grievances, sufferings, and revolt of the broad masses, whose voluntary and conscious adhesion they sought to win.[31]

Finally, during the revolutionary struggles of the years II and III in France, the same kind of conflict occurred between the representatives of the most combative *sans-culottes* and the Jacobin dictatorship. In criticizing "the Incorruptible" himself, the *"Enragés"* (J. Roux, Leclerc, Varlet, etc.), whose theme was "People, save thyself," were inciting the masses to expect salvation not from the "constituted authorities" but from a "revolutionary upheaval," a "spontaneous movement."[32]

---

[29] Engels, *Anti-Dühring*, CW, X, 19.
[30] Engels, *The Peasant War*, CW, X, 426.
[31] Cf. T. C. Pease, *The Leveller Movement* (Chicago: 1916), p. 360; D. M. Wolfe, *Leveller Manifestos of the Puritan Revolution* (New York: 1944), p. 98; V. Gabriel, introduction to *Puritanismo e Libertà* (Einaudi, 1956), pp. L, LI.
[32] D. Guérin, *La lutte de classes sous la première Republique – Bourgeois et "bras-nus" (1793–1797)* (Paris: 1946), p. 84 (reprinted 1969).

In these three movements we find, of course, only a crude egalitarianism and a very vague sketch of the idea of self-liberation. Between them and the *Communist Manifesto* there lies all the difference between the urban *plebs* of the 16th, 17th, and 18th centuries – a heterogeneous and imprecise category wherein poor craftsmen, journeymen, hired hands, lower clergy, unemployed, vagrants, etc., are all mixed up together – and the modern proletariat which begins to take shape in the 19th century. It is only with the appearance of this class, after the Industrial Revolution, that the structural foundation arises for a coherent and rigorous conception both of communism and of self-emancipation, yet the role of the conjuncture continues to be determining: as a general rule, it is only during great revolutionary crises that the broad masses of the proletariat identify themselves with this conception.

The very nature of the proletariat and of the proletarian revolution constitutes the structural foundation for the theory of workers' self-liberation. In the first place, the common bond, union, community does not appear to the workers as something external and transcendental (as it does for the bourgeois competing among themselves) but as an attribute of the masses or the result of common action: "solidarity" is the immediate psychological relation among the workers, at the level of the factory, the trade, and the class. The bourgeois ideologist Hobbes saw social life as a "war of all against all," but the naïve craftsmen of the London League of Communists had as their motto: "All men are brothers." For the proletariat, which has no private property (in means of production, etc.), the "social," the "public" no longer needs to be incarnated in a Higher Being over against the particularism of individuals. It becomes immanent in "the people," it presents itself as a quality intrinsic in the workers as a whole. Insofar as he is not a property-owner and is not drawn into "free competition," the proletarian *can* escape from bourgeois political alienation and its myths. Looked at in another way, the historical significance of the proletarian revolution is essentially different from the "taking of power" by the bourgeoisie: it will be a self-liberation or it will be nothing. The bourgeoisie can become the "ruling class" even without a conscious historical action, because the bourgeois revolution belongs to the Kingdom of Necessity. Even if this action is alienated, oriented towards illusory objectives, and inspired by myths, the "cunning of reason" of economic and social liberation will give it victory. The bourgeois revolution is the immediate realization of the bourgeoisie's social being. The barriers in the way of this realization are purely external. It does not presuppose any "self-changing" by the class. This "automatic," alienated, and necessary process can easily assume the mythological form of a personal Liberator from without. The proletarian revolution, on the contrary, has to be the first *conscious* transformation of society, the first step in the "Kingdom of Freedom," the historical moment when individuals who have hitherto been objects and products of history come forward as subjects and producers. It does not realize the immediate condition of the proletariat but, on the contrary, implies for it a "transcendence of self" through coming to consciousness and revolutionary action.³³ As Engels wrote in his "political testament" (the 1895 preface to *The Class Struggles in France 1848–1850*):

> The time of surprise attacks, of revolutions carried through by small conscious minorities at the head of masses lacking consciousness is past. When it is a question of a complete transformation of the social organization, the masses themselves must also be in on it, must themselves already have grasped what is at stake, what they are fighting for, body and soul.³⁴

It must nevertheless be observed that in some periods, for a number of reasons which need to be studied concretely in each case, certain leaders, the vanguard, or even a large part of the mass take over the bourgeois mythology or return to past forms of organization and action (utopianism, conspiracy, etc.). We see, for instance, in the 19th century, the reappearance in some sectors of the working class of the myth of the man sent by Providence: the "flirtation" of Proudhon, Weitling, and some worker groups with Napoleon III, of Lassalle with Bismarck, and so on. Furthermore, utopia and the secret society reappear after 1848 and persist in diverse forms (Proudhonism, Blanquism) right down to the Commune of 1871. And ought one not to interpret similarly what is conventionally called "the cult of personality" in the working-class movement in the 20th century?

The most favorable conditions for the appearance of these phenomena of "ideological regression" are:

a) weakness, immaturity, low level of consciousness in the working-class movement;
b) defeats of the proletariat, setbacks to the revolution, disappointment and discouragement of the masses;
c) isolation of the vanguard, bureaucratization, gap between leaders and mass. To the revolutionary conjuncture corresponds the tendency to self-emancipation; to the victory of the counterrevolution corresponds the return to messianic myths, utopia, and Jacobino-Machiavellism.

c) *Marx's "communism of the masses"*

The economic and social consequences of the Industrial Revolution were more and more felt in Europe during the period 1830–1848: growth of towns, development of industry and commerce, concentration and numerical increase of

---

³³ Cf. Lukács, *History and Class-Consciousness*, p. 71; A. Gorz, *La morale de l'histoire* (Paris: 1959), p. 175; R. Luxemburg, "Masse et chefs," in *Marxisme contre dictature* (Paris: 1946), p. 37. [From "Gekwickte Hoffnungen" ("Hopes dashed"), *Die Neue Zeit* 1903–1904, I Bd, Nr. 2].
³⁴ *CW*, XXVII, 520.

the proletariat, pauperization, and proletarianization of craftsmen, etc. These changes brought about, directly or indirectly, a great reinforcement and reorientation of the labor movement. We thus see, in France, the formation of independent working-class groups and tendencies, separate from republicanism and purely bourgeois Jacobinism. This was the time of the rise of "workers' unions," societies for resistance, secret societies made up of workers and with a working-class ideology, neo-Babouvist communism, a wave of combinations, strikes, riots, and popular insurrections. In England, trade unions develop, the worker masses organize themselves politically (Chartism), strikes and uprisings follow one after another. In Germany, the first workers' associations appear, and also the first workers' revolts. In exile, German craftsmen form Babouvist secret societies. In general, Europe's working class appears on history's scene, begins to act through its own organizations and also to sketch out a program of its own.

Marx was able to grasp the common feature of these experiences and to develop into a coherent theory the more or less vague and fragmentary tendency towards communism and self-emancipation, and he could grasp and give expression to the real movement of the proletariat because, since 1843, he had been concerned with "making the world aware of its own consciousness, . . . *explaining* to it the meaning of its own actions,"[35] and not inventing and imposing a new ready-made dogmatic system.

The central idea of Marx's "communism of the masses" was self-liberation by the masses through the communist revolution. This idea, or, rather, this significant constellation of ideas, was made up of three dialectically linked ideas, three perspectives that were mutually implicit:

a) recognition of the potentially revolutionary nature of the proletariat;
b) the proletariat's tendency towards communist consciousness, by way of its revolutionary praxis;
c) the role of the communists in developing this tendency towards total coherence.

In this threefold approach, the critical practical structure of Marx's thought appears clearly: on the basis of critical reflection about reality, a possibility emerges, and upon this possibility he builds a project for transforming action.

Marx's doctrine of the communist revolution is a *realistic* political theory because it is based on a "critico-scientific" analysis of capitalist society: the possibility of changing social reality is present within reality itself.[36] The hypothesis of the potentially revolutionary and communist nature of the proletariat is the link, the organic connection, between Marx's political theory

---

[35] Marx, "Letter to Ruge," *CW*, III, 144.
[36] Cf. Lefort, *op. cit.*, p. 117.

and his sociology, economics, philosophy of history, and so on. "Communism of the masses" presupposes Marx's entire *Weltanschaung*; it is a partial totality articulated within this longer totality.

In this conception, the role of the *communists* (a broad term which, for Marx, embraces the ideologists, the political leaders, and the vanguard of the proletariat) is qualitatively different from that of the Jacobin heroes or the revolutionary conspirators. They are the "catalysts" of the totality within the labor movement: their function is to link every limited demand, every national struggle, every partial moment, to the total movement (the ultimate aim, the international struggle, etc.).[37] Contrary to the ideologists of the "Savior" or the supporters of conspiratorial societies, for whom the separation between "the general interest" and the masses is institutionalized, because people are necessarily particularist, corrupt, or ignorant, Marx refuses to dig a ditch between the communists and the proletariat, because their separation is provisional, because the proletariat tends towards the totality, towards communism, towards revolution. The bourgeois doctrinaire alienates the "totality" in an individual or an institution because he regards civil society as essentially particularist. The conspirator sees in the secret sect the only bearer of the "totality," because the working-class mass seems to him to be doomed to obscurantism so long as the capitalist regime survives. Marx sees his role and that of the communists as an instrument of self-liberation of the masses, because he is witnessing the birth of an independent labor movement, and he believes this to be capable of attaining consciousness of its historic task.

---

[37] Cf. V.I. Lenin, *What Is To Be Done? CWL*, V, 423: "The Social Democrat's ideal should not be the trade-union secretary, but the *tribune of the people*, who is able to react to every manifestation of tyranny and oppression, no matter where it appears, no matter what stratum or class of the people it affects; who is able to generalize all these manifestations and produce a single picture of police violence and capitalist exploitation; who is able to take advantage of every event, however small, in order to set forth *before all* his socialist convictions and his democratic demands, in order to clarify for *all* and everyone the world-historic significance of the struggle for the emancipation of the proletariat."

Chapter One
The Transition to Communism (1842–1844)

I. The *Rheinische Zeitung*

The *Rheinische Zeitung* was the product of a brief marriage between Left Hegelianism and the liberal bourgeoisie. If the Hegelian Left was born from the Rhineland bourgeoisie, their association in a common organ would call for no further explanation. However, we know that the Young-Hegelian intelligentsia was recruited above all from the middle strata (with only a few exceptions, the most notable being the industrialist Mevissen, who, besides, always stayed somewhat on the edge of the movement), that its philosophical and theological speculations were remote from the concrete and material preoccupations of the Rhineland's industrialists and merchants, and that its Hegelian conception of the state was quite the opposite of the free-trader liberalism of a Camphausen.

Nevertheless, despite these differences – which were to give rise to serious frictions within the *RZ* and to lead, after 1843, to a complete break – the two groups managed to find common ground in opposition to the feudal-bureaucratic Prussian state (for one group a "critical" opposition, for the other a moderate, "constructive" opposition) and in defense of the liberties threatened by royal absolutism (freedom of the press for the Hegelians, freedom of industry for the bourgeois). Thus, in a sense, the evolution of the Prussian state and the dashing of the hopes that had been placed in the "liberalism" of King Friedrich Wilhelm IV brought about a development which caused the two groups to come together in the *RZ*.

In the period 1838–1840, most of the Young Hegelians busied themselves in the celestial realm of theological criticism: the most "politicized" group, represented by Ruge and the *Hallischen Jahrbücher*, took its stand under the sign of unity between philosophy and Protestantism and sought to be the ideologist of the national Prussian state and its struggle against Ultramontanist Catholicism. The accession of Friedrich Wilhelm IV in 1840 was welcomed by the neo-Hegelians as the first step towards the transformation of Prussia into a national state. "Spring grows green again in all hearts" and "a dawn of hope is reflected in everyone's countenance," wrote Bruno Bauer about this event.[1] Very soon, however, the new King showed his true face – pietistic, romantic, and reactionary. His hatred of Hegelianism found expression in the banning of journals of that tendency (suppression of the *Hallischen Jahrbücher* in June 1841 and of the *Athenäum* in December) and in the eviction of Hegelian professors from the universities. The culmination was reached with the dismissal of Bruno Bauer in March 1842. The Young-Hegelian movement was thus sharply brought down to earth and found that the state had closed its traditional means of expression (philosophical journals, university chairs), which, for some of them at least, were also their means of existence. Three possibilities alone were left to them:

1. To surrender, abandon the political struggle, support the government, disappear;
2. To emigrate to France or Switzerland and carry on the fight from abroad, as Heine and Börne had done after 1830 (and as many of them were to do in 1843);
3. To ally themselves with a powerful class in society, through the mediation of a concrete political movement able to resist Prussian absolutism and to open channels of expression for them. This movement was the bourgeois liberalism of the Rhineland.

Thus, the Prussian state's reactionary intervention dislodged the Left Hegelians from the literary, theological, and philosophical criticism to which they had confined themselves until 1840 and thrust them into political opposition, into the arms of the Rhineland bourgeoisie.

On their part, the Rhineland liberals, whose hopes for a constitution and illusions concerning the new King's liberalism had been bitterly disappointed in 1840,[2] felt the need for ideological instruments (juridical, economic, philosophical) to use in the "constructive" opposition with which they aspired to confront the Prussian state.

Marx's evolution took place within this general setting. As a member of the Berlin "Doctors' Club," a friend of Bruno Bauer, and the author of a brilliant

---

[1] B. Bauer, *Der Aufstand und Fall des deutschen Radikalismus von Jahre 1842* (Berlin: 1840), 2nd edn., p. 5. Cf. A. Cornu, *Karl Marx et Friedrich Engels* (Paris: P. U.F., 1958), Vol. I, p. 165.

[2] J. Droz, *Le Libéralisme rhénan, 1815–1848* (Paris: Sorlot, 1940), pp. 223–225.

doctoral thesis, he was irresistibly disposed to pursue a university career. And while it is true that, from September 1842, he had participated in the discussions which preceded the foundation of the *Rheinische Zeitung*,[3] and in February 1842 had written a politico-philosophical article on censorship[4] (published in 1843 in the *Anekdcta*), he did not plunge decisively into journalism and political life until after Bauer's dismissal. It is hard to imagine what would have happened if the Prussian government had not dismissed Bauer and if Left Hegelianism had not been diverted, "sublimated," and neutralized by university life. Of one thing we can be sure: that brutal dismissal, which the Young Hegelians treated as an historic event and a symbol of the reactionary policy of the Prussian state,[5] was decisive for the radical "politicization" of Left Hegelianism in general and of Marx in particular.[6] By consummating the breach between neo-Hegelianism and the government and closing the university's doors against it, that measure forced philosophy "into the editorial offices of newspapers," to "become worldly,"[7] and to concern itself with concrete political and social problems.

The *Rheinische Zeitung* period was a phase of decisive importance in the evolution of young Marx. It marked both this entry into political life, and his first confrontation with "material questions." In a well-known commentary on this period, composed in 1859, Marx wrote:

> In the year 1842–1843, as editor of the *Rheinische Zeitung*, I first found myself in the embarrassing position of having to discuss what is known as material interests. The deliberations of the Rhine Province Assembly on thefts of wood and the division of landed property, the official polemic started by Herr von Schaper, then Oberpräsident of the Rhine Province, against the *Rheinische Zeitung* about the condition of the Mosel peasantry, and finally the debates on free trade and protective tariffs caused me in the first instance to turn my attention to economic questions.[8]

Engels goes further than this, declaring in a letter to R. Fischer of April 15, 1893, that "I always heard Marx say that it was through study of the law on theft of wood and the situation of the Moselland peasants that he was led to go over from pure politics to the study of economic questions and thereby even to socialism."[9] Lenin, summing up the significance of this episode, went

---

[3] Cornu, *op. cit.*, Vol. II (1958), pp. 8–9.
[4] *Karl Marx, Chronik seines Lebens in Einzeldaten*, (henceforth *Chronik*), Marx-Engels Institute, Marx-Engels Verlag (Moscow: 1934), p. 10.
[5] Cornu, *op. cit.*, Vol. II, p. 34.
[6] Marx was directly involved with the University of Bonn, for which, so late as January 1842, he was preparing an expanded version of his thesis, in order to obtain his qualification for an appointment in higher education. Cf. *Chronik*, p. 10.
[7] *CW*, I, 195.
[8] *CW*, XXIX, 261–262.
[9] *Marx-Engels Werke*, Dietz-Verlag, Berlin, Vol. 39 (1968), p. 466.

so far as to say that "Here we see signs of Marx's transition from idealism to materialism and from revolutionary democracy to communism."[10]

While these remarks were broadly correct, they have inspired some misleading works in which attempts are made to find in certain sentences taken out of context a content which is *already* communist or *already* materialist. But, although it is true that one can find in Marx's articles in the *Rheinische Zeitung* some signs that help us to understand his later development (and comparison with his "mature" writings is a valid tool to use in that research) ,it is no less important to perceive in these texts everything that is *still* neo-Hegelianism, *still* "the German ideology." It is above all necessary to consider these writings as relatively coherent structures, unities that must be treated as such, and from which one cannot isolate certain elements without depriving them of all meaning.

My task here will be to determine, through these articles, what Marx's attitude was to certain problems – private interest, poverty, communism, the relations between philosophy and the world – the attitude which enables us to understand not only his future adherence to communism, but also the *particular form* which his communism assumed at the beginning of 1844.

a) *The state and private interest*

In his first article for the *Rheinische Zeitung* about the debates in the Rhenish Diet on freedom of the press, the whole distance that separated Marx from Rhineland bourgeois liberalism is clearly apparent. His criticism is aimed not merely at the bourgeois deputies of "the urban estate" (*Stand der Städte*) who were opposed to freedom of the press – he treats them as *bourgeois*, not *citizens*, and calls them "urban reaction" (*städtischen Reaktion*).[11] He furthermore notes that indecision and "half-heartedness" (*Halbheit*) are typical of this estate,[12] since the bourgeois pseudo-defenders of press freedom do not differ, in the basic content of their speeches, from its foes. They want only three-eighths of freedom and are an example of "the natural impotence of a half-hearted liberalism."[13]

This indecision and impotence are not accidental. In his article on thefts of wood, Marx writes that private interest, the soul of which is "petty, wooden, mean [*geistlos*] and selfish,"[14] is "always cowardly, for its heart, its soul, is an external object which can always be wrenched away and injured."[15] This statement is essential for understanding Marx's evolution because it contains, in

---

[10] *CWL*, XXI, 80.
[11] *CW*, I, 169, 171.
[12] *CW*, I, 171.
[13] *CW*, I, 179–180.
[14] *CW*, I, 235.
[15] *CW*, I, 236.

germ, a corollary that was to be made explicit in the *Introduction to the Contribution to the Critique of Hegel's Philosophy of Law*: the private-property owner is always cowardly and selfish; only those who own nothing, who "have nothing to lose," are capable of courage, revolutionary energy, and identifying themselves with the general interest.

Marx's principal rebuke to private interest (represented in this article by the forest-owners), "the paltry soul of which was never illuminated and thrilled by thought of the state,"[16] is its claim to make the state an instrument for its own use, the state authorities its servants, and the state's organs so many "ears, eyes, arms, legs, by means of which the interest of the forest owner hears, observes, appraises, protects, reaches out and runs."[17] Whereas, in the article on press-freedom, we might still suppose that Marx was contrasting a "true liberalism" to the "semi-liberalism" of the bourgeois representatives in the Rhenish Diet, we can now see that Marx's conception is inspired by Hegel and is wholly contrary to the idea of the "policeman" state typical of classical liberalism. This conception is clearly developed in the article on representation by estates (*Ständische Ausschüsse*), where Marx contrasts "the organic life of the state" to the "non-state spheres of life," "state need" to "need of particular interest," "political intelligence" to "particular interests," "elements of the state" to "something passive... what is material, spiritless, unable to rely on itself," and he ends by saying that,

> in a true state there is no landed property, no industry, no material thing, which as a crude element... could make a bargain with the state; in it there are only *spiritual forces*, and only in their state form of resurrection, in their political rebirth, are these natural forces entitled to a voice in the state.[18]

Maximilien Rubel, who strives (in vain) to prove that Marx was, already at this time, "almost entirely freed" from the Hegelian conception of the state,[19] sees in these last lines only a "real sleight-of-hand" whereby Marx "negates the state by sublimating it" and "allows to political representation only the attribute of a spiritual function," dialectics in face of which "censorship should find itself disarmed."[20]

However, the truth of the matter is quite otherwise. For Marx, emphasis on the spiritual nature of the state is neither "sleight-of-hand" nor a trick to cheat the censor, and still less is it a sly "negation" of the state, but, on the contrary, assertion of the superiority of the "state spirit" over selfish "material

---

[16] *CW*, I, 241.
[17] *CW*, I, 245.
[18] *CW*, I, 297, 303–306.
[19] Rubel, *op. cit.*, pp. 42–43.
[20] *Ibid.*, p. 49.

interests" and even, generally, of "spirit" over "matter." Thus, we observe in most of his articles in the *Rheinische Zeitung* a formulation which "transforms material struggles into intellectual struggles and idealizes their crude material form,"[21] the most typical being that wherein he criticizes *"abject materialism, this sin against the holy spirit of the people and humanity,"* because it tries to "solve each material problem in a *non-political way*, i.e., without any connection with the whole of the reason and morality of the state."[22]

We thus perceive here a politico-philosophical schema which assumes two fundamental spheres (the second, of course, being the "truth" of the first): on the one hand, Matter – passivity – civil society – private interest – bourgeois, and, on the other, Spirit – activity – state – general interest – citizens. The inspiration of this schema is *essentially Hegelian*[23] – and without that basic admission we are indeed doomed to see here merely examples of sleight-of-hand. Nevertheless, on certain specific problems, Marx already separates himself from Hegel. First, he obviously rejects, along with most of the Left-Hegelians, identification of the existing Prussian state with the realized rational state, and inclines towards a resolutely democratic position. Also, however, and this seems to me very important, we find in his articles a virulent and radical criticism which we would look for in vain in Hegel: denunciation of particular interests and private-property-owners (selfish, cowardly, mean, etc.), and pessimism regarding the possibility of making them harmonize with the general interest of the state. This difference can easily be explained by:

(a) the considerable development of bourgeois "private interests" in Germany since the time when Hegel wrote his *Principles of Philosophy of Law* (1820);
(b) Marx's rejection of Hegel's solutions for the conflict between state and civil society: corporations, bureaucracy, etc.;

---

[21] CW, I, 165.
[22] CW, I, 262.
[23] Cf. Hegel, *Philosophy of Right* (Oxford: 1905), p. 189: Property and the private interest of particular spheres "must be subordinated to the higher interests of the state ... The maintenance of the state's universal interest, and of legality, in this sphere of particular rights, and the work of bringing these rights back to the universal, require to be superintended by holders of the executive power ..." And, on p. 156, "If the state is confused with civil society, and if its specific end is laid down as the security and protection of property and personal freedom, then the interest of the individuals as such becomes the ultimate end of their association, and it follows that membership of the state is something optional. But the state's relation to the individual is quite different from this." (Hegel's paras. 289 and 258).
This schema was also adopted by Ruge, Feuerbach, and others. It was from this standpoint that Ruge was to criticize the communist artisans of Paris in 1844 and the weavers' revolt in Silesia: the artisans' suffering was a private evil, a "partial injury," and the weavers' movement lacked "political spirit." Cf. his letter to Fleischer, July 9, 1844, in Ruge, *Briefwechsel und Tagebuchblätter 1825–1880* (Berlin: Weidmannsche Buchhandlung, 1886), I, p. 359. In a certain sense, Marx's break with Ruge in 1844 was also his final break with Hegel's philosophy of the state.

(c) the influence upon him of French socialism and of Moses Hess (critique of property, egoism, etc.).

In short, while still remaining attached to the Hegelian conception of the rational state, Marx has already, by way of his criticism of the Prussian bureaucratic and feudal state, taken the path that will in 1843 lead him to break completely with Hegel and, through criticism of "private egoism," onto the path bringing him to communism.

What interests us in the present work, however, is not the Marxian conception of the state, as such, but the relation between this conception and Marx's attitude to the proletariat (or, rather, to "the poor," since the proletariat in the strict sense does not figure in the articles studied). This attitude can be grasped only in the light of the contradiction between the state and civil society as Marx saw it.

b) *The suffering of the poor*

Hegel saw in the existence of two poles, luxury and poverty, in civil society a consequence of the development of the "system of needs," that is, of *bürgerliche Gesellschaft* itself.[24] Marx, after criticizing the selfishness of the rich property-owners, contemplates the problem of poverty in Germany, but. unlike Hegel,[25] he directly defends the poor and their threatened rights. And yet, despite all his sympathy for the "wood-thieves" and winegrowers of the Moselland in their distress, Marx views their situation in accordance with the same neo-Hegelian categories he uses for criticizing the private interests of the property-owners: this distress (*not:* want) belongs to the system of needs, to civil society, to the private sphere. These are "private interests which suffer," and it is only through the generalizing action of the free press that this "private misfortune" (*Privatleiden*) becomes a "misfortune for the state" (*Staatsleiden*), and this particular interest becomes a general interest.[26] Moreover, already in his first article (on press freedom), he noted that the absence of a truly free press has a demoralizing effect, diverting the people from political life and turning them into "a rabble of private individuals" (*Privatpöbel*).[27]

"Private misfortune," "particular interest," "rabble of private individuals" – these are all expressions that show us that Marx is on the side of the poor (his entire article on the thefts of wood is a courageous, burning, and angry

---

[24] Hegel, *op. cit.*, pp. 123, 128, 149, 150 (paras 185, 195, 243, 245).
[25] Hegel, *op. cit.*, (para 245), p. 150: "In Britain, particularly in Scotland, the most direct measure against poverty and especially against the loss of shame and self-respect – the subjective bases of society – as well as against laziness and extravagance, etc., the begetters of the rabble, has turned out to be to leave the poor to their fate and instruct them to beg in the streets."
[26] *CW*, I, 348.
[27] *Ibid.*, I, 168.

defense of poor people persecuted and exploited by the owners of forests), but that he is still a prisoner of the Hegelian schema of the superiority of the spiritual and general concerns of the state over the material and particular concerns of the private sphere.

Also, Marx sees in the poverty of the peasants its passive aspect only: their distress, their needs, their suffering. Furthermore, the German word itself that he constantly uses in relation to the poor, *Leiden*, can mean both "suffering" and "passivity," and he uses it to indicate all the passive forms of suffering: "to endure, to tolerate, to suffer," etc. One can account for this attitude by his neo-Hegelian beginnings ("active spirit" against "passive matter"), but one must also emphasize that the actual object of Marx's attention in these articles was *peasant* poverty, which was and remained throughout the 19th century essentially passive, and not *workers'* poverty, the *active* side of which was already making itself felt, at least in France and Britain. It is notable that the word "proletariat" appears in *none* of Marx's articles in *Rheinische Zeitung*.

Having said that, one has nevertheless to point out that Marx already notes in these "poor" people some essential characteristics which apply also to the proletariat. They are a "species" which "has only numerous arms with which to pluck the fruits of the earth for higher races,"[28] and "which has not found an appropriate place in the conscious organization of the state,"[29] which is "politically and socially propertyless" and "possesses nothing,"[30] and, finally, which, through its representatives in the Rhenish Diet, has shown itself to be the only serious defender of freedom.[31]

We thus see how an idea could appear that would eventually be central in Marx's transition to communism: the selfishness of the *property-owners* causes them to fall into the swamp of "impotent semi-liberalism"; only the "dispossessed (*besitzlose*) are radically libertarian. But it is probable that, in 1842, Marx had not yet developed all the implications of what he observed in the Diet debates, and that he looked on poverty not as a ferment of emancipatory revolt but as an "object" (*Gegenstand*), a "situation" (*Zustand*), which had to be reorganized and which the state had to do something to correct.[32]

c) *Communism*

The first fact that has to be taken into account when studying Marx's attitude towards communism in 1842 is his comparative ignorance of the

---

[28] *Ibid.*, I, 231. Marx is obviously referring to the serfs of the soil and not to the industrial proletariat.
[29] *Ibid.*, I, 234.
[30] *Ibid.*, I, 230.
[31] Apart from the commission's spokesman, Marx mentions as true defenders of press freedom in the Diet debates only some deputies of the peasantry, or "the fourth estate." *CW*, I, 171, 177, 179.
[32] *Ibid.*, I, 347–349, 342.

subject, which he admits in the relevant article itself in the *Rheinische Zeitung* and confirms in his brief "intellectual autobiography" of 1859:

> At that time, when good intentions "to push forward" often took the place of factual knowledge, an echo of French socialism and communism, slightly tinged by philosophy, was noticeable in the *Rheinische Zeitung*. I objected to this dilettantism, but at the same time frankly admitted in a controversy with the *Allgemeine Zeitung* that my previous studies did not allow me to express any opinion on the content of the French theories.[33]

What could Marx have known at that time about socialist and communist theories? To be mentioned first, of course, is the feeble German "echo," which was sounded in the *Rheinische Zeitung*, especially by Moses Hess, whose influence on Marx must not be underestimated. Among the contemporary French writers, the only one who is mentioned several times and with approval is Proudhon, for his "sharp-witted work."[34] Marx readily makes use of Proudhon's most original formulations; for example, when he demands, in the article on wood-thefts, whether all private property ought not to be regarded as theft.[35] As for the two other writers mentioned in the article on communism, Leroux and Considérant, the mention of their names can be explained by the fact that they were present at the *Congrès des Savants* at Strasbourg, the review of which in the *Rheinische Zeitung* led to the polemic with the *Augsburger Allgemeine Zeitung*,[36] as well as by the frequent quotation from their writings and discussion of their views by Proudhon in *What is Property?* Mere mention of their names is not enough to prove that Marx had direct contact with their works. Finally, in January 1843, the first references to strictly communist theoreticians appear. In an article of January 12, Marx quotes a sentence of Dézamy's (which presupposes that Marx had read his work),[37] and, in an editorial note of January 7, there is mention of the journal *La Fraternité*, which was the organ of a Babouvist communist tendency (Lahautière and Choron).[38]

---

[33] *Ibid.*, XXIX, 262.

[34] *Ibid.*, I, 220.

[35] "If every violation of property without distinction, without a more exact definition, is termed theft, will not all private property be theft? By my private ownership do I not exclude every other person from this ownership? Do I not thereby violate his right of ownership?" *CW*, I, 228.

[36] F. Mehring, *Geschichte der Deutcher Sozialdemokratie* (Berlin: Dietz Verlag, 1960), I, p. 140.

[37] *CW*, I, 358: "Let Monsieur Cabet take heart: with so many titles, he cannot fail to obtain his *disability pension* soon." This comes from *Calomnies et politique de M. Cabet* (Paris: 1842), p. 7.

[38] MEGA, I, 1/2, pp. 141–142; On *La Fraternité*, cf. Volgin, "Socialist and Communist ideas in the secret societies, 1835–1840" [in Russian], *Voprosy istorii* (1954), No. 2, pp. 27–28.

From these indices, it would seem that Proudhon and Dézamy were the only French socialists of whom we can say with some assurance of probability that they were read by Marx when he was at the head of the *Rheinische Zeitung*. This choice is significant in that they were thinkers standing to one side of the utopian and dogmatic sects (Saint-Simonians, Fourierists, Cabetists, etc.), and, what marks them sharply off from most of the French socialists, they were *materialists* and opposed to religion. Now, if we consider that:

(a) utopianism and mystical "neo-Christianity" were the aspect of the French theories most criticized by the atheistic Young Hegelians in general and by Marx in particular; and
(b) between 1842 and 1845 these two writers remained, for Marx, the ones most deserving of interest and the closest to a "scientific socialism" in France, we can form the hypothesis that, already, in the *Rheinische Zeitung* period, Marx was not altogether hostile to communism and that he followed with interest the work of the less dogmatic French socialists.

Actually, the article on communism reveals Marx's profound *ambivalence* regarding the socialist theories. At first he seems to reject them altogether:

> The *Rheinische Zeitung*, which does not admit that communist ideas in their present form possess even *theoretical reality*, and therefore can still less desire their *practical realization*, or even consider it possible, will subject these ideas to thoroughgoing criticism.[39]

However, if we look closer, we note a first distinction being made between the German manifestations of communism – the demagogy of some reactionary groups or the empty phraseology of scribblers[40] – and the French theories of Leroux, Considérant, and, above all, Proudhon. *These* theoretical works have to be taken seriously: they "cannot be criticized on the basis of superficial flashes of thought, but only after long and profound study," and it will not do to think of "disposing by a *single* phrase of problems which *two* nations are working to solve."[41] This differentiation appears also in a letter from Marx to Ruge, written in the same period (one month after the article), in which he severely criticizes the literary "communism" of the group of "the Free" in Berlin and demands that the socialist conception of the world be discussed

---

[39] *CW*, I, 220.
[40] Ibid. "Would otherwise the surprising fact have escaped you that communist principles are being disseminated in Germany not by liberals but by your *reactionary* friends?"
"Who is it that talks of *artisans' corporations*? The reactionaries.... Who carries on a polemic against *parcellation of landed property*? The reactionaries. In a quite recent work (Kosegarten on parcellation) written in a feudalistic spirit, the author goes so far as to call *private property* a *privilege*. That is Fourier's basic principle. Once there is unity on basic principles cannot there be any dispute over consequences and application?"
[41] *Ibid.*, I, 219–220.

"thoroughly."[42] But it is the last paragraph of the article which is most remarkable from this standpoint. It seems to suggest a veritable *conflict of consciousness* in Marx between a "subjective" tendency towards communism and the rejection thereof which his reason dictates. The text speaks literally of "pangs of conscience" (*Gewissensangst*) created by a "rebellion of man's subjective wishes against the objective views of his mind" (*Verstand*), and of the power of communist ideas, "demons" which, though vanquished by the intelligence, nevertheless enchain our hearts, and which "human beings can vanquish only by submitting to them."[43] True, Marx speaks of "men" in general and not of himself, but the contempt he shows for those who, like the *Augsburger Zeitung*, have never felt such "troubles" tends to indicate that he was one of the "human beings" grappling with the communist "demons." In spite of that, I do not at all seek to prove by these hypotheses that Marx was, in 1842, already a communist or "almost" one. It is merely a matter of showing that his transition to communism in 1844 was a "qualitative leap" that had been prepared for by a certain previous evolution.

In the last paragraph of the *Rheinische Zeitung* article, we see clearly apparent a fundamental feature of the conception of communism that Marx had at that time. This is of particular interest because that feature is still partly present in the texts of early 1844 and conditions the way in which Marx sees the role of the proletariat in the *Introduction to the Contribution to the Critique of Hegel's Philosophy of Law*. In 1842, Marx sees communism as, above all, a system of dogmas, a set of ideas, even a *Weltanschauung*,[44] which are important, serious, penetrating, etc., as *theoretical works*, worthy of "long and profound study." True, Marx is not unaware that the demands of "the estate that today owns nothing" are a fact which is "obvious to everyone in Manchester. Paris and Lyons," that this is a problem "which two nations are working to solve," and that communism may provoke dangerous "mass practical attempts" that only cannon can check.[45] For him, though, the "real danger" – that is,

---

[42] Marx to Ruge, November 30, 1842: "I stated that I regard it as inappropriate, indeed even immoral, to smuggle communist and socialist doctrines, hence a new world-outlook, into incidental theoretical criticisms, etc., and that I demand a quite different and more thorough discussion of communism." CW, I, 394.

[43] "We are firmly convinced that the real *danger* lies not in *practical attempts*, but in the *theoretical elaboration* of communist ideas, for practical attempts, even *mass attempts*, can be answered by cannon as soon as they become dangerous, whereas *ideas*, which have conquered our intellect and taken possession of our minds, ideas to which reason has fettered our conscience, are chains from which one cannot free oneself without a broken heart, they are demons which human beings can vanquish only by submitting to them. But the Augsburg newspaper has never known the *pangs of conscience* called for by the rebellion of man's subjective wishes against the objective views of his mind, *since it has neither a mind of its own, nor views of its own, nor even a conscience of its own.*"CW, I, 220–221.

[44] *Ibid.*, I, 394.

[45] *Ibid.*, 216, 220–221. The reference to cannon shows that he does mean revolutions and not peaceful attempts to practice communism (settlements, etc.).

the real importance – lies not in these "practical attempts" but in the *theoretical* development of communism, in the communist *ideas*, those invincible demons, and so on. Here we have once more the Young-Hegelian thesis of the hegemony of the "activity of the spirit" over "crude material practice" that we find in Bruno Bauer, for whom theory constituted "the most powerful practical activity,"[46] as well as in Ruge, who believed that thoughts are "the weapons most certain to conquer, the impregnable batteries" and that determine action and history,[47] and, above all, in the "philosophical communism" of Hess, for whom the "great mistake" of L. von Stein was to consider communism as a material aspiration of the proletariat and not as a struggle between "the principle of communism" and "the principle of private property."[48]

Marx was not to rid himself definitively of neo-Hegelianism, of "philosophical communism" and the structure of relations between thought and the proletariat which follows from it, until the period which begins with the article against Ruge in *Vorwärts* in 1844. I shall come back to this problem.

d) *Philosophy and the world*

This Left-Hegelian "idealism" is expressed also in the theory of relations between philosophy and the world, which would in 1844 become the theory of relations between philosophy and the proletariat, and which is outlined in the article against the *Kölnische Zeitung*. In order to grasp the essential features of this theory, we must go back for a moment, to Marx's preparatory

---

[46] Letter from Bauer to Marx, March 31, 1841: "It would be absurd for you to take up a practical career. Theory is now the most powerful practical activity, and we cannot yet foresee the extent to which it will take on that character." MEGA, I, 1/2, p. 250.

[47] Ruge, "The Hegelian philosophy and the philosophy of the *Augsburger A. Zeitung*," *Deutschen Jahrbücher*, August 12, 1841: "Thoughts are free and action is, in the last analysis, determined by thought. This implies that we must, of our own free will, reflect upon the great questions of politics and theology, so as not to be overtaken and submerged by the thoughts of this world and the next. Thoughts are the weapons most certain to conquer, the impregnable batteries. What alone remains is the truth, which reforms and develops itself. There is no history other than that of the movement which advances into the future and which is determined by the thinking spirit." Cornu, *op. cit.*, I, p. 234. Compare the image of "impregnable batteries" with that of Marx, who asserts the superiority of ideas over practical attempts, which "cannon can check."

[48] Cf. Moses Hess, "Sozialismus und Kommunismus," *21 Bogen aus der Schweiz* (1843) in *Sozialistische Aufsätze 1841–1847* (Berlin: Welt-Verlag, 1921). This would also be the position of the "True Socialists," whom Marx was to criticize in *The German Ideology* because they "regard foreign communist literature not as the expression and the product of a real movement but as purely theoretical writings which have been evolved – in the same way as they imagine German philosophical systems to have been evolved – by a process of 'pure thought.'" *CW*, V, 455.

work for his doctoral thesis, composed in early 1841. Here we find formulations which are amazingly similar to the Eleventh Thesis on Feuerbach: "There are moments when philosophy turns its eyes to the external world, and no longer apprehends it, but, as a practical person, . . . throws itself on the breast of the worldly Siren."[49] However, we soon perceive that we are still far from the theory of praxis, since "the *practice* of philosophy is itself *theoretical*: it is the critique that measures the individual existence by the essence, the particular reality by the idea."[50] But what is most important is the result of this "struggle," which ends in the "becoming-worldly" of philosophy and the "becoming-philosophical" of the world: "The result is that as the world becomes philosophical, philosophy also becomes worldly (*Weltlich-Wenden*) and that its realization is also its loss"[51] – a formulation that again reminds us of the *Deutsch-Französischen Jahrbücher*, in which the issue is the abolition and realization of philosophy through the abolition of the proletariat.

These themes were taken up again by Marx in his attack in the *Rheinische Zeitung* on an editorial in the *Kölnische Zeitung*. First comes this statement which seems apparently very "materialistic": "Philosophies do not spring up like mushrooms out of the ground: they are products of their time, of their nations, whose most subtle, valuable and invisible juices flow in the ideas of philosophy . . . every true philosophy is the intellectual quintessence of its time . . ."[52] However, this was an idea dear to Hegel, who wrote already in his *Philosophy of Law*: "Every individual is a child of his time; so philosophy too is its own time apprehended in thought."[53] Finally, in connection with philosophy's entry into "the editorial office of newspapers," Marx speaks of "interaction with the real world of its day" and, once more, says that "philosophy has become worldly and the world has become philosophical."[54]

What interests me in these texts is not, abstractly, their degree of "materialism" or "idealism." I prefer to draw from them a key idea: the "theoretical-practical" activity of philosophy and its "becoming worldly," an idea which enables us to understand why Marx, at the beginning of 1844, saw in the proletariat only the "passive basis" or the "material instrument" of philosophy.

II. Break and Transition: 1843

The year 1843 was the one that saw the definitive break by the Young Hegelians with the Prussian state and bourgeois liberalism. This break was the

---

[49] *CW*, I, 491.
[50] *Ibid.*, I, 85.
[51] *Ibid.*
[52] *Ibid.*, I, 195.
[53] Hegel, *op. cit.*, p. 11.
[54] *CW*, I, 195.

common starting point for the diverging way in which the different tendencies within the group evolved. Actually, the very terms in which this break was conceived showed already what their respective subsequent evolutions would be.

The position of the Hegelian Left in relation to the Prussian state passes through various phases: "critical support" until 1840 (Ruge), deluded enthusiasm when Friedrich-Wilhelm IV came to the throne, "critical opposition" getting sharper and sharper between 1841 and the emigration of 1843.

Marx himself had been opposed to the existing state from the beginning of his political life. We must see in his "loyalist" declarations in the *Rheinische Zeitung*, if not a concession to the censorship, at least a formal way of expression designed to protect a radically critical content. Yet the very fact that he was willing to make this concession shows that he had not, so far, reached the point of complete break. It was his experience of the fight with the censorship during 1842, when the reactionary and "irrational" nature of the Prussian state and the mean, narrow-minded spirit of the bureaucracy were revealed in a particularly crude fashion, that brought Marx to this radical break, expressed in January 1843 in a letter to Ruge in which he criticized all the concessions made in the past by the *Rheinische Zeitung* and refused to make any more.

This concrete experience of the true nature of the state and also of the power of private interests, and of the difficulty of harmonizing these with the general interest, were probably the factors that made Marx realize the need to apply the principles suggested by Feuerbach in the *Preliminary Theses* to his critique of Hegel's philosophy of the state. It was not just the Hegelian identification of the rational state with the Prussian state that was to be questioned (as in 1842), but the entire theory of relations between the state and civil society, etc.

Regarding the Left Hegelians' break with liberalism, a comment by Marx in the *Deutsch-Franziosischer Jahrbücher* allows us to perceive the essential reason for the conflict: "We are *philosophical* contemporaries of the present without being its *historical* contemporaries."[55] There was, indeed, a veritable *ideological time-lag* between the philosophers, who stood at the level of the most up-to-date French thought, and the German bourgeoisie, who were backward historically and politically, a gap between the ideological "overdevelopment" of Germany and the country's economic and social "underdevelopment." This lack of a sound social basis and this "advanced" appearance of the German ideology doubtless contributed to giving it its abstract and speculative character, sustaining among the thinkers the illusion that "the idea" was the driving force of history. The gap was to some extent mitigated

---

[55] *CW*, III, 180.

in the Rhineland, owing to the comparatively developed condition of that province and the "French" traditions of its bourgeoisie, which made possible temporary harmony within the *Rheinische Zeitung*. Nevertheless, there was still an element of misunderstanding, especially with the most "philosophical" sectors (the Berlin group), and conflicts within the editorial department occurred continually. Right at the start there was a struggle over who should be editor-in-chief, a struggle that revealed the tendencies of the two sides: on the one hand Moses Hess, the candidate of the Hegelians, representing philosophical radicalism, and on the other, Hoffken, a follower of the economist F. List, the victorious candidate of the bourgeois shareholders of the *Rheinische Zeitung* (Oppenheim, Schramm, etc.) – in other words, critical theory confronting concrete defense of the bourgeoisie's economic interests. To be sure, Hoffken's triumph did not last long, but his ousting was probably not only a result of his refusal to accept the collaboration of the Left Hegelians, which offended the rich sympathisers with that tendency in Cologne (Jung). Account must be taken also of the opposition from a considerable section of the Rhineland bourgeoisie, represented in the *Rheinische Zeitung* by L. Camphausen, to List's protectionism. Rutenberg's accession to the post of editor-in-chief was a victory for the philosophers, but after a few months the abstract phraseology of the Berlin "Free" became unacceptable to the clearer-minded of the Young Hegelians. In a conversation with Hess, Mevissen deplored the "negative tendency" of the journal and its taste for philosophical speculation.[56] In a letter to Oppenheim, Marx spoke out against "general theoretical arguments" and declared that "the correct theory must be made clear and developed within the concrete conditions."[57] All the same, despite the more realistic tendency given to it by Marx from October onward, the journal's orientation was not to the liking of the Rhenish bourgeois, who accused it of having "broken the law, slandered and ridiculed our institutions and sought to raise up the people against the government," thus substituting "the spirit of violence for the spirit of truth."[58]

All this enables us to understand both the lukewarm reaction of liberal circles to the banning of the *Rheinische Zeitung* (restricted to the sending of a few platonic petitions to the government) and the indignation of the Young Hegelians, who considered that they had been betrayed by the "liberal cowards." If we recall that the Press Ordinances were decisive in triggering the 1830 Revolution in France, we can appreciate the disappointment felt by the Left Hegelians, who now realized that, after all, the German bourgeoisie was not the revolutionary class capable of liberating Germany. Ruge gives admirable expression to this feeling in his letter to Marx of March 1843 (published in

---

[56] Droz, *Le Libéralisme rhénan*, pp. 259–260.
[57] *CW*, I, 392 (Letter to Oppenheim, August 25, 1842).
[58] Letter from the Cologne merchant R. Peill to Mevissen, January 1843. Droz, *op. cit.*, p. 263.

the *Deutsch-Französische Jahrbücher*: "Who would not have expected that this outrageous relapse from speech to silence, from hope to despair, from the state of a free man to that of an absolute slave would stir up all vital spirits, bring a rush of blood to everyone's heart and provoke a general shout of indignation?"[59] Similarly, the publisher Froebel wrote in a letter of August 1843 to Wigand that "the most pitiful and most repugnant individuals are the so-called liberals. Anyone who has learnt to know thoroughly what these poltroons are like needs to have a well-tempered soul to be able to go on fighting together with such a wretched crew."[60]

After trying in vain to play the role successively of ideologist of the "Protestant" state and of the liberal bourgeoisie, the Young-Hegelian group found itself in 1843 in a situation of "ideological availability." It broke up into several tendencies, each of which crystallized the differences which had become apparent in 1842, with, as common denominator, rejection of the Prussian state and of bourgeois liberalism. These tendencies were:

(a) the group of "the Free," some of whom came together to establish, after December 1843, the *Allgemeine Literatur-Zeitung* (the Bauer brothers, etc.): interpreting the liberals' defeat as a "retreat of the masses," this tendency withdrew more and more from the concrete political struggle, taking refuge in the purely theoretical "activity" of the "critical spirit";

(b) a tendency that might be called "democratic-humanist" (Ruge, Feuerbach, Froebel, Wigand, Herwegh) and which was keen to confuse communism with humanism; we find Feuerbach, for example, saying of Herwegh that he was, "like me, a communist fundamentally though not formally," and taking care to explain that their communism was "noble," not "vulgar."[61] Thus, Froebel, in a letter of March 5, 1843, to the communist Becker, wrote that he was "with my heart alone with the communists" and that he "divides people into egoists and communists." Ruge himself, in a letter to Cabet, declared that "in principle we are with you, we affirm, like you, that real man constitutes the foundation and the purpose of society";[62]

(c) a "philosophical communist" tendency (Hess, Bakunin, Engels), whose communism appeared as a category opposed to egoism, which made possible a certain confusion with the anti-liberal "humanists," and, consequently, common work with them in an organ, the *Deutsch-Französische Jahrbücher*.

Marx's evolution in this period was similar to that of the democratic group. Like most of the members of this tendency, he broke openly with the liber-

---

[59] MEGA, BD I, 1/1, p. 559.
[60] Cornu, *op. cit.*, II, p. 115.
[61] Letter from Feuerbach to Kriege about Herwegh. Cornu, *op. cit.*, II, 233.
[62] Cornu, *op. cit.*, II, pp. 116, 234.

als owing to their attitude in "the press affair." From the beginning of his activity at the head of the editorial board of the *Rheinische Zeitung*, he had clashed not only with the "radical" verbiage of "the Free," but also with the timid "moderation" of the bourgeois shareholders. In a letter to Ruge of November 30, 1842, in which he announces his break with the Berlin group, Marx also complains about having to put up, "from morning to night," with "howls from shareholders."[63] Finally, the managers of the journal decided, at a meeting held at the beginning of January, to steer clear of conflict with the government,[64] a decision with which Marx was very probably not in agreement. In fact, on January 25, 1843, in another letter to Ruge, he wrote:

> Moreover, I had begun to be stifled in that atmosphere. It is a bad thing to have to perform menial duties even for the sake of freedom; to fight with pinpricks instead of with clubs. I have become tired of hypocrisy, stupidity, gross arbitrariness, and of our bowing and scraping, dodging, and hair-splitting over words . . . I can do nothing more in Germany. Here one makes a counterfeit of oneself.[65]

Here Marx is making not only a critique of the "moderate" tendencies in the journal, but also what is almost a "self-criticism" of his tactics in the editorial board, and he proclaims his refusal to continue thenceforth a policy of "flexibility" in relation to the Prussian state, a policy which would lead, from one concession to the next, eventually to self-corruption. We can therefore easily understand Marx's opposition, at the general meeting of shareholders of the *Rheinische Zeitung* on February 12, 1843, to the majority tendency (Oppenheim, etc.) which sought once more to save the journal from the government's ban of January 24 by "moderating" its contents.[66] It is significant that these conflicts caused him to leave the editorial board before the date on which, according to the government's decree, the *Rheinische Zeitung* had to cease publication (April 1, 1843). On March 13, he wrote to Ruge that he would not, for anything, stay with the *Rheinische Zeitung*,[67] that is, even if the shareholders were to secure, by making more concessions, a lifting of the ban. On March 18, he announced publicly his decision to leave the editorial board.

Having already criticized the "semi-liberalism" and indecision of the bourgeois deputies in the Rhenish Diet during the debates on press freedom, Marx now watched the surrender of the bourgeois shareholders of the *Rheinische Zeitung*, their attempt at conciliation with the Prussian state, and the indifference of the Rhineland bourgeoisie to the suppression of the liberal press.

---

[63] *CW*, I, 395.
[64] J. Hansen, *Rheinische Briefe und Akten* I (Essen: 1919), p. 401.
[65] *CW*, I, 397–398.
[66] *Chronik*, p. 16.
[67] *CW*, I, 400.

This experience proved to him that the attitude of the bourgeoisie in Germany was not that of "revolutionary citizens" but of "cowardly property-owners," and, consequently, they could not be allotted the role that the French bourgeoisie had played in 1789. If, however, one ruled out the bourgeoisie, the question then arose: *who* could liberate Germany? For Bauer it was "critical thinking": for Ruge, nobody – Germany was doomed to remain in servitude, "our people has no future," he wrote to Marx in March in 1843.[68] Marx's striving to find a concrete answer to this central and essential question made him turn his attention as early as 1843 to "suffering mankind"; but it was his arrival in Paris that provided him with a clear and coherent answer which asserted itself as vivid, irrefutable proof: it was the proletariat that would play this revolutionary role.

Between his break with the liberal bourgeoisie at the beginning of 1843 and this "discovery" of the proletariat at the beginning of 1844 there lay, for Marx, a period of "democratic-humanist" transition, a phase of ideological loss of bearings and of feeling his way which would bring him eventually to communism.

a) *The critique of Hegel's philosophy of the state.*

In Marx's critique of paragraphs 261–313 of Hegel's *Principles of the Philosophy of Law,* which seems to have been drawn up during 1843,[69] his starting point is "anthropological" (Feuerbach), but his point of arrival is political and close to Moses Hess. This critique is a decisive stage in his transition to "philosophical" communism, a transition completed in his article on the Jewish question, which takes up and develops the themes of the 1843 manuscript.

Why, and to what extent, was Marx's break with Hegel to play a part in his adhesion to communism?

The main reproach which the "democratic" Young Hegelians in general, and Ruge in particular, aimed at communism was its "apolitical," purely social character. In a letter of July 8, 1844, Ruge writes that the communism of the German artisans is "a dreary activity lacking political interest," and that this "apolitical communism" is "a stillborn product,"[70] a proposition which follows rigorously from the Hegelian conception of the state as representative of the general interest, in relation to which any movement that remains at the level of civil society can be only private, partial, secondary, and inferior.

Marx breaks precisely with this Hegelian schema, showing that the universality of the state is abstract and alienated, that it constitutes "the *religion* of national life, the heaven of its generality over against the *earthly existence*

---

[68] MEGA, BDI, 1/2, p. 560.
[69] *Chronik*, p. 18.
[70] Ruge to Fleischer, July 9, 1844, in *Briefwechsel*, p. 359.

of its actuality," and that "the people alone is what is concrete."⁷¹ By this de-bunking of the sphere of politics, in 1843, he is already going beyond Ruge and turning no longer to the state as "the truth" of social problems (poverty, etc.), the position he still held in his articles in the *Rheinische Zeitung*, but to the real people, to social life. In so doing, he takes up a position very close to that of Hess, in which the *leitmotiv* was, precisely, the primacy of "the social" over "the political," the thesis which Marx was to defend in the *Deutsch-Französische Jahrbücher*.

In 1842, the main political *problem* for Marx was: how to ensure the universality of the state against assault by the private interests that seek to enslave it? Having given up the Hegelian philosophy of the state, the *question* that he puts in 1843 is quite different: why is universality alienated in the abstract state and how is this alienation to be "overcome and abolished"? The answer that he sketches leads also to communism: it is the *private essence* of civil society, that is, its atomistic individualism centered on private property, that is the basis for the "exteriorization" of the universal into a "political heaven."⁷² For this reason the existence of the political constitution is linked historically with freedom of trade and property, with the independence of the private spheres: the Middle Ages did not know the abstract political state.⁷³

It is in the light of these considerations that one must see the meaning of the solution proposed by Marx, namely, "true democracy." This was not at all bourgeois republican democracy, but a radical transformation which implied abolition of the alienated political state and of "privatized" civil society. The word "democracy" had for Marx a specific meaning: abolition of the separation between the social and the political, the universal and the particular. It is in this sense that he speaks of the Middle Ages as "the democracy of unfreedom."⁷⁴ His attitude to the bourgeois republic is clear: the North-American republic and the Prussian monarchy are alike simple political forms that protect the same content, namely, private property. In the state established by the French Revolution, the individual members of the nation are "*equal* in the heaven of their political world, but unequal in the earthly existence of *society*."⁷⁵ The implicit conclusion that follows is that what has to be changed is not the political *form* (republican or monarchical) but the social *content*: private property, inequality, and so on. This conclusion was also drawn by the French communists, and Marx is aware of this agreement

---

⁷¹ *CW*, III, 31, 28.
⁷² *Ibid.*, III, 31: "The particular spheres do not realize that their private nature coincides with the other-worldly nature of the constitution or of the political state, and that the other-worldly [*jenseitig*] existence of the political state is nothing but the affirmation of their own estrangement."
⁷³ *Ibid.*, III, 32.
⁷⁴ *Ibid.*, III, 32.
⁷⁵ *Ibid.*, III, 31, 79.

between him and them: he expresses his approval of the fact that "the French have recently interpreted this as meaning that in true democracy *the political state is annihilated*."⁷⁶

As for the proletariat, it is not mentioned in the 1843 manuscripts, except for one phrase, which, however, is highly significant: "*lack of property* and *the estate of direct labor*, of concrete labor, form not so much an estate of civil society as the ground upon which its circles rest and move."⁷⁷ This statement involves two implications which would be developed in the *Introduction to the Contribution to the Critique of Hegel's Philosophy of Law*, as features of the proletarian condition and basis of the proletariat's role as liberator:

> (a) the workers are propertyless; lack of property is the essential feature of their estate (along with the concrete nature of their labor). So, since private property is the main obstacle in the way of identification of the particular with the universal, it is enough to carry the argument through to the end in order to see (in the *Introduction*) the proletariat as the bearer of society's universal interests;
>
> (b) the propertyless workers constitute an estate which is not an estate of civil society, but something underneath that society ("the ground upon which," etc.), a basis for the activity of its higher spheres. Once again, this brings us directly to the *Introduction*, in which the proletariat appears as "a class of civil society which is not a class of civil society" (*CW*, III, 186). What does this mean? Quite simply, that Marx dissociates the propertyless workers from egoistic, particularistic bourgeois civil society. In other words, he abandons his position of 1842, in which poverty belongs to the system of needs, to civil society, to the *private sphere*. He now sees in propertylessness no longer a "particular matter" but a "general matter" which is the foundation of civil society and yet is situated outside of that society.

b) *The correspondence with Ruge*

The first feature to strike the attention of the reader of the correspondence exchanged between Marx and Ruge in 1843, as this was published in the *Deutsch-Französische Jahrbücher*, is the contrast between Ruge's deep pessimism and Marx's "revolutionary optimism." Was this difference due solely to the different "temperaments" of the correspondents? Does it not imply causes that are significant in other ways, namely, differences in outlook? It seems to me that this contrast can only be explained in accordance with the following hypothesis – that, already in 1843, Marx and Ruge were turning towards *different social classes*.

---

⁷⁶ Ibid., III, 30.
⁷⁷ Ibid., III, 80.

In his reply to Marx's first letter (March 1843), where mention was made, vaguely, of "the impending revolution,"[78] Ruge asks: "Shall we live long enough to see a political revolution? *We*, the contemporaries of these Germans?"[79] The key word in this sentence, which is central to the difference of outlook in 1843 and was to be central to the break in 1844, is the adjective attached to the revolution: 'political." Ruge, in fact, thinks always in terms of a *political* revolution, that is to say, a *bourgeois-democratic* revolution, and as he notes "the imperishable sheep's patience" of the German bourgeois, their passivity in the face of the "outrageous relapse from speech into silence," and, finally, "the degree of political indifference and decline into which we have fallen," it is perfectly logical that he can envision no prospect of revolution in Germany: "Oh! That German future? Where has its seed been sown?"[80]

Marx did not believe, any more than Ruge, in a revolution led by the German bourgeoisie. In his reply to Ruge (May 1843), he writes that "the philistines" (*Spiessbürger*) do not want to be "free men, republicans," but, like animals, want only to "live and reproduce themselves."[81] Unlike Ruge, however, he thinks that, in view of the failure of its alliance with the liberal bourgeoisie, philosophy must and can find other allies: the "seed of the future" has been sown not among the "bourgeois sheep," but among "suffering human beings." The revolution of which he dreams is based on "a rupture within present-day society," which is due to "the system of industry and trade, the ownership and exploitation of people"[82] – a formula that is still vague but in which Marx, for the first time, makes reference to the modern class struggle and its economic causes. This makes quite comprehensible the "optimism" of this letter compared with Ruge's "funeral song."[83] Let down by the "cowardly liberal property-owners," Marx redirects his hopes towards the suffering people, propertyless and exploited. True, the aim to be reached in this "social" revolution is, apparently, still "political": the letter speaks of the "democratic state," "the human world of democracy," etc.[84] However, in order to grasp the true meaning of the term "democracy," we need to refer to the 1843 manuscripts (*Contribution to the Critique of Hegel's Philosophy of Law*) written at more or less the same time. As mentioned earlier, Marx means by "democracy" not just a change in the *political form* (such as the establishment of a bourgeois republic would be), but a change in the very foundations of *civil society* (private property, etc.).

---

[78] *Ibid.*, III, 134.
[79] MEGA, BDI, 1/1, pp. 553–560.
[80] *Ibid.*
[81] CW, III, 134.
[82] *Ibid.*, 141.
[83] *Ibid.*, III, 134: "Your letter, my dear friend, is a fine elegy, a funeral song, that takes one's breath away."
[84] *Ibid.*, 137, 139.

A biographical detail provides a certain degree of support for this assumption. Immediately after his resignation from the *Rheinische Zeitung*, towards the end of March 1843, Marx paid a short visit to Holland, where, as we learn from his letter to Ruge, he had the opportunity to read the French newspapers – for the first time, seemingly, since he is surprised by the views they express about Germany.[85] It is possible, and even highly probable, that he would have found in these newspapers some echoes of the French workers' movement much more concrete than the "feeble echo" of the *Rheinische Zeitung*: for example, reports of the strikes which succeeded one another in between January and April 1843 (carpenters at Bourges, textile workers at Roubaix, roofers at Rennes, dockers in Paris, etc.), strikes which led to clashes, arrests and so on.[86] He may even have read articles on the development of workers' communism, the secret societies, and so on. And we must emphasize that at this moment Marx was in a particularly "receptive" situation: the break with the *Rheinische Zeitung* had left him in a state of availability that was not merely professional but also *ideological*.

It remains, however, to measure the whole distance that separates this idea of an agreement between "the enemies of philistinism, in short, all people who think and who suffer,"[87] and the terms in which Marx was to present, in 1846–1848, the problem of the relations between intellectuals who break with the bourgeoisie, on the one hand, and, on the other, the labor movement. In the first place, there is nothing here about clearly defined social classes, but only about two very vague categories which lack objective definition: those who "think" and those who "suffer." It is only thanks to the phrase that follows immediately after, referring to a rupture caused by the system of profit and exploitation, that we may believe that the "suffering" mentioned is indeed that of the proletariat. Again, no hierarchy of importance is established as between the two groups. It is not a matter of the adherence of a few "thinkers" to the proletariat's class struggle – Marx's formula in the *Communist Manifesto* – but of an agreement on an equal footing between all whose very existence is opposed to "the animal world of the philistines." Finally, what is most important, the fact that the proletariat is perceived only as "suffering human beings" makes it appear as the *passive* partner in the agreement, while the *active* partner is "thinking mankind." This brings us back, once again, to the Young-Hegelian schema: activity of mind against passivity of matter. I have already mentioned the double meaning of the German word *Leiden* ("suffering" and "passivity"), and it seems that in this text the ambiguity is such that M. Molitor [the translator of the works

---

[85] *Ibid.*, 133: "I am now travelling in Holland. As far as I can judge from the Dutch and French newspapers, Germany is sunk deep in the mire . . ."

[86] J. P. Aguet, *Les Grèves sous la Monarchie de Juillet, 1830–1847* (Geneva: E. Droz, 1934), pp. 237–257.

[87] *CW*, III, 141.

of Marx – *Oeuvres* – which the author has used for his quotations and references – B.P.] has seen fit to render *leidenden Menschheit* sometimes as "passive humanity" and sometimes as "suffering humanity." But there are proofs which are more conclusive than Molitor's translation. Marx's text itself suggests a basis of "passivity" in the suffering: "The existence of suffering human beings who think, and thinking human beings who are oppressed, must inevitably become unpalatable and indigestible to the animal world of philistinism which passively and thoughtlessly consumes."[88] One is familiar with the young Marx's fondness for reversals of form ("weapon of criticism" – "criticism by weapons," etc.), which he used without fear of making his text sometimes rather obscure. In the passage quoted, the "reversal" is there, but it is *broken*: "suffering human beings who think – thinking human beings who are oppressed." Why does Marx not place in relation to "suffering human beings who think," "thinking human beings who *suffer*"? The only possible explanation is that suffering, because of its passive nature, cannot be associated with thinking, which is essentially an activity (an activity oppressed by the world of philistinism). It is quite obvious that this Young-Hegelian conception is the opposite of the real situation. Concretely, it is the active rebellion of the worker masses that is oppressed and repressed by the authorities, whereas the "moral suffering" of the discontented intellectuals remains passive. It is in the particular situation of Germany – confrontation between the Left Hegelians and the state, absence of a labor movement – that we must seek the social origin of this illusion, and in the situation that existed in France, the starting point of Marx's evolution after 1844.

In any case, we must not forget that, in this letter, Marx nevertheless attributes a role to the "suffering" masses in the advent of the new world, and thereby places himself ahead of Ruge and most of the neo-Hegelians: "The longer the time that events allow to thinking humanity for taking stock of its position and to suffering mankind for mobilizing its forces, the more perfect on entering the world will be the product that the present time bears in its womb."[89] It would be very interesting to determine the exact meaning of that "mobilization," but we have to be content with guesses. He probably meant either the concentration of the proletariat by modern industry, a process the revolutionary consequences of which are discussed in the *Manifesto*, or else the union of the workers in coalitions, workers' associations, etc.

The main interest of Marx's last letter (September 1843) lies in the details it offers concerning his attitude to communism, just a bare few months before he joined it. It shows us a Marx who is ideologically confused, who, after his break with the Prussian state and the liberal bourgeoisie has not yet "found"

---

[88] *Ibid.*
[89] *Ibid.*

the proletariat and communism (except in the vague, ambiguous forms of "suffering humanity" and "true democracy"). The point of departure was clear, the point of arrival not yet determined.

> Although no doubt exists on the question of 'whence,' all the greater confusion prevails on the question of 'whither.' Not only has a state of general anarchy set in among the reformers, but everyone will have to admit to himself that he has no exact idea what the future ought to be.[90]

It was this absence of any doctrinaire *a priori*, and, especially, of any precise utopian notions about the future that enabled him, moreover, to avoid the dogmatism of the socialist sects:

> On the other hand, it is precisely the advantage of the new trend that we do not dogmatically anticipate the world, but only want to find the new world through criticism of the old one.[91]

The criticisms levelled by Marx at communism in this letter can be grouped under two headings: on the one hand, reservations which were to be abandoned during the years 1844–1845, and, on the other, criticisms of utopian socialism which were always to remain among the essential features of his political writing.

In the first category we find the following criticisms:

(a) Socialism is one-sided, it considers human life exclusively in its material aspect, totally overlooking men's spiritual activity:

> And the whole socialist principle in its turn is only one aspect that concerns the reality of the true human being. But we have to pay just as much attention to the other aspect, to the theoretical existence of man, and therefore to make religion, science, etc., the object of our criticism.[92]

This remark has a clearly "Young-Hegelian" flavor, and it is enough to compare it with Marx's fourth thesis on Feuerbach to measure the distance that separates March 1843 from March 1845. Feuerbach is accused of limiting himself to criticism of religion, of "the heavenly family," while forgetting the main thing, namely, the *earthly family*, to which true theoretical criticism and revolutionary practice needs to be directed. True, Marx's intellectual program would always be simultaneous criticism of theories and of reality, but his gravest reproaches, after 1845, would be addressed to those who confined themselves to purely theoretical "critical criticism," and not to those who applied themselves to analysis of reality.

---

[90] CW, III, 142.
[91] Ibid.
[92] CW, III, 143. Here "reality" (*Realität*) means "material being."

(b) For the "crude" socialists political questions are of no interest. Criticism can and must concern itself with these questions,[93] because "the *political state* – in all its *modern* forms – . . . even where it is not yet consciously imbued with socialist demands, contains the demands of reason." Nevertheless, Marx observes that

> everywhere it assumes that reason has been realized. But precisely because of that it everywhere becomes involved in the contradiction between its ideal function and its real prerequisites. From this conflict of the political state with itself, therefore, it is possible everywhere to develop the social truth.[94]

These fragments show that Marx was in a transitional stage between the criticism of the political state contained in the manuscript of 1843 (*Contribution to the Critique of Hegel's Philosophy of Law*) and the assertion of the primacy of the social in the *Deutsch-Französischen Jahrbücher*. This stage would soon be left behind, and, subsequently, Marx would no longer blame the socialists for being "apolitical."

(c) Communism, in particular, is a dogmatic abstraction, in which connection, however, I am not thinking of some imaginary and possible communism, but actually existing communism as taught by Cabet, Dézamy, Weitling, etc. This communism is itself only a special expression of the humanistic principle, an expression which is still infected [*Infiziest*] by its antithesis – the private system [*Privatwesen*]. Hence the abolition of private property and communism are by no means identical, and it is not accidental but inevitable that communism has seen other socialist doctrines – such as those of Fourier, Proudhon, etc. – arising to confront it because it is itself only a special, one-sided realization of the socialist principle.[95]

This criticism was to be repeated by Marx in his *Manuscripts of 1844*, where he counterposes his conception of "the real *appropriation* of the *human* essence by and for man" to "crude communism," characterized by envy of those wealthier than oneself, leveling-down, negation of culture, etc. This communism is still "infected by private property."[96] We shall come back to the significance of these remarks when we analyze the *Manuscripts*.

---

[93] *CW*, III, 143–144.
[94] *CW*, III, 143.
[95] *CW*, III, 142–143. It appears that, at this time still, Marx's chief source of information about French socialism was Proudhon's work. In a letter to Feuerbach of October 3, 1843, Marx speaks of "weak, eclectic Cousin" and "gifted Leroux" (*CW*, III, 350). Now, Proudhon, in *Qu'est ce que la propriété?*, speaks of "M. Cousin's usual eclectic tricks." *Oeuvres complètes*, Vol. IV (Paris: Marcel Rivière, 1926), p. 175; *Deuxième mémoire sur la propriété* gives high praise to Leroux, "the anti-eclectic, the apostle of equality," etc. *Oervres complètes* (Paris: A. Lacroix, 1873), p. 311.
[96] *CW*, III, 295–296.

The second category of criticism is the one that presents the greatest interest, because it was to determine Marx's entire political evolution and constitute one of the central axes of Marxist socialism. Already in 1843, Marx is refusing to construct "some ready-made system such as, for example, the *Voyage en Icarie*." He rejects the attitude of the philosophers who "had the solution of all riddles lying in their writing-desks," and for whom "the stupid, exoteric world had only to open its mouth for the roast pigeons of absolute knowledge to fly into it." In short, Marx was "not in favor of raising any dogmatic banner."[97] His program was quite different and was expounded in the following terms, in the form of a proposal for an "ideological platform" for the *Deutsch-Französische Jahrbücher*:

> We do not confront the world in a doctrinaire way with a new principle: Here is the truth, kneel down before it! We develop new principles for the world out of the world's own principles. We do not say to the world: Cease your struggles, they are foolish; we will give you the true slogan of struggle. We merely show the world what it is really fighting for, and consciousness is something that it *has* to acquire, even if it does not want to.
>
> The reform of consciousness consists *only* in making the world aware of its own consciousness, in awakening it out of its dream about itself, in *explaining* to it the meaning of its own actions . . .
>
> In short, therefore, we can formulate the trend of our journal as being: self-clarification (critical philosophy) to be gained by the present time of its struggles and desires. This is a work for the world and for us. It can only be the work of united forces.[98]

The theme which here appears for the first time would recur constantly in Marx's writings, right up to the *Communist Manifesto*, which was to establish definitively the opposition between "scientific socialism" and "utopian socialism." But one must not forget that this letter was written a few weeks before Marx left for Paris. It enables us to understand Marx's attitude to the French labor movement and helps to explain why he did not join any of the utopian schools (and did not found a new one), why he did not become one more doctrinaire among all those who swarmed in Paris – a new creator of political and philosophical dogmas.

Contrary to the utopian or "philosophical" socialists, Marx refuses to counterpose a finished system to men's actual struggles. His starting point is the concrete actions and aspirations of "the world," and he sees his role, the role of the critical philosopher, *as explaining to men the meaning of their own struggles*, instead of inventing new "principles."

---

[97] *CW*, III, 142–143.
[98] *CW*, III, 144–145.

It was thus that, in Paris, on the basis of the workers' actual struggles and of the aspirations of the proletariat and its communist vanguard – partially and confusedly expressed by the most advanced among the doctrinaires: Dézamy, Weitling, Flora Tristan – Marx was to discern the historical significance of this striving of theirs, the essential tendency towards which this nascent movement was heading: self-liberation through communist revolution.

Contrary to the utopians, whose abstract ideal was arbitrarily set up over and against the real world, Marx rejected the moralizing separation between being and should-being and sought the rationality of reality itself, the immanent sense of the movement of history. Thereby Marx, a disciple of Hegel's "realism," distinguished himself from the other Left Hegelians (especially Moses Hess and the "true socialists" whose "bad transcendence" of Hegel was basically just a disguised return to the moralism of Fichte and Kant).[99] This was, perhaps, the reason why it was Marx who was the first to grasp, in 1844, the revolutionary significance of the proletariat's struggles and aspirations.

Similarly, unlike most of the Left Hegelians, he did not believe that this task of "becoming conscious of our epoch" was incumbent solely on the intellectuals. It had to be, he wrote in his letter of September 1843, "the work of united forces." These forces were, on the one hand, "us," the critical philosophers, and, on the other, the struggling people. Here we find, again, the theme of the alliance between "thinking human beings" and "suffering human beings."

III. Marx's adhesion to communism

Analyses of Marx's transition to communism usually fail to distinguish between the three stages this process passed through, and, in particular, take no account of the qualitative leap accomplished between the second and third stages.

The first stage is that of Marx's adhesion to "philosophical communism" *à la* Moses Hess. This adhesion became concrete in the article on the Jewish question published in the *Deutsch-Französische Jahrbücher*, which marks the culmination of Marx's ideological evolution during 1843. The influence of Hess and Feuerbach is clearly apparent in this work, while that of the French workers' movement is barely noticeable.

The second stage, on the contrary, is that of Marx's "discovery" of the proletariat as the liberating class and real base of the communist revolution. It needs to be emphasized, though, that this discovery was still "philosophical." To be sure, as soon as he arrived in Paris Marx was "gripped" by the communist workers' movement, and his second article for the *Jahrbücher*

---

[99] Cf. Lukács, "Moses Hess and the Problems of Idealist Dialectics," in *Political Writings 1919–1929* (London: 1972), pp. 193–204.

(*Introduction to Contribution to the Critique of Hegel's Philosophy of Law*) expresses the veritable "ideological shock" caused by this first impression. But Marx's experience of this movement was at that time very limited. He had not yet made direct contact with the secret societies: all the evidence points to these contacts having begun only after the *Jahrbücher* began publication.[100] His knowledge of the workers' struggles in France was still abstract, and, consequently, the proletariat appears in the *Introduction* almost as a Feuerbachian philosophical category. One could, of course, assume that Marx was able to learn something from the works of the French socialists and communists. But the only work of that kind that we are sure he read in this period was Louis Blanc's *Histoire de dix ans*.[101] That work would not have helped him to appreciate the concrete significance of the workers' movement since, while Louis Blanc acknowledges the fundamental importance of the "social question" and of the proletariat's struggles, he nevertheless remains still a "political idealist." For example, he writes regarding the revolt of the silk-weavers in 1831 that, in order to overthrow those in power, "ideas, more formidable weapons of war than cannon, were necessary" – a phrase astonishingly similar to Marx's in his article on communism for the *Rheinische Zeitung* – and that in Lyons "the people, for whom to obey is the strongest of all necessities, was stupefied when it found itself without masters."[102] However, and this is what is most important, Louis Blanc considers that the solution to the social problems, the evils caused by competition, will not be brought about by an emancipatory proletarian revolution but by "repentance" on the part of the bourgeoisie, to whom he addresses, in the final pages of his work, an emotional appeal: "Who can believe that the bourgeoisie will obstinately persist in its infatuation? The natural guardian of the people, can it possibly persevere in distrusting it as an enemy? . . . Instead, therefore, of standing aloof from the people, it must unite with it indissolubly, by taking the first steps towards a system which should make association, not competition, the rule of trade . . ."[103] I do not wish to say that these illusions were shared by Marx but merely to suggest that, at the beginning of 1844, he could not, for lack of direct connections or of "appropriate" reading, have formed a concrete

---

[100] My working hypothesis when I began this research was that the great ideological break in Marx's evolution took place between 1843 and the *Jahrbücher*. Accordingly, I thought that Marx was decisively influenced by the French proletariat during the first months of his stay in Paris, and I hunted long and in vain for traces of contact between him and the communist secret societies between October 1843 and February 1844. A more thorough analysis of the texts showed me, however, that there was comparative "philosophical" continuity between 1843 and the *Jahrbücher* articles, and a crucial break between these articles and Marx's writings after August 1844. Moreover, historical research has shown that close contacts between Marx and the French and German communists did not begin until April 1844.

[101] *Chronik*, p. 20.
[102] L. Blanc, *History of Ten Years 1830–1840*, Vol. I, 1884, pp. 536 and 539.
[103] *Ibid.*, Vol. II, 1885, p. 658.

idea of the workers' movement in Paris – and hence the "philosophical" nature of his first discovery of the proletariat.

Furthermore, this "discovery" was not a break, something happening suddenly when considered in relation to previous development. Basically, it could be said, Marx would not have been able to "discover" the proletariat and its role in Paris if he had not already "found" it, in a certain sense, in 1843, in the still vague form of "suffering human beings," "propertylessness," etc.

To conclude, the conception of the proletariat we find in the *Introduction* is at once the starting point of a politico-ideological evolution closely linked with thinking about the European workers' movement and the end-point of a philosophical evolution "in search of the universal." It is consequently a kind of "hinge," which at once accounts for its *ambiguity*: on the one hand revolutionary and concrete, on the other Left-Hegelian and abstract, seemingly very precise in contrast to the vague notions of 1843 ("suffering," "propertyless"), yet, in fact, still very close to them.

The third stage, which begins with the article against Ruge in *Vorwärts*, is that of a new discovery, concrete this time, of the revolutionary proletariat. This was a decisive moment in the evolution of Marx's political thought. This "second discovery" led to the stage of *Communism of the masses*, which I will examine later.

a) *"The Jewish Question"*

A very widespread interpretation of this article of Marx's published in the *Deutsch-Französische Jahrbücher* treats it as an anti-Jewish pamphlet, which is then explained "psychologically" as an example of "Jewish self-hatred."[104] While it is true that in this article Marx identifies Judaism with trade, money, egoism, etc. – an identification made by all the Young Hegelians, both Jewish (Moses Hess) and non-Jewish – we have only to go beyond appearances to realize that it is basically a defense of the Jews, for two very simple and clear reasons:

(a) against the anti-Semite Bauer, for whom the Jews, unlike the Christians, are incapable of becoming free, Marx asserts the equality of the two groups from the standpoint of human emancipation;

(b) Marx shows that egoism, money, etc., are not blemishes *specific* to Judaism but essential characteristics of *all* modern and Christian society (a theme already outlined by Feuerbach and Hess).

Once this misunderstanding is removed, it is possible to perceive the general significance of "The Jewish Question." This article is the moment when Marx's ideological evolution joins the "philosophical communism" of Moses Hess.

---

[104] Rubel, *op. cit.*, p. 88.

The critical remarks contained in *The German Ideology* applied equally to Hess's theses of 1842–1845 and to Marx's writings in the *Jahrbücher*:

> The relation between German socialism and the proletarian movement in France and England is the same as that which we found . . . between German liberalism, as it has hitherto existed, and the movement of the French and English bourgeoisie . . . They [the "True Socialists"] detach the Communist systems, critical and polemical writings from the real movement, of which they are but the expression and force them into an arbitrary connection with German philosophy.[105]

Indeed, the "communism" of "The Jewish Question," like that of Hess, looks at social problems through "German spectacles," in an abstract way, because it "reinterprets" French communism, its "reinterpretation" being conditioned by the situation in Germany (absence of a workers' movement, etc.). Marx had begun the article during his stay in Kreuznach and finished it in Paris. On the one hand he takes up and develops as far as they will go the theses of his 1843 manuscripts while, on the other, he incorporates new themes inspired by Hess (who was in Paris and collaborating in the *Jahrbücher*). We are able, moreover, very easily to distinguish between the parts of the text written in Kreuznach and in Paris. In the earlier part the subjects dealt with are those of the *Contribution to the Critique of Hegel's Philosophy of Law* – the citizen's imagined sovereignty in the state, the religious-type alienation of political life, defense of democracy, etc. In the latter part of the article, however, we find quite new problems discussed, the origin of which is undoubtedly to be sought in the article on the essence of money that Hess had submitted to the editors of the *Deutsch-Französische Jahrbücher* (but which was destined to get published only in 1845, in the *Rheinische Jahrbücher*) – criticism of monetary alienation, of "huckstering," of the egoism of the rights of man, and so on.[106] "The Jewish Question" is essentially – beneath its form as a polemic with Bruno Bauer – a radical critique of "modern civil society," that is, of *bourgeois society* (in the present sense of the word) as a whole, in all its philosophical presuppositions, its political structures and its economic foundations:

> (a) Critique of the juridico-philosophical ideology of bourgeois liberalism, meaning "the rights of man" (property, etc.) separate from the rights of the citizen, that is, the rights of egoistic man considered as an isolated monad, turned in on himself, of man as member of civil-bourgeois society, in which the only bond of union is private interest, the conservation of "individual" (egoistic) property and rights.[107]

---

[105] *CW*, V, 455–456.
[106] Cf. the very precise comparison between Hess's article and "The Jewish Question" carried out by Cornu in *Karl Marx and Friedrich Engels*, Vol. II, pp. 323–328.
[107] *CW*, III, 162–164.

(b) Critique of purely political emancipation, which is the "revolution of civil society" that transforms political life into a mere means at the service of civil-bourgeois life and man as "citizen" into a servant of man as egoistic "bourgeois." Consequently, this emancipation cannot be confused with total, human emancipation. Critique also of the outcome of this revolution: the political state, the "heavenly," imaginary alienated life of the member of civil-bourgeois society.[108]

(c) Critique of civil-bourgeois society itself, as a sphere of egoism, of the war of all against all, which rends all the generic bonds between men and substitutes selfish need, decomposing the human world into a world of isolated individuals.[109]

(d) Critique of the economic foundations of the *bürgerliche Gesellschaft* and the political state: money (the essence of man separated from man, an alien entity which dominates alienated man and which he adores), "huckstering" (*Schacher*) and private property.[110]

True universal emancipation, *human emancipation*, is alone capable of overcoming the contradictions of civil-bourgeois society, because it is the *Aufhebung* (sublation) of the conflict between tangible individual existence and the generic existence of human beings. It is realized only "when man has recognized and organized his *forces propres* [own powers] as *social* forces, and consequently no longer separates social power from himself in the shape of *political power*." This total emancipation obviously requires the abolition of the economic foundations of civil society and political alienation: money, trade, private property.[111]

In what sense do these theses belong to "philosophical communism"? First of all, it is clear that both the critique of bourgeois society and the solutions contemplated are communist in character, even if what is stressed is circulation (money, trade, etc.) rather than production (something that was frequently observable among the French socialists themselves). Yet, behind the political and economic appearance, Marx's critique is essentially *philosophical*: the great sin of the rights of man, of political emancipation, of civil society, and of money is *egoism*. True, the problematic of egoism does not bear, in this text, the moralizing character given it by Feuerbach and Hess ("egoism" – "love"). Here, the point of departure is Hegel himself, who, in his *Philosophy of Law*, rejects the liberal point of view according to which "the interest of individuals as such becomes the end of their association" and stresses that "unification pure and simple is the true content and aim of the individual, and the

---

[108] Ibid., 151–154; 164–166.
[109] Ibid., 155, 173.
[110] Ibid., 154; 170–174.
[111] Ibid., 168.

individual's destiny is the living of a universal life."[112] This premise was adopted by Feuerbach and Hess, but "mixed" with the neo-Christian theme of "love," whereas Marx gives back to it its politico-philosophical meaning, stripped of all moralism:

> We see that the political emancipators go so far as to reduce citizenship [*Staatsbürgertum*], and the political community, to a mere *means* for maintaining the so-called of rights of man, and that therefore the egoistic *citoyen* [citizen] is declared to be the servant of egoistic *homme* [man], that the sphere in which man acts as a communal being is degraded to a level below the sphere in which he acts as a partial being.[113]

The conclusion which is forced upon us, but which may seem somewhat surprising, is that the critique of bourgeois society by Marx and, consequently, his communism, have directly Hegelian origins...

The abstract and "philosophical" character of "The Jewish Question" results not merely from what is *in* the text but, above all, from what is *not in* it. Like Hess, Marx assigns the task of human emancipation to no concrete class of society: the proletariat is absent, everywhere what is spoken of is "man." In this sense, the second article in the *Deutsch-Französische Jahrbücher*, the *Introduction to the Contribution to the Critique* was to constitute an important step forward along the path that led Marx from Feuerbachian humanism to revolutionary proletarian communism.

b) *Introduction to the Contribution to the Critique of Hegel's Philosophy of Law.*

The structure of this article is nothing but an illustrated description of Marx's politico-philosophical journey, that is to say, critical thinking in search of a concrete foundation, a "head" looking for a "body." The starting point is the moment when "criticism appears no longer as an end in itself [*Selbstweck*], *but*, only as a means," otherwise than as with Bauer – the moment when it becomes "criticism in *hand-to-hand combat.*"[114] Consequently, it turns to *practice*: the weapon of criticism becomes criticism with weapons, theory becomes a material force. To become such a force, however, critical theory needs a material foundation, a "passive element": it needs to penetrate the masses:

> The weapon of criticism cannot, of course, replace criticism by weapons, material force must be overthrown by material force; but theory also becomes a material force as soon as it has gripped [*ergreift*] the masses... For revolutions require a passive element, a *material* basis. Theory can be realized in a people only insofar as it is the realization of the needs of that people.[115]

---

[112] Hegel, *Philosophy of Right* (Oxford: 1965), p. 156.
[113] CW, III, 164.
[114] Ibid., 177–178.
[115] Ibid., 182–183.

In other words: "As the revolution then [the Reformation] began in the brain of the *monk*, so now it begins in the brain of the *philosopher*." "But will the enormous discrepancy between the demands of German thought and the answers of German reality be matched by a corresponding discrepancy between civil society and the state and between civil society and itself?"[116] The entire second half of the article tries to answer that question and to find in the contradictions of civil society a social class which can play the role of material foundation for revolutionary thought.

The first half appears to have been written in Kreuznach and its terminology is still vague ("mass," "people"), but the second bears already the mark of Paris; the word "proletariat" appears for the first time in Marx's writings. In the second half, he pursues his journey: revolutionary philosophy in search of material instruments turns first to the German bourgeoisie, but very soon finds that no "particular class" in Germany possesses "the consistency, the severity, the courage or the ruthlessness that could mark it out as the negative representative of society." What they lack, above all, is "that revolutionary audacity which flings at the adversary the defiant words: *I am nothing and I should be everything.*"[117] Here, Marx is summing up his experience in 1842 and comparing the cowardice of the German bourgeois with the boldness of the French Third Estate. The phrase quoted, "I am nothing . . .," is obviously an allusion to the opening words of Sieyès's "What is the Third Estate?" However, Marx does not confine himself to recording but tries to *explain* this difference between the French bourgeoisie in 1789 and that of Germany in 1844. The explanation he offers forms the first sketch of the theory of *permanent revolution*:

> Every section of civil society goes through a defeat before it has celebrated victory, develops its own limitations before it has overcome the limitations facing it, and asserts its narrow-hearted essence before it has been able to assert its magnanimous essence. Thus the very opportunity of a great role has on every occasion passed away before it is to hand, thus every class, once it begins the struggle against the class above it, is involved in the struggle against the class below it. Hence the princes are struggling against the monarchy, the bureaucrats against the nobility, and the bourgeois against them all, while the proletariat is already beginning to struggle against the bourgeoisie. No sooner does the middle class dare to think of emancipation from its own standpoint than the development of the social conditions and the progress of political theory pronounce that standpoint antiquated or at least problematic.[118]

Marx shows in this way the impossibility of a partial, "political" revolution. One cannot carry through a bourgeois revolution with a bourgeoisie which is not revolutionary: the German bourgeoisie suffers from historical belated-

---

[116] *Ibid.*
[117] *Ibid.*, 185.
[118] *Ibid.*, 185–186.

ness. Unlike its French equivalent in 1789, it is already threatened by the proletariat at the moment when it begins its struggle against the *ancien régime*. It becomes conservative and timid at the very instant when it ought to be revolutionary and bold. Consequently, "it is not the *radical* revolution, not the *general human* emancipation which is a utopian dream for Germany, but rather the partial, the *merely* political revolution, the revolution which leaves the pillars of the house standing." In Germany "universal emancipation is the *conditio sine qua* of any partial emancipation."[119]

These remarks, based on the disappointing experience of the alliance with the bourgeoisie in the *Rheinische Zeitung*, are almost prophetic of the events of 1848–1849. Marx was to repeat in the *Neue Rheinische Zeitung* his experience of 1842, but the timorous, hesitant and conciliatory behavior of the bourgeoisie, who were eventually to "betray" the popular movement, would compel him to revive in 1850 his 1844 theses on permanent revolution. The evolution from the *Rheinische Zeitung* to the "Introduction" was to be reproduced, more intensely and clearly, in the transition from the "democratic" themes of the *Neue Rheinische Zeitung* to the call for proletarian revolution in the *Circular* of the Communist League in March 1850.

In short, the German revolution would be human, universal – that is to say, communist (we have seen the meaning Marx gives to "human emancipation" in "The Jewish Question") or would not be at all. But such a revolution could be accomplished only by a class that was not a "particular class" of civil society, but a *universal* class, which had not privileges to defend, which had no other class beneath it, namely, the proletariat.

The essential characteristics of the proletarian condition, providing the basis for its emancipatory role, are set forth as the precise opposite of the bourgeoisie's characteristics:

(a) the proletariat is outside bourgeois society: it is "a class of civil society which is not a class of civil society";
(b) it possesses a universal character by its "universal suffering" because it "claims no *particular* right" and because it does not stand in "one-sided antithesis" to the consequences but in "all-round antithesis to the premises of the German state";
(c) it is "a class with *radical* chains"; "only a revolution of radical needs can be a radical revolution"; the proletariat, "in a word, is the *complete loss* of man and hence can win itself only through the *complete rewinning* of man."[120]

---

[119] Ibid., 184, 186. Cf. also p. 187. "In Germany emancipation from the *Middle Ages* is possible only as emancipation from the *partial* victories over the Middle Ages as well. In Germany *no* kind of bondage can be broken without breaking every kind of bondage... The emancipation of the German is the emancipation of the human being."
[120] Ibid., 186; CW, III, 183.

Young Marx's journey had reached its end. Critical philosophy, no longer considering itself to be an end in itself, had turned to practice. It sought a concrete foundation, thought it had found this in the bourgeoisie, but was soon disappointed. It had found at last in the proletariat the universal emancipatory class and its material weapons.

The example provided by the French proletariat was decisive for the final stage of Marx's evolution. It served as a model that he "projected" into German reality, believing that the workers' revolution in France would give the signal for the uprising of the German proletariat: "the day of German resurrection will be proclaimed by the ringing call of the Gallic cock."[121]

The problematic of the relations between proletariat and philosophy in the "Introduction" is the expression of this journey, that is, the interpretation given by a Young Hegelian of his path to communism and of the general relations between revolutionary thought and the masses. For Marx the revolution is born in the philosopher's head before, in a second stage, it "takes hold" of the worker masses. He forgets that he would not have been able to announce "the day of German resurrection" in communist terms if he had not already heard "the ringing call of the Gallic cock" – in other words, that neither he, nor Hess, nor Engels, nor Bakunin would have become what they were in 1844 if French socialism and the French workers' movement had not existed. And that was what Marx himself wrote a little later in *The German Ideology*.

In the face of this *active* philosophical thinking, which *takes hold* of the masses, which *strikes* like lightning the "ingenuous soil of the people,"[122] the proletariat is looked at only in terms of its suffering and needs, as a "material *foundation*," as the "*passive* element" of the revolution, which serves as philosophy's material weapon, *letting itself* be taken hold of and "thunderstruck" by philosophical thought.

This perspective and this terminology show clearly the extent to which the article in question still belongs in the universe of Left Hegelianism and "philosophical communism." It is a work in which Feuerbach's influence is very noticeable, and this needs to be stressed in order that the full political significance of the break with Feuerbach in 1845 may be appreciated. A key phrase in the text enables us to understand the role of Feuerbach's influence in the formulation of this theme of the "passive proletariat": "the head of this emancipation [of the human being] is philosophy, its heart is the proletariat."[123]

---

[121] *Ibid.*, 187.
[122] *Ibid.* "And once the lightning of thought has squarely struck this ingenuous soil of the people the emancipation of the *Germans* into *human* beings will have begun."
[123] *Ibid.*

We find, in fact, in Feuerbach's *Preliminary Theses for the Reform of Philosophy* (1842), a work greeted with enthusiasm by the Young Hegelians generally and Marx in particular, a whole theory of the contrast between the *head*, which is active, spiritual, idealistic, political, free, and the *heart*, which is passive, sensitive, materialistic, social, suffering, and "necessitous" (subject to its needs). This contradiction becomes, at the philosophical level, that between *German* metaphysics and *French* materialism: it has to be transcended by a synthesis within the "new philosophy" of "Gallo-German blood."[124]

Why is this Feuerbachian heart passive? This question enables us to understand the passivity of the proletariat, the heart of the revolution, in Marx's writings. According to Feuerbach:

1. The heart is prey to passions (*Leidenschaft*) and sufferings (*Leiden*), to which it is subject in a *passive* (*Leiden*) way. (I have already mentioned the double meaning of the word).
2. The heart has *needs*, that is to say, it depends on a being outside itself. Its essential object, which defines it, is the other. The thinking being, on the contrary, "relates to itself, being its own object, having its essence in itself."[125]
3. The heart is sensitive, that is, receptive, contemplative. Feuerbach even speaks of the "feminine principle of sensual contemplation," in contrast to the "masculine principle of thought."[126]
4. The heart is "materialist." "The essential determination of matter, as distinguished from the mind, from the activity of thinking" is "the determination making it a passive being."[127]

The Paris proletariat appeared to Marx at the beginning of 1844 as the concrete expression, the "incarnation," of the Feuerbachian partner of German philosophical thinking: the "French" and "materialistic" heart, with its "needs" and its "suffering," counterpose to spiritual activity by an essential attribute – *passivity*.

To appreciate the full significance of this passivity, we need to notice that, for Feuerbach, this does not rule out *practice*, "passive practice," which must not be confused with *self-activity*, the exclusive right of the mind, because it is mere material *movement*, pure response to extreme stimulation, an *egoistic* reaction to sense-impressions (pleasure, pain) and needs. For this reason Feuerbach writes in *The Essence Of Christianity* that egoism is "the most prac-

---

[124] In *Anekdota zur neuesten deutschen Philosophie und Publizistik*, ed. Ruge (Zurich: 1843), Vol. 2, p. 76.
[125] Feuerbach, *Principles of the Philosophy of the Future* (New York: 1966), p. 8.
[126] The second quotation is in *Das Wesen des Christianismus* (Berlin: 1973), pp. 508–10. The first is a misquotation from *ibid.*, p. 475.
[127] Feuerbach, *Principles*, p. 32.

tical principle in the world,"¹²⁸ and Marx declares, in "The Jewish Question" that "practical need, the rationale of which is self-interest, is passive."¹²⁹

The Feuerbachian thesis had an implicit political corollary which was developed by Ruge: the social sphere is egoistic and practical, politics is spiritual and active. Already in his articles in the *Deutsch-Französische Jahrbücher*, Marx rejected this corollary, but his break with Ruge was not yet complete because he accepted its premises. It would not be till the *Vorwärts* article that he abandoned the idea of the "passive proletariat." This final break with Ruge led at once to Marx's settlement of accounts with Feuerbach. A few months later, he was to write his "Eleven Theses" and *The German Ideology*, in which he would overcome the Feuerbachian dilemma of "passive practice" – "spiritual activity" – through the category of *revolutionary praxis*.

Modern interpreters of this text are not always very aware of the distance that separates it from the writings of 1845–1846. They situate the great break between 1843 and the appearance of the *Deutsch-Französische Jahrbücher*, and ascribe a "Marxist" meaning to the articles in the latter. From the standpoint of the theory of workers' self-emancipation, however, the truth is rather the opposite of this. There is a certain continuity between the manuscripts and letters of 1843 and the *Jahrbücher* – the big jump comes at the end of 1844, *after* Marx has made direct contact with the workers' movement – which enables us to give a sociological explanation of the "leap." Some examples show us that the interpretation which assimilates the "Introduction" to the later, "Marxist" works (*The Holy Family*, *The German Ideology*, etc.) ends by making Marx say *precisely the contrary* of what he writes.

Auguste Cornu, though he realizes very well the "transitional" character of this article, nevertheless writes, in summing up Marx's thought: "What is lacking in Germany, for this revolution to be accomplished, is a material foundation, a revolutionary mass which, *penetrating itself* with the radical criticism of the existing state of affairs, sets this to work." (My italics – M. L.)¹³⁰ In a footnote, Cornu translates Marx's own phrase thus: "Theory itself becomes a material force when *it penetrates* the masses." The difference between the two versions is the difference that separates the Marx of the *Jahrbücher* from the post-1844 Marx. For the one, the activity is on the part of philosophical criticism, which penetrates, takes hold of the masses; for the other, it is the masses themselves who, by their revolutionary activity, attain consciousness, become communists, and appropriate the theory for themselves. Cornu's "summary" is "Marxist," but Marx's text is not yet Marxist.

---

[128] Feuerbach, *The Essence of Christianity*, p. 114.
[129] *CW*, III, 173.
[130] Cornu, *Karl Marx*, op. cit., I, p. 282.

As for M. Rubel, whose merit it is to emphasize the importance of the idea of self-emancipation in Marx's work, he falls into the same trap when he wants to find this concept in the "Introduction," regarding which he writes:

> What is most striking in this conception of the workers' movement that Marx sets out is the absence of any allusion to a *political party* which would represent the class consciousness of the proletariat. Here is a precious pointer to the way we should understand the ideas that Marx was to formulate later concerning the proletarian party. He will *never* say that any party can play the role of "head" or "brain" of the working class, with the latter reduced to being the organ for executing the decisions of a sovereign authority.[131]

Now, what is most striking in this commentary of Rubel's is the absence of any allusion to the fact that for Marx in this article there *is* an "authority" which plays *precisely* the "role of head and brain" of the proletariat: namely, philosophy (or the philosophers). Does Marx not write, *in so many words*, that philosophy is the *head* of the revolution, that this revolution is born in the *brain* of the philosopher, and that, for this "authority," the proletariat is nothing but a "material weapon," that is to say, an executive organ?

Actually, there is a remarkable analogy between the themes of the "Introduction" and the conceptions of the most brilliant ideologist of the theory of "the party as head of the working class," namely, the Lenin of 1902–1904. Like Marx in 1844, Lenin in *What Is To Be Done?* writes that socialism is born in the brain of the intellectuals and has subsequently to penetrate the working class by an "introduction from without." Here, the party plays the same role as the philosophers in Marx's work. The images themselves are similar: the "lightning" of revolutionary thought becomes in Lenin the "spark," a striking image which assumes the presence of a center of vigorous energy, kindling an inert mass which provides the "foundation," the "matter" for the liberating fire. This vision, which was to be abandoned by Marx and by Lenin in the light of the concrete development of the revolutionary workers' movement, is highly attractive because it is not wholly false. It is merely partial,

---

[131] Rubel, *op. cit.*, p. 102. I can understand this type of proceeding all the better for having myself attempted it. Because my first hypothesis located the fundamental break before the "Introduction," I sought in vain for

(a) proofs of contact between Marx and the Paris workers' movement earlier than February 1844, and
(b) a "Marxist" meaning for the inconvenient phrases in the "Introduction."

Having failed in both tasks, I realized that I had to reconsider the hypothesis itself, and to locate the break *after* the *Deutsch-Französische Jahrbücher*.

forgetting the dialectical play between theory and the masses. Coherent revolutionary thought cannot appear otherwise than from out of the problems, aspirations, and struggles of the class itself. Employing the same image, let us say that lightning can burst forth only from the clashing of clouds loaded with storm . . .

Chapter Two
The Theory of Communist Revolution (1844–1846)

I. Marx and the workers' movement (1844–1845)

The traditional conception of the relations between Marx's theory and the workers' movement of his time is that which Karl Kautsky set forth in 1908 in his pamphlet *Die historische Leistung von Karl Marx* ("Karl Marx's Historical Achievement"): Marx and Engels brought about "union between socialism and the workers' movement," "socialism" being understood as the set of utopias conceived on the fringe of the working class and "workers' movement" as the purely corporative, demand-making activity of the workers' organizations. Starting from these premises, Kautsky and Victor Adler had no difficulty in showing that "socialism was introduced into the working class from without." True, Kautsky acknowledged that in the 1840s there were already workers who were socialists, but, he said, these workers had merely taken up bourgeois socialism.[1] However, this was not the view of Engels, who, in his 1890 preface to the *Manifesto* wrote: "socialism in 1847 signified a bourgeois movement, communism a working-class movement." The socialists were

> people who stood outside the labor movement and who looked for support rather to the "educated" classes. The section of the working class, however, which demanded a radical reconstruction of society, convinced that mere political revolutions were not enough, then called itself *communist* ... And since we were very decidedly of the opinion as early as then that

---

[1] K. Kautsky, *Die historische Leistung von Karl Marx* (Berlin: 1919).

"the emancipation of the workers must be the act of the working class itself" we could have no hesitation as to which of the two names to choose [for the *Manifesto*].[2]

Thus, according to Engels, the decisive political features of Marxist communism – social revolution and self-emancipation by the proletariat – had as their point of departure not "bourgeois" socialism but *workers'* groups and tendencies.

Indeed, it was not among the various utopian-socialist sects (Saint-Simonians, Owenites, Fourierists, Cabetists, etc.) or among the "state socialists" (Louis Blanc), who rejected the idea of an egalitarian revolution and looked for social changes through bourgeois philanthropy or the miraculous intervention of a king, that Marx would have been able to discover the germs of his conception of communist revolution. This conception was the product not of a "union between socialism and the workers' movement," but of *a dialectical synthesis which started from the various experiences of the workers' movement itself* in the 1840s. These experiences were not created by the influence of "bourgeois" socialism but resulted above all from traditions and activities peculiar to the working class.

I shall try here to provide not a history of the workers' movement in the 1840s but a schematic picture of the tendencies in that movement which served as the "social settings" for Marx's ideological evolution. Consequently, I shall concern myself particularly with those groups or movements which Marx knew, either directly or indirectly, as they were described and defended in the works of historians and ideologists that were, either certainly or probably, read by Marx. In other words, I shall try to depict the workers' organizations and ideologies *as Marx saw them* in 1844–1845. As I pointed out in my introduction to this book, the setting of a political doctrine is never given us in "the raw state." What is essential for understanding, for instance, the role of the workers' communism of 1840–1844 in the formation of Marx's theory of revolution is not what might be written in 1970 about that communism, but what was thought about it by men like Dézamy, Heine, L. von Stein, authors who were read, analyzed, and criticized by Marx.

a) *The communist secret societies in Paris (1840–1844)*

There can be no doubt that Marx not only knew about the secret societies of the Paris workers but personally attended meetings of communist artisans. In 1860, he wrote in *Herr Vogt*:

> During my first stay in Paris, I established personal contact with the leaders of the "League" living there, as well as with the leaders of the majority

---

[2] *CW*, XXVII, 60, 59–60.

of the secret French workers' associations, without, however, becoming a member of any of them.³

But his testimony of the year 1844 is much more precise and shows the deep impression made on him by these workers' meetings, the atmosphere of which differed radically from that of the meetings of the "cowardly" shareholders of the *Rheinische Zeitung*. In a letter of August 11, 1844, to Feuerbach, Marx voices his admiration unequivocally:

> You would have to attend one of the meetings of the French workers to appreciate the pure freshness, the nobility which burst forth from these toil-worn men . . . It is among these "barbarians" of our civilized society that history is preparing the practical element for the emancipation of mankind.⁴

What was the situation of the Paris secret societies in 1844? All contemporary evidence agrees in indicating the year 1840 as the starting point of large-scale diffusion of communist ideas in the Paris proletariat.⁵

---

³ *CW*, XVII, 79. What were the French secret societies with which Marx made contact during his residence in Paris? This question can be answered only with suggestions and hypotheses. For example, it is probable that Marx knew the editors of the communist journal *La Fraternité*, because this, with *La Réforme*, was the only one to protest against his expulsion from Paris. In its issue of March 1845, *La Fraternité* noted that "the Prefect of Police has just expelled several German socialist writers who had ceaselessly preached, in the journal *Vorwärts*, the holy alliance between our two peoples. Among them is the communist philosopher M. Charles Marx, of Trèves [Trier]." There is something else to support this hypothesis. The periodical mentioned is quoted, quite favorably, in a letter from Engels to Marx dated September 16, 1846:

> At the *Fraternité* there has been a tremendous dispute between materialists and spiritualists . . . But that has not stopped the *Fraternité* from publishing a very nice article on the various stages of civilization and their ability to continue developing in the direction of communism. *CW*, XXXVIII, 66.

Marx's choice of *La Fraternité* is very significant because this journal brought together the *materialist communists* and the *followers of Flora Tristan*, that is, the two trends among the workers that were closest to his own conceptions and whose union in *La Fraternité* foreshadows, to some extent, the synthesis of these tendencies that Marx was to accomplish (while transcending them).

⁴ *CW*, III, 355. The same attitude is apparent in a famous paragraph of the *Manuscripts of 1844*, probably composed at the same time as the letter to Feuerbach:

> When communist *artisans* associate with one another, theory, propaganda, etc., is their first end. But at the same time, as a result of this association, they acquire a new need – the need for society – and what appears as a means becomes an end. In this practical process the most brilliant results are to be observed whenever French socialist workers [*ouvriers*] are seen together . . . The brotherhood of man is no mere phrase with them, and the nobility of man shines upon us from their work-hardened bodies. *CW*, III, 313.

⁵ This year saw the Belleville Banquet, organized by Dézamy and J.-J. Pillot, the

The opinions which probably caught Marx's attention were those of Heine and Lorenz von Stein, which marked the upsurge of communism after 1840 and its character as a "mass movement." Heine, whose friendship with Marx during his stay in Paris is well-known, wrote in a correspondent's report to the *Augsburger Zeitung* of December 11, 1841, that, in Paris, there were "400,000 hard fists which await only the signal to put into effect the idea of absolute equality which smolders in their hard heads." and that "communist propaganda uses a language that everyone understands: the elements of this universal language are as simple as hunger, desire and death."[6] In another report, published on June 15, 1843, Heine even speaks of the communists as "the only party in France that deserves positive attention"! And he adds: "sooner or later, the whole scattered family of the Saint-Simonians and the entire headquarters of the Fourierists will join the growing army of communism."[7]

What with Heine remained a poet's intuition was developed as a serious sociological analysis by Lorenz von Stein in his 1842 work *Der Socialismus und Communismus des heutigen Frankreichs*. Marx probably did not study Stein's book until 1844–1845. Before then, we find no mention of the work in his writings, nor any trace of influence by its themes. The first reference to Stein appears in *The Holy Family*. In *The German Ideology*, it figures in several passages of the chapter directed against Grün, where Stein's book appears in a rather sympathetic light: "Grün's fabrication is on a much lower level than the work by Stein, who at least tried to explain the connection between socialist literature and the real development of French society."[8]

---

first independent and public manifestation of the "Communist Party." It was in 1840, too, that the society of "Egalitarian Workers" was formed, made up exclusively of workers and with a clearly communist program. In 1840, furthermore, a real "general strike" took place in Paris, the "ringleaders" of which seem to have been "inspired by communist ideas." Cf. De la Hodde, *Histoire des sociétés secrètes et du parti républicain de 1830 à 1848* (Paris: Julien, Lanie et Cie, 1850), p. 278.

According to the *agent provocateur* de la Hodde, who had infiltrated the secret societies, "about 1840 Paris began to be seriously infected by communism." Bourgeois liberal writers like Duvergier de Hauranne observed, with alarm, in 1841, that "although, only a few years ago, insurrections took place in the name of the Republic, today their slogan is common ownership of property." And democratic publicists such as Thoré claimed that "nearly all the workers in Paris, Lyons, Rouen, etc., adhere more or less to the sect of communists or egalitarians." Cf. De la Hodde, *Histoire des sociétés secrètes*, p. 267; Talmon, *Political Messianism* (London: Secker and Warburg, 1960), p. 391; Thoré, *La vérité sur le parti démocratique* (Paris: Desessart, 1840), p. 22.

[6] Heine, *Lutezia*, in *Mein Wertvollstes Vermächtnis* (Zurich: Manesse Verlag, 1950), p. 256.
[7] *Ibid.*, p. 278.
[8] *CW*, V, 492.

Stein's great merit, in fact, which brought upon him criticisms from the "philosophical communists" like Hess, was to have shown French communism not as an abstract "principle" but as a concrete historical movement, the expression of the revolutionary aspirations of a new class – the modern proletariat, this element which is "dangerous not only by its numbers and by the courage it has often demonstrated but also by its consciousness of unity and the feeling it has that it can realize its plans only through revolution."[9]

According to Stein, after the revolt in 1839 of the Society of the Seasons (Blanqui, Barbès), which was thoroughly repudiated by the bourgeoisie and "the grocers," a new period began

> which was marked off, outwardly, from those preceding it by the resolute separation of the republicans from everything bearing the name of communism, and, inwardly, by the rapid progress made by the communist movement, from 1839, in all parts of France and in all the propertyless classes, whereas previously it had been shut up in the narrow circle of the associations. And one can rightly say that whereas before this time communism appeared in connection with the associations, today the associations appear in connection with communism. This gives the latter an effective importance which, already, is denied by no-one. All the questions and problems [of communism – M. L.] are no longer the business of a small select section of this social class, listened to by the rest with the fanaticism of believers: everyone now considers himself competent to think for himself and judge for himself. The communist ideas and theories have found their way into all the workshops and all the workers' dwellings and agitation about the future has affected even the least significant of them . . . It is as though, since the last revolt, the proletariat has felt that, from now on, it is on its own and must cope with its hard tasks through thinking together.[10]

For Stein the first overt symptom of this development was the attempt on the King's life made by the communist worker Darmès on October 15, 1840:

> Here things came out into the open; the revolutionary seed had taken – the proletarian thought, the proletarian acted, and without any impulse or influence from the democrats or liberals . . . This entry on the stage by the independent proletariat had until then been considered impossible, even by the conservatives and the government . . . One could no longer hide the fact: the people itself had begun to live a life of its own [*eigenthümlich*], creating new associations, dreaming of new revolutions and daring to raise its hand against the life of the King himself. Darmès belonged to the society of

---

[9] L. von Stein, *Der Socialismus und Communismus des heutigen Frankreichs* (Leipzig: O. Wigand, 1848), p. 9.
[10] Stein, *op. cit.*, p. 507.

"Egalitarian Workers": this society existed, it was fanatical, and perhaps it was numerous and powerful.[11]

We thus see appearing in Stein's analyses *certain key ideas the influence of which on Marx's transition from "philosophic" communism to "proletarian" communism must not be underestimated: the revolutionary tendency of the proletariat, its consciousness of unity, the communist movement as independent expression of the worker masses* (and not of a small minority). These themes were entirely absent from the "utopian" or "philosophical" socialist literature. Marx had to discover them through reading Stein's book and *through his direct contacts with the workers' societies.*

The secret societies in Paris had, in fact, since 1839–1840 undergone fundamental changes, in the sense of a rise in their ideological level and also in the proletarian character of their membership. We must, of course, reject the distorted presentation given by the police reports on the communist societies ("lairs of regicides," of "criminals," etc.). An entire work of education went on in the societies' meetings, effected through reading, commentary, and discussion of the journals and pamphlets of the socialists, Babouvists, and communists, work which subsequently had repercussions in the workshops.[12]

The tremendous proliferation of communist literature after 1840 did not take place outside the working class; workers participated in the editing of communist journals (e.g., *l'Humanitaire* in 1841), and the communist ideologists were in close contact with some of the workers' secret societies.[13] Along with this striving for ideological self-education, this "thirst for knowledge" on the part of the communist workers which struck all observers, starting with Marx himself, who mentions it several times in *The Holy Family*, went a process of "proletarianization" in the social makeup of the secret societies.[14]

---

[11] Stein, *op. cit.*, pp. 509, 510, 511.

[12] Cf. Tchernoff, *Le Parti républicain sous la Monarchie de Juillet* (Paris: A. Pedone, 1901), pp. 370–371. Heinrich Heine lists the books most widely read among the Paris workers: "... new publications of the speeches of old Robespiérre, pamphlets by Marat in two-sou editions, Cabet's *History of the Revolution*, Cormenin's venomous lampoons, Buonarotti's *The Conspiracy of Babeuf*." Heine, *Lutezia*, April 30, 1840, in *Mein Wertvollstes Vermächtnis*, p. 280.

[13] The most interesting example of this is provided by the Revolutionary Communist Society, made up entirely of workers, which had broken away from the Society of Egalitarian Workers because of the latter's blind discipline and, above all, because of the *lack of discussion* within it. A direct link was very soon established between the new society and the materialist communists Dézamy, May, Savary, Charassin, Pillot, and Lahautière. The leaders of the Revolutionary Communists were among the 1,200 invitees at the communist banquet in Belleville organized by Dézamy and Pillot. Cf. De la Hodde, *La Naissance de la République* (Paris: 1850), p. 19.

[14] After the laws of 1834 banning the republican societies ("Society of the Rights of Man," etc.) the period of secret associations began. These were gradually abandoned by the bourgeois or "moderate" elements. In the first of such societies, that of "The

It must, however, be kept in mind that the "proletarians" who were members of these secret societies were journeymen artisans rather than industrial workers.[15]

At the ideological level the two predominant trends in the secret societies were neo-Babouvism (Buonarroti) and "materialist" communism (Dézamy).

Families" (1833–1836), formed by Blanqui from the ruins of "The Rights of Man," we still find groups that belong to the middle classes. In the "Society of the Seasons" (1837–1839: Blanqui, Barbès, Martin Bernard), soldiers and students were excluded from membership, being considered suspect, and the society's composition was wholly working class. According to De la Hodde, "at that time the membership of the secret societies was almost completely renewed: instead of drawing recruits form the bad elements of the bourgeoisie, they took their members now exclusively from the dregs of the people" – the class which, he adds, has "this big advantage that it has nothing to lose in an upheaval." Tchernoff, *Le Parti républicain*, p. 383; De la Hodde, *Histoire des societés secrètes*, pp. 217–218.

This proletarian character was even more clearly manifested in the Society of Egalitarian Workers, not only in the association's name and the names of its hierarchical subdivisions ("Trades," "Workshops," "Factories," instead of "Weeks," "Months," and "Seasons") but also in the program, which contained typically working-class demands (wages fixed by law, mutual schools, etc.) along with the traditional Babouvist formulations (egalitarian society, popular dictatorship), and its activity linked with mass movements such as the 1840 strike. G. Sencier, *Le Babouvisme après Babeuf (1830–1848)* (Paris: M. Rivière, 1912), pp. 270–271.

[15] I have tried to draw up a table showing the social and occupational composition of the membership of the communist associations between 1838 and 1847, a table based on the following groups:

a) Political prisoners in Mont St-Michel arrested between 1838 and 1841;
b) Known leaders of the Egalitarian Workers and the Revolutionary Communists;
c) Invitees at the Belleville Communist banquet (1840);
d) Founders of the journal *l'Humanitaire* arrested in 1841;
e) Members of the society of "materialist communists" arrested in 1847.

Among the 67 communists thus assembled, 53 (79 percent) had an artisan background: 9 shoemakers or boot-makers, 6 cabinet-makers or carpenters, 5 printers or typographers, 4 tailors, 3 founders, 2 jewellers, 3 mechanics, 2 hatters, 2 building workers, 2 copper-workers, 2 hosiers, 2 hairdressers, 2 "workers" (trade unknown), 1 cardboard-maker, 1 maker of inlaid ware, 1 locksmith, 1 draughtsman, 1 courier, 1 gilder, 1 cook, 1 clockmaker, 1 bookbinder; 14 (21 percent) belonged to the middle classes: 5 merchants, 3 journalists, 2 students, 1 lawyer, 1 officer, 1 manufacturer, 1 professor. The sources for this table are: A. Zevaes, "Une révolution manquée" [The insurrection of May 12, 1839], *Nouvelle Revue Critique*, 1933; Sencier, *Le Babouvisme après Babeuf. Le premier banquet communiste, le 1er juillet 1840*). If we compare these figures with those obtained by A. Soboul for the "Babouvists" of Paris (based on the Paris subscribers to Babeuf's *Tribun du Peuple*), we get some indications of the difference and the continuity between the Babouvism of the year IV and the "neo-Babouvism" of 1840. According to Soboul, artisans and shopkeepers made up 72.3 percent of the subscribers to the *Tribun du Peuple*, minor office-workers and civil servants 9.5 percent, traders 7.4 percent, manufacturers 3.1 percent, and members of the liberal professions 7.4 percent. (A. Soboul, "Personnel sectionnaire et personnel babouviste," in *Babeuf, Buonarroti* (for the bicentenary of their birth), Societé

Marx probably studied Buonarroti's book on *The Conspiracy of Babeuf* in or around 1844. He mentions Babeuf and Buonarroti for the first time in *The Holy Family*, and in his notebook we find this list in a preparatory outline for his book: "Morelly, Mably, Babeuf, Buonarroti," alongside *"Cercle social*, Hébert, Leroux, Leclerc." Also, in this notebook we find, at the head of a list of books to be translated into German, drawn up in 1845: "Buonarroti, 2B" ("2 Bände," i.e., two volumes).[16]

Babouvism brought into the 19th century the features given it by Buonarroti in his work published in Brussels in 1828. The central themes of this book, which had a profound effect on the revolutionary movement before 1848, and even after (through Blanqui) were:

(a) Taking of power by an insurrectionary conspiracy of a secret society. The decisive role is allotted to the enlightened élite of conspirators, and a victorious putsch is substituted for the revolutionary experience of the masses. It may be that Buonarotti put into the movement of the Equals some features of his own conspiratorial activity in the 19th century, thereby giving it a more "sectarian" character than it had had in reality.[17] However, it was in this form that Babouvism was spread in the workers' movement and the secret societies.

(b) The necessity of a "revolutionary dictatorship" of the Jacobin type after the victory of the insurrection. In Buonarroti's words:

> The experience of the French Revolution and, more especially, the troubles and waverings of the National Convention have sufficiently proved, it seems to me, that a people whose opinions have been formed under a regime of inequality and despotism is poorly capable, at the beginning of a regenerative revolution, of choosing by its votes the men who must lead and consummate this revolution. That hard task can be carried out only by wise and courageous citizens who, full of love for their country and mankind, and having long studied the causes of public evils, have shaken off the common prejudices and vices, surpassed the enlightenment of their

---

des études Robespierristes, Nancy, pp. 91–92. But if we remove from the first group the "merchant" shopkeepers, the percentage of artisans and small shopkeepers becomes 60.6 percent, whereas among the communists of the 1840s it reached 79 percent. The reasons for this change are these: the *"sans-culotterie"* of the 18th century was beginning to break up; political expression for the "grocers," the merchants, the shopkeepers, small traders, and minor office-workers was provided by *La Réforme* and Ledru-Rollin, while for the journeymen artisans and workers it was provided by communism. This must not cause us to forget the relative continuity between the two phenomena – continuity both of social basis among the artisans and of "Jacobin-egalitarian" ideology, between 1796 and 1840.

[16] "Marxens Notizbuch," MEGA, BD5, 1 Abt. (1932), pp. 549–550.

[17] C. Mazauric, *Babeuf et la Conspiration pour l'Egalité*, Ed. Sociales (Paris: 1962), p. 180.

contemporaries and, despising gold and vulgar grandeur, have identified their happiness with becoming immortal through ensuring the triumph of equality.[18]

This Jacobin conception of dictatorship has as its philosophical presupposition the thesis of the mechanistic materialists of the 18th century, for whom "circumstances or education shape men's character and opinions," with an implicit political corollary: the masses will remain corrupt and plunged in obscurantism so long as present circumstances have not been changed – hence the need for a revolutionary force *above* the masses, a Legislator, an Incorruptible, or, for Buonarroti, an élite of "wise and courageous citizens" who have "surpassed the enlightenment of their contemporaries" and have "shaken off the common prejudices and vices."

The idea of the secret society and that of the dictatorship of the "wise citizens" are the two sides of the same ideological superstructure, which is situated, as I have already shown, between the bourgeois myth of the savior from on high and the project of workers' self-emancipation.[19]

> (c) The aspiration to an egalitarian revolution which abolishes private property and ends the reign of the rich. With the development of industry in France this aspiration evolved substantially between Babeuf's time and 1848. "Sharing" communism gradually gave way to "communitarian" communism and the contrast between "poor" and "rich" was replaced by that between "proletarians" and "bourgeois." In fact, while egalitarian revolution had been the centuries-old dream of the propertyless masses, from the end of the Middle Ages, it was only in the 19th century, with the appearance of the industrial proletariat, that egalitarianism was wholly identified with society's appropriation of the means of production.

The second trend observable in the secret societies and the vanguard of the workers was that of "materialist communism," represented by Dézamy, Pillot, Gay, Charavay, May, and others, and expressed in popular pamphlets and in ephemeral journals persecuted by the police (*l'Egalitaire, le Communautaire, l'Humanitaire, la Fraternité*).

We have seen how interested Marx was, in 1843, in Dézamy and the tendency he represented. In *The Holy Family*, Dézamy and Gay are mentioned as "the more scientific French communists,"[20] and in the plan for this book

---

[18] Buonarroti, *Conspiration pour l'Egalité, dite de Babeuf*, Ed. Sociales (Paris: 1957). p. 111.
[19] The neo-Babouvism of the 1840s represented, in this sense, an advance compared with Babeuf and Buonarroti. The Jacobin dictatorship was no longer considered the model for the revolutionary dictatorship. Blanqui, Dézamy, and Pillot took Hébert and the Hébertists as their models rather than Robespierre and the Jacobins
[20] *CW*, IV, 131.

which is in Marx's notebook there are references to "Dézamy, Gay" and to *"Fraternité, l'Egalitaire, l'Humanitaire,"* while, in the list of books included in this notebook, Marx has noted, after "Buonarroti, 2B," "Dézamy Code, id. Lamennais réfuté, id. *l'Egalitaire 2 Hefte."*[21]

Dézamy's work sought to transcend the opposition between conspiratorial Babouvism and Cabet's "peaceful propaganda." From this standpoint, his most interesting book is *Calomnies et politique de M. Cabet* (1842), which Marx quoted in his article of January 12, 1843, in the *Rheinische Zeitung*.

In this pamphlet, Dézamy opposes to the neo-Christian dream of a general conciliation of the classes through "conversion" of the rich to communism, as preached by Cabet (an ideology which put him close to the "bourgeois" utopian socialists), independent *action* by *proletarian* communism: "It is a capital error to believe that co-operation by the bourgeoisie is indispensable for the triumph of the community." And he adds, criticizing Cabet's refusal to participate in the Belleville communist banquet: "You refused to attend this banquet ... You seemed from the start very unhappy because the proletarians were allowing themselves to raise the communist flag on their own, without having at their head some *bourgeois*, some *well-known name."*[22] His main concern is, in contrast to the "fraternization between rich and poor" proposed by the Icarians, that *proletarian unity* be consolidated: "It is more than ever necessary to lose no time in finding common ground on which the proletariat can unite and, first and foremost, before proceeding further, establish its own unity."[23]

However, he still had something in common with Cabet, namely, unlimited confidence in propaganda: "That is why I will never stop crying: 'propaganda, propaganda, propaganda.' Truth and propaganda, and liberation will be won."[24] He repeated this theme in all the speeches, as, for example, the toast at the Belleville banquet: "Citizens! The shortest road to arrive at common well-being is *egalitarian education*: that is our firm conviction."[25]

Finally, Dézamy resolutely condemned the myth of the savior and the Jacobin dictatorship (which Cabet, who thought that he, too, was a second Christ, eulogized). Contrasting with Robespierre the "teachers of real equality" – the *Cercle Social*, Chaumette, Hébert, supporters of "materialism and the abolition of property" – Dézamy stresses that "the salvation of all can never depend on a man, whoever he may be, but only on a principle."[26] The book ends

---

[21] "Marxens Notizbuch," *op. cit.*, pp. 549–550.
[22] T. Dézamy, *Calomnies et politique de M. Cabet. Réfutations par des faits et par sa biographie* (Paris: Prévost, 1842), pp. 4, 8.
[23] *Ibid.*, p. 3.
[24] *Ibid.*, p. 37.
[25] *Le Premier Banquet communiste*, 1er juillet 1840, p. 5.
[26] Dézamy, *op. cit.*, pp. 38, 41, 42, 45.

with a warning both passionate and prophetic:

> Proletarians! It is to you that I address these reflections, to you who, a thousand times already, have been *betrayed, sold, handed over, slandered, tortured and mocked* by alleged saviors! If you again submit to the cult of individuals, expect to experience once more cruel and poignant illusions!!![27]

b) *The League of the Just in Paris*

It was probably Dr. G. Mäurer, who resided, like Marx and Ruge, at No. 38 rue Vaneau, or else Dr. Ewerbeck, who introduced Marx to the League of the Just, whose principal leaders in Paris they were. Marx's first contacts with the artisans of the League took place in April or May 1844. The first explicit evidence of this that we have is dated May 19: in a letter to his mother, Ruge wrote that Marx "has merely won over him (Herwegh) and the German artisans so as to have a party and people at his service."[28] In another letter, dated July 9, to his friend Fleischer, he mentions the fact again, with a different "explanation," no less "penetrating" than the first: "Marx has thrown himself into the German communism of this city – from sociability, that is, because it is not possible that he can find their dreary activity politically important."[29] As for Marx himself, the only evidence we have, apart from a brief mention in *Herr Vogt*, is his letter of August 11, 1844, to Feuerbach, which shows us both his sympathy and his reservations regarding the communist artisans of the League: "I must not forget to emphasize the theoretical merits of the German artisans in Switzerland, London and Paris. The German artisan is still, however, too much of an artisan."[30] Finally, there is a police report of February 1, 1845, which confirms the "active presence" of Marx in the meetings of the Paris section of the League.[31]

The German societies in Paris evolved in parallel with the French republican associations, with which they were always in close contact.[32] Founded in

---

[27] *Ibid.*, p. 47.
[28] Ruge, *Briefwechsel und Tagebuchblätter aus den Jahre 1825–1888*, P. Nerrlich (Berlin: Weidmannsche Buchhandlung, 1886), p. 350.
[29] *Ibid.*, p. 359.
[30] *CW*, III, 355.
[31] In Cornu, *op. cit.*, III, p. 7.
[32] The year 1830 saw the creation in Paris of the *Pressverein*, an association of the German press in exile, which was linked with the French "Association of the Patriotic Press." The *Pressverein* became soon afterward the German People's Society (*Deutschen Volksverein*), linked with the Society of the Rights of Man. The dissolution of the latter in 1834, under the laws banning public associations, was followed by the break-up of the *Volksverein* and the appearance of a conspiratorial society, the League of the Proscribed (*Bund der Geächteten*), led by Venedey and Th. Schuster. An ideological struggle was waged between a "patriotic German" tendency, led by the former, and another, close to French socialism, preached by the latter, a conflict which was similar to the one that divided the Society of the Rights of Man and led to a split in 1836

1836, the League of the Just quickly became a secret society, neo-Babouvist in tendency, with about a thousand members,[33] and in fraternal association with the Society of the Seasons (Blanqui, Barbès, M. Bernard).[34]

The writings of Wilhelm Weitling are the most faithful expression of the aspirations and ideological tendencies of the "proletarianized" artisans whose vanguard was represented by the League.

Weitling's work – according to Engels "the first independent theoretical stirring of the German proletariat"[35] – was included by Marx, in the preface to his *Manuscripts of 1844*, among the "*original* German works of substance," along with those of Hess and Engels.[36] Marx's interest in and admiration for Weitling are even more apparent in his article in *Vorwärts*, where he writes of Weitling's "brilliant works," "this *vehement* and brilliant literary début by the German workers," "these gigantic *infant shoes* of the proletariat."[37]

Weitling, a tailor, was a real "organic intellectual," a "prophet of his estate" (*Prophet seines Standes*), as Feuerbach called him,[38] whose work reflected, both in its brilliant intuitions and in its utopian limitations, the "ideological universe" of the German journeymen artisans of the 1840s. His first book, *Mankind As It Is and As It Ought To Be* (1838), had been produced at the request of the central committee of the League of the Just, to satisfy the members' desire to see proof of the possibility of common ownership of property. In his second

---

and the formation of the League of the Just (*Bund des Gerechten*), made up solely of workers. This evolution resembled that undergone by the societies of "the Families" and "the Seasons." See on this subject A. W. Fehling, *Karl Schapper und die Anfänge der Arbeiterbewegung bis zur Revolution von 1848*, Inaugural Dissertation, typescript, University of Rostock: 1922, pp. 41–42; A. Ewerbeck, *L'Allemagne et les Allemands* (Paris: Garnier Frères, 1851), p. 589; Engels, "On the History of the Communist League,"preface to Karl Marx, *Revelations concerning the communist trial in Cologne*, 1853, in CW, XXVI, p. 313.

[33] Ruge's estimate in *Zwei Jahre in Paris* (Leipzig: W. Jurany, 1846), p. 338.

[34] The League of the Just took part in the "Blanquist" coup of May 12, 1839, alongside the French workers, and suffered the consequences, its chief leaders being arrested and expelled from France. After 1839–1841, the center of the League's activity was in London, where Schapper, Moll, and Bauer lived. But the French section continued to exist, led by Ewerbeck. In 1836–1839, the ideology of the Just was very close to that of the Paris Babouvists. Engels speaks of the League as having been "originally . . . a German offshoot of the French worker-communism, reminiscent of Babouvism," and it appears that works like *Ni châteaux ni chaumières*, by J.-J. Pillot (1840) were very popular with the German artisans generally and the League's members in particular. Later, under the influence of Ewerbeck, who was an "Icarian communist," Cabet's ideas also came to have a certain influence among the Just.

[35] CW, XXVI, 315.

[36] CW, III, 232.

[37] CW, III, 201.

[38] Fr. Mehring, *Geschichte der Deutschen Sozial-Demokratie* (Berlin: Dietz Verlag, 1960), p. 107.

work, *Guarantees of Harmony and Freedom* (1842), he wrote: "This work is not mine but ours: without the help of others I would not have accomplished it ... I have brought together in this work all the powers, material and spiritual, of my brothers."[39]

The *Guarantees*, undoubtedly Weitling's richest book, is at once filled with revolutionary realism and impregnated with utopian messianism. In the ideological history of the workers' movement, it represents a transitional stage between the "utopian socialism" of Fourier or Cabet and proletarian communism, between the appeal to Tsar Alexander I and the self-liberating workers' revolution. Its contradictory character results from the situation, itself contradictory, unstable and fluctuating, of the proletarianized artisans faced with growing industrialization.

The "revolutionary side" of the book is expressed in these themes of the *Guarantees*:

(a) The present state of things bears within itself the causes of its revolutionary destruction: "All that exists bears within it the seed and the nutrient element of revolutions."[40]

(b) Progress is possible only through revolution: "Where have we seen those persons [who possess power and money] listen to reason? Ask history, if you will ... England, France, Switzerland, America, Spain, Sweden, Norway, Holland, Belgium, Greece, Turkey, Haiti, and all nations owe every increase in their political liberty to revolution."[41]

(c) The revolution must be social, not political, because founded on the interests of the masses: "Some philistine politicians say that ... a political revolution should come first ... I answer: if we must sacrifice ourselves, it is better that we do this for what is most necessary, for us and for society ... He [the German peasant] hardly knows what a Republic is ... If he sees that his interests are involved he can be won for the movement. It is only through their interests that we can win the masses of the people."[42] And when the people has won, it will want to go to the end and not stop at half-measures: "Imagine a situation in all countries as wretched as it is in England; imagine that social revolution breaks out in this situation; will the victorious people be satisfied with

---

[39] W. Weitling, *Garantien der Harmonie und der Freiheit* (Berlin: Buchhandlung Vorwärts, 1908), pp. 7, 8.
[40] Weitling, *op. cit.*, p. 248.
[41] Weitling, *op. cit.*, p. 226. This is an idea already present in *Mankind As It Is*: "Do not believe that you are going to succeed in anything through negotiations with your enemies. Your hope lies solely in your swords ... The best work on plans for social reform will be written with our blood." Weitling, *Die Menschheit, wie sie ist und wie sie sein sollte* (Paris: 1838), pp. 31–32.
[42] Weitling, *Garantien*, pp. 246–247.

progressive measures?"⁴³ Finally, the coming social revolution will be "of mixed nature": it will employ both physical violence and "spiritual violence," and it will be "the last [revolutionary] storm" in Europe.⁴⁴

The theme which provides the link between the revolutionary perspective and the utopian tendency, and which thus gives the whole a certain coherence, is Jacobino-Babouvist in origin:

> Wanting to wait until we are all suitably enlightened (*aufgeklärt*), as is usually recommended, means abandoning the matter altogether, because never will a whole people possess an equal degree of enlightenment, so long, at least, as inequality and conflict in society between private interests continues.⁴⁵

This is only a variant of the old theme of "the obscurantism of the people," who will not become enlightened until after the regime of equality has been established. This ideology is fiercely opposed to Icarian communism, *but both have the same notion of "enlightenment," inherited from the 18th century: "education of the people" as a theoretical and passive apprenticeship.* Buonarroti and Weitling deny that it is possible to enlighten the people by such an "education" under the existing regime: Cabet puts blind trust in "peaceful propaganda": but for all of them, *"enlightenment" is conceived as the product of "instruction" and not of coming to consciousness through praxis.*

Since the revolution is not to be the work of a conscious proletariat, the way is open for all the Jacobin or Messianic speculations. Weitling compares the people, in a revolutionary situation, to a "machine" that a "master" has to "skilfully set going," and he draws a parallel between "the Dictator who organizes the workers" and "the Duke who commands his army."⁴⁶ After all, why should the revolution not be the work of a monarch? Weitling considers that such an event is not at all impossible, and invokes an example from history to support this possibility: "In Sparta the Kings twice introduced community of property. Is no one to be found in 3,000 years to follow their example?"⁴⁷

Finally, we find in the *Guarantees* all the messianic dreams of utopian socialism, all the "neo-Christian" themes of Lamennais, Cabet, Saint-Simon, etc.: "A second Messiah will come, to fulfill the teaching of the first. He will destroy the rotten edifice of the old social order, divert the springs of tears into the sea of oblivion and transform the earth into a paradise."⁴⁸

---

⁴³ *Ibid.*, p. 231.
⁴⁴ *Ibid.*, p. 247.
⁴⁵ *Ibid.*, p. 247.
⁴⁶ *Ibid.*, pp. 234, 253.
⁴⁷ *Ibid.*, pp. 247, 258.
⁴⁸ *Ibid.*, p. 253.

c) *Chartism*

It was probably from Buret's *De la Misère des classes laborieuses en Angleterre et en France* (1840), numerous extracts from which are to be found in his notebooks of 1844,[49] that Marx obtained his first information about Chartism. However, it was obviously Engels's work on *The Condition of the Working Class in England* (1845) that provided the reference point for his thinking about the British workers' movement. Already in 1844, he knew the main themes of this work, through Engels's articles in the *Républicain Suisse*, the *Deutsch-Französische Jahrbücher* and *Vorwärts*: nevertheless, it was only in July–August 1845, during his first stay in England, that he was to have the opportunity to make direct contact with the leaders of the "Chartist Left" (Harvey, Jones).[50] Allusions to the Chartist party are frequent in *The German Ideology* (i.e., after Marx's visit to London) as a concrete example of a mass movement of workers, contrasted with the empty lucubrations of the "critical spirit."

Marx's (unpublished) notebook containing extracts from Buret, which is in the *Marx-Engels Archief* of the International Institute of Social History in Amsterdam, was compiled in 1845 in Brussels. The extracts deal mainly with the profound disturbances of social relations caused by the industrial revolution. "In the contemporary industrial system there is no moral bond of any kind between master and workman, and these two agents of production are completely alien to one another as *men* [Marx's emphasis]." The machine "divides the population taking part together in production into two distinct classes with opposed interests: the class of capitalists, owners of the instruments of labor, and the class of wage-workers." Are these agents of production not "separated, isolated from each other, unknown and indifferent to each other, enemies?" Consequently, "there prevails between workers and employers a sullen hostility which breaks out at the slightest opportunity, and with redoubled violence each time."[51] The passages on Chartism (read by Marx but not transcribed) show that Buret recognized in the class struggle – which he calls "social war" – in the proletariat's revolutionary tendency, and in the Chartist movement so many inevitable products of industrial development.[52]

---

[49] MEGA, I, 3, pp. 411–412 (Description of the notebooks only: the notebooks themselves are in the International Institute of Social History in Amsterdam.)

[50] D. B. Ryazanov, "Introduction to Marx and Engels," *The Communist Manifesto* (London: 1930), p. 16. In a letter to Marx and Engels, October 20, 1845, from Bradford, Weerth writes of "our friend Harvey." G. Weerth, *Samtliche Werke*, Bd. 5 (Berlin: Aufbau Verlag, 1957), p. 182.

[51] *Marx-Engels Archief*, International Institute of Social History, shelf-mark B28. The edition used by Marx was E. Buret, *De la misère des classes laborieuses en Angleterre et en France*, in *Cours d'economie politique*, Ed. Vahlen (Brussels: 1843). The extracts are from pp. 557, 579, 598.

[52] "In the most advanced countries they [the workers] see their poverty as oppression and the idea of resorting to violence in order to free themselves from it has

In another notebook of the same period, we find extracts from Carlyle's *Chartism* (1840), with the same themes: new social relations engendered by industry, workers' revolt against the blind economic mechanism, "catastrophic" nature of future workers' uprisings:

> How is he [the worker] related to his employer; by bonds of friendliness and of mutual help; or by hostility, opposition and chains of mutual necessity alone? . . . If men had lost belief in a God, their only resource against a blind No-God, of Necessity and Mechanism, that held them like a hideous World-Steamengine, like a hideous Phalaris' Bull, imprisoned in its own iron belly, would be, with or without hope – *revolt!* . . . The speaking classes speak and debate, each for itself; the great dumb, deep-buried class lies like an Enceladus who, in his pain, if he will complain of it, has to produce earthquakes![53]

Engels, too, shows the relation between the progress of industry and the progress of class-consciousness in the English proletariat.[54]

In his 1845 book, he sketches a history of the evolution of Chartism, from its origin in the democratic party in the 1780s which, with the coming of peace, became the radical party. In 1835, the People's Charter was drawn up by the committee of the London Workingmen's Association (William Levett), the six points of which, "harmless as they seem, are sufficient to overthrow the whole English constitution." In 1839 came the great insurrectionary strikes in Wales, when the Chartists revived the old idea of the "sacred month" and the general strike. Then the strike of 1842, betrayed by the bourgeoisie, which resulted in the decisive separation of the Chartist proletariat from bourgeois radicalism at the Birmingham congress (1843).[55] Of this strike, Heine said that the

---

already occurred to them." "England, the country of large-scale industry, is also the country of social war, expressed in [workers'] combinations and, in the last two years, in the Chartists' Union." Buret mentions, "the rapid progress among the lower classes of the spirit of revolt expressed in Chartism" and paints a "catastrophic" picture of England's social crisis: "At the time of writing the disaffection and separation between the two classes, workers and capitalists, has reached its climax in England: it amounts, as all agree who have seen this state of affairs, to a veritable secession and preparation for civil war." E. Buret, *op. cit.*, pp. 563–565.

[53] *Marx-Engels Archief*, shelf-mark B35; T. Carlyle, *Chartism* (London: James Fraser, 1840), pp. 12–13, 37, 89.

[54] "Lancashire, and especially Manchester, is the seat of the most powerful unions, the central point of Chartism, the place which numbers most Socialists. The more the factory system has taken possession of a branch of industry, the more the workingmen employed in it participate in the labor movement; the sharper the opposition between workingmen and capitalists, the clearer the proletarian consciousness in the workingmen . . . [The latter] form a separate class, with separate interests and principles, with a separate way of looking at things in contrast to that of all property-owners . . ." *CW*, IV, 528–529.

[55] *CW*, IV, 518–523.

union between the Chartists and the factory-workers "was perhaps the most important phenomenon of our time."[56]

Engels thought that it was inevitable that Chartism and socialism would come together, "especially when the next crisis directs the workingmen by force of sheer want to social instead of political remedies," but he severely criticized the Owenite socialists, for their dogmatism, their abstract and metaphysical tendencies, their philanthropic and "peaceable" illusions, and he prophesied that, "in its present form, socialism can never become the common creed of the working class." The future belonged, on the contrary, to "true proletarian socialism, having passed through Chartism, purified of its bourgeois elements, assuming the form which it has already reached in the minds of many Socialist and Chartist leaders (who are nearly all Socialists)." The Owenite socialists, "proceeding originally from the bourgeoisie, are for this reason unable to amalgamate completely with the working class. The union of Socialism with Chartism, the reproduction of French Communism in an English manner, will be the next step, and has already begun."[57]

This remark shows us that Engels conceived the future "Chartist socialism" in terms comparable to the French communism as L. von Stein had seen it, that is, as a mass movement with a working-class basis and a socialist program, qualitatively different from the utopian sects of bourgeois origin. Engels's analyses of the English proletarian movement thus followed the same line as those of Stein in France: the two together probably oriented Marx's work in the same direction, namely, *the communist movement considered as an independent expression of the worker masses.*

Although we cannot regard her theories as an ideology peculiar to Chartism, it was doubtless on the basis of this movement and of the attempts at reforming the system of journeyman service in France[58] that Flora Tristan developed her ideas about workers' self-organization and self-emancipation.

It was during her fourth visit to England, in 1839, that Flora Tristan discovered Chartism, an enthusiastic account of which she gives in her *Promenades*

---

[56] Heine, *Lutezia* (September 17, 1842), in M. W. *Vermächtnis, op. cit.,* p. 284.
[57] CW, IV, 524–527.
[58] The movement for "reform of abuses in the system of journeyman service," expressed in the writings of workers like Adolphe Boyer, Agricole Perdiguier, and Pierre Moreau, was still impregnated with the artisan spirit, but at least one strong idea emerged from it, namely, that the workers constitute a community and ought to *unite*, regardless of all occupational or sectarian disputes, against their common foes. Cf. A. Boyer, *De l'état des ouvriers et de son amélioration par l'organisation du travail,* Dubois Editeur (Paris: 1841). pp. 48, 50; P. Moreau, *De la réforme des abus du compagnonnage et de l'émancipation du sort des travailleurs* (Paris: Prévot, 1843), p. 163; A. Perdiguier, *Le Livre du compagnonnage* (Paris: published by the author, 1840), p. 217.

dans Londres (1840).⁵⁹ She grasped remarkably well the essentially social character of Chartism, and its nature as a proletarian organization of the masses opposed not only to the aristocracy but also to "mercantile privileges" and to "shopkeepers." Moreover, she wrote in the same book:

> The great struggle, the struggle which is destined to transform the social order, is that which pits property-owners and capitalists – who control everything, wealth and political power . . . – against the workers of city and countryside, who have nothing, neither land, nor capital, nor political power . . .⁶⁰

It was the "organizational" experience of Chartism rather than its "political" program that inspired her *Union Ouvrière* [Workers' Unity].

The two central themes of *Union Ouvrière* were:

1. Unification of the proletariat. Flora Tristan began by criticizing radically the artisans' associations (journeymen's societies, mutual benefit societies, etc.), her criticism being inspired by "reformers" like Perdiguier, Moreau, and Gosset but going far beyond them.⁶¹ She saw them as *"particular societies whose sole aim is to relieve individual suffering,"* societies which "cannot (and do not claim to be able to) change in any way or even improve *the material and moral position of the working class."* She criticized corporatism, too, "this spurious, petty, egoistic and absurd form of organization which divides the working class into a multitude of small, particular societies . . . this system of fragmentation which decimates the workers."⁶² To this division of the proletarians, "the true cause of their woes," Flora Tristan counterposes *workers' unity*, the essential aim of which is to "create compact and indissoluble *unity* of the *working class"*: "Workers, you can see that, if you wish to save yourselves, there is only one means open to you: you must *unite."* "Workers, put aside, therefore, all your petty rivalries and form, alongside your particular associations, a compact, solid, indissoluble *union."*⁶³

---

⁵⁹ "The most formidable association yet formed in the United Kingdom is that of the Chartists . . . The association's ramifications extend everywhere: in every mill, every factory, every workshop Chartist workers are to be found; there are Chartists in country cottages; and this holy alliance of the people, who have faith in their future, grows greater and stronger with each day . . . All, without exception, want the suppression of aristocratic, religious or mercantile privilege . . . No half-measures can hope to satisfy the Chartists; they will never put their trust in a party whose object is to transfer to shopkeepers the privileges of the aristocracy." *Flora Tristan's London Journal, 1840* (London: 1980), pp. 40–41.
⁶⁰ *Ibid.*, p. 39.
⁶¹ F. Tristan, *Union Ouvrière* (Paris: Prévot, 1843), pp. 12–13: "I don't know how to account for the fact that the three worker-writers . . . did not dream of proposing a plan for *general union* . . ."
⁶² *Ibid.*, pp. 15–17.
⁶³ *Ibid.*, pp. 8, 17, 18, 25.

2. Self-emancipation by the proletariat. Flora Tristan deduced this from a comparison between the bourgeois revolution of 1789 and the future emancipation of the proletariat: "Actually, while the bourgeois were 'the head' they had for 'hands' the people, whom they knew how to skilfully make use of. Whereas you, proletarians, have nobody to help you. Therefore you have to be both 'head' and 'hands.'" She deduced this also from the indifference of the authorities to the workers' lot: "Workers, stop waiting any longer for the intervention promised you for 25 years past. Experience and facts are enough to tell you that the government *cannot* or *does not want to* concern itself with improving your lot. It depends on you alone, if you firmly wish it, to break out of the maze of poverty, sorrow and humiliation wherein you languish."[64]

L. von Stein sums up in a clear and concise phrase the importance of Flora Tristan's work:

> It is in her, perhaps, that is manifested, with greater power than in the other reformers, the consciousness that the working class is a single entity, and that it should know this and act in solidarity, with common will and power, in pursuit of a common aim, if it wants to escape from its condition.[65]

Engels, who read *Union Ouvrière* in 1844, defended Flora Tristan against the attacks of "critical criticism," which treated her "*en canaille*," in a short passage in *The Holy Family*.[66]

d) *The revolt of the Silesian weavers*

Here we are concerned not with an organization or an ideology but with a precise historical event, the revolt of the weavers in Silesia in June 1844, an event which served Marx as "catalyst," as theoretico-political overturn, as

---

[64] *Ibid.*, pp. 4, 27.
[65] In Rubel, "Flora Tristan et Karl Marx," *La Nef* (Paris: January 1946), p. 71.
[66] CW, IV, 19. Having said this, it remains the case that the theories of the "pariah" were still deeply coloured with "utopian socialism." The influence of Owen, of Considérant's Fourierism (the "workers' palaces"), and of Louis Blanc ("the organization of labor") is noticeable in her *Union Ouvrière*. The traditional appeal to the philanthropy of the King, the clergy, the nobility, the "factory chiefs," and even of the financiers and bourgeois is also present. The social program of the *Union* is very vague ("ownership by the hands," "right to work") and revolutionary methods are strictly ruled out: "Since 1789 *many governments* have been overthrown, and what have the workers gained from these revolutions? Were they not always made at the workers' expense? . . . Precious little advantage for them [the people] in making revolutions." Flora Tristan, *Union Ouvrière*, pp. 81–87, 118–119.

In his article on "Flora Tristan and Karl Marx" Maximilien Rubel emphasizes, probably with justification, the influence upon Marx of the theme of self-emancipation contained in *Union Ouvrière*. but he leaves aside some "differences" which are not negligible: revolution, communism. Rubel, "Flora Tristan et K. Marx," pp. 74–76.

the concrete and violent demonstration of what was already emerging from his reading and his contacts in Paris, namely, the potentially revolutionary tendency of the proletariat.

For some writers, including Nicolaievsky and Maenchen-Helfen, Marx

> overestimated the desperate revolt of the Silesian weavers . . . This was no rising of organized industrial workers against the capitalists but wild rioting by desperate, impoverished home-workers who smashed machines as they had done in England half a century before.[67]

However, as Marx pointed out in *Capital*, "This modern 'domestic industry' has nothing except the name in common with old-fashioned domestic industry," since it "has now been converted into an external department of the factory, the manufacturing workshop, or the warehouse." The exploitation of labor-power "is carried out in a more shameless manner in modern manufacturing than in the factory proper."[68]

But a brief analysis of the events is enough to show that this was indeed a clash between *proletarians and capitalists* and not a "Luddite" movement by artisans opposed to machinery.[69] It was against the *bourgeois*, and not against

---

[67] Nicolaievsky and Maenchen-Helfen, *Karl Marx, Man and Fighter* (London: 1936), p. 73. Cf. also Mehring, in *Aus dem literarischen Nachlass von Karl Marx, Friedrich Engels und Ferdinand Lassalle*, Bd 2 (Stuttgart: 1902), p. 29: "As regards content, too, his polemic seems sometimes exaggerated, especially in his historical judgment concerning the revolt of the Silesian weavers, which, as we see the matter today, was judged more correctly by Ruge, in so far as he perceived it as a mere hunger riot that constituted an obstacle rather than an aid to political development."

[68] *Capital*, I, Harmondsworth (Penguin), 590–591. On the standard of living of the "workers at home," see pp. 595–599.

[69] At the beginning of the revolt, we find a song that was created spontaneously by the weavers of the Silesian village of Peterswalden. This song would be quoted by Marx in *Vorwärts* as one of the proofs of the level of consciousness in the insurrection (CW, III, 201), and it was to inspire a famous poem by Heine. It gives clear expression to the weavers' revolt against capitalist exploitation:

> You are the source of the poverty
> That here oppresses the poor man,
> It is you who snatch
> The dry bread from his mouth
> . . . . .
> But your money and your property
> Will one day disappear
> Like butter in the sunshine.
> What will become of you then?

Cf. K.Obermann, *Einheit und Freiheit 1815–1849* (Berlin: Dietz Verlag, 1950), p. 206; Mehring, *Geschichte der Deutschen Sozial-Demokratie*, pp. 227–228.

On June 4, 1844, the police arrested a weaver from among a group of people who

the *machines* that the revolt was aimed. Moreover, the repercussions of the event throughout Silesia and Bohemia, in Prague and even in Berlin, where strikes and riots followed one another all through June, July and August 1844, show that this was no mere local event but the explosive manifestation of widespread feeling. Hence the apprehension felt by the German bourgeoisie, who set about forming, everywhere, "associations for the welfare of the working class."

Among the German democrats in Paris the importance and the radical nature of the insurrection were recognized. On July 6, *Vorwärts* published the following note (which was probably one of Marx's sources of information:

> One day in June 1844, at Peterswalden and Langebielau in Silesia, 5,000 weavers rose up, gripping sticks, knives and stones in their lean fists, and fought a brave battle with several battalions of soldiers! They sacked the palaces of the princes of industry, destroying the records of debts and the letters of credit, but stealing nothing ... In short, for the first time on the soil of our German fatherland, in this Silesia that is normally so tranquil, there appeared a forewarning of the social transformation which is taking the world irresistibly towards a higher development of mankind.[70]

On July 10, Heine published, also in *Vorwärts*, his poem "The Poor Weavers," in which he depicts workmen weaving the shroud of the old Germany and cursing the false God, the King of the rich and the false fatherland. On July 13, another note appeared in *Vorwärts*, in which the revolt of the weavers was described as "the cock-crow that announces the coming of the new world." Finally, Ruge himself, who had so despised the insurrection, spoke, in a letter to his friend Stahr, on July 19, of the "*communist* riots in Silesia."[71]

---

were singing this song under the window of the manufacturer Zwanziger (who paid starvation wages and was in this region the embodiment of the oppression by the rich). This was the drop which made the cup run over. That afternoon, a rebellious crowd sacked the industrialists' houses and destroyed their account books. Some proposed setting fire to the houses, but the majority refused to do this, "because the owners would receive compensation, and we want to ruin them, so that they may learn in their turn what hunger is like." On June 5, a crowd of 3,000 weavers marched to a neighboring village (Langebielau), where similar scenes occurred. But the army had been alerted and intervened already, firing on the unarmed crowd: 11 workers were killed and 24 wounded. The desperate crowd reacted, and with stones and sticks forced the soldiers to quit the village. This victory did not last long. On June 6, three companies of infantry and a battery of artillery arrived and crushed the revolt. The survivors took refuge in the nearby mountains and forests, whither they were pursued by the troops: 38 weavers were arrested and given heavy sentences of hard labor. Cf. Mehring, *Geschichte der Deutschen Sozial-Demokratie*, pp. 228–230.

[70] *Vorwärts*, Pariser Deutscher Zeitung, July 6, 1844, p. 4.
[71] Ruge, *Briefwechsel, op. cit.,* p. 364.

A report sent by a correspondent of *Vorwärts* in Silesia[72] confirmed both the high level of consciousness of some strata of the German proletariat, their solidarity with the weavers, and the possibility that the conflict might have spread if the rebels had resisted for a little longer.[73]

e) *Marx's theoretical synthesis*

It was the weavers' revolt that, in a sense, "unleashed" in Marx the process of theoretical work which resulted, in 1846, in his definitive break with all the implications of Young Hegelianism, Feuerbach included. During this process, the Marxist conception of the revolutionary communist movement gradually developed in its various aspects.

This theoretical work did not begin *ex nihilo*, but started out from the actual tendencies in the European workers' movement and their ideological expressions. It started out also, however, from a scientific and critical analysis of bourgeois society and of the proletarian condition, an analysis which, while criticizing them, profited from the achievements of contemporary science and philosophy: classical political economy, the "sociology" of the utopian socialists, Hegel's dialectics.

Marx effected the dialectical synthesis, the transcending of the fragmentary, scattered, and partial elements, the various experiences and ideologies of the workers' movement, and the production of a coherent and rational theory appropriate to the proletariat's situation by:

---

[72] *Vorwärts*, "Schlesische Zustände," December 4, 1844, p. 3. The (anonymous) correspondent writes: "I have recently spoken with some railway workers and am really surprised by their clear conception of our social situation, its basis and the principles of a new order of things." In his last report, on December 7, he adds: "One may privately be convinced that the anger of Peterswalden and Langebielau was only the start of a prologue the end of which will follow sooner or later ... In order that the contrasts between property-owners and propertyless, rich and poor, may disappear from among us it will perhaps be necessary for the drama of which we have seen the foreshadowing to be carried through to the end by the worker masses."

[73] The correspondent reports (literally) statements made by a railway worker: "So long as we work here we make a living for ourselves, but we know very well that we are being skinned, mainly for the financiers' benefit. They are in the town, in the market-place, and are doing well out of our sweat ... We shall be the last to use the trains that we build ... Our only advantage is that, huddled together in thousands, we have got to know each other, and, through that long mutual relationship, most of us have grown more intelligent. Only few among us still believe the old fables. We now have devil a bit of respect for the eminent and the rich. What people hardly dared to think silently at home we now say aloud: it is we who maintain the rich, and it would be enough for us to will it for them to beg their bread from us or else die of hunger, if they don't want to work. Believe me, if the weavers had resisted longer there would have been trouble among us. The weavers' business is, at bottom, our business too. And as we are 20,000 men working on the trains in Silesia, we should have had something to say as well." *Vorwärts*, December 4, 1844, p. 3.

(a) transcending the social (artisanal, petty-bourgeois), national, or theoretical limitations of those experiences and ideologies; and
(b) confronting them with the socioeconomic reality of capitalism and bourgeois society.

In this process of "conserving and transcending," the tendencies which constitute the historical and concrete point of departure are several: the revolutionary tradition of Babouvism, the "materialist communism" of the 1840s (Dézamy), the efforts of self-organization and self-emancipation by the workers themselves (Chartism, Flora Tristan), and the praxis of revolutionary action by the masses (the Chartist riots, the revolt of the Silesian weavers).

But this synthesis could be accomplished only by transcending mechanistic materialism, the artisanal heritage, the conspiratorial habits, the Jacobin and messianic tendencies, the confusion with petty-bourgeois radicalism – in short, all the features inherited from the past or from bourgeois ideology that were inappropriate to the proletarian condition.

It must be added that Marx's theory was, to a large degree, anticipatory, in view of

(a) the backward state of Europe's economy and the predominance of craft occupations among the working masses;
(b) the weakness of the workers' movement, its organizational and theoretical immaturity;
(c) the relations of strength between the classes of society, which made a victorious proletarian revolution impossible.

II. The break: theory of revolution, 1844–1846

a) *The Manuscripts of 1844*

In the evolution of Marx's theory of communism, the economic and philosophical manuscripts of 1844 clearly represent "progress" in relation to the articles in the *Deutsch-Französische Jahrbücher*. Under the influence of his readings in history and economics and of his first contacts with the labor movement in Paris, Marx finally came to communism (the Manuscripts of 1844 are his first writings in which he calls himself a "communist"), abandoned the Young-Hegelian thematic of "active philosophy," and outlined an economic analysis of the proletarian condition. Nevertheless, this text is still somewhat "Feuerbachian," in so far as the schema of the critique of religious alienation in *The Essence of Christianity* is applied to economic life. God becomes private property and atheism is transformed into communism. Moreover, this communism is presented, in a rather abstract way, as the transcending of alienations, and the concrete problems of revolutionary praxis are hardly looked at.

In the 1844 Manuscripts, the proletariat is considered, above all, as an "alienated class." Marx's analysis depicts a "factual situation," the paradoxical position of the workers in relation to the products of their labor:

> We proceed from an *actual* fact.
>
> The worker becomes all the poorer, the more wealth he produces, the more his production increases in power and size. The worker becomes an ever cheaper commodity the more commodities he creates. The *devaluation* of the world of men is in direct proportion to the *increasing value* of the world of things.[74]

For Marx, the essence of this phenomenon is the process of *alienation of labor*:

> This fact expresses merely that the object which labor produces – labor's product – confronts it as *something alien*, as a *power independent* of the producer... The *alienation* of the worker in his product means not only that his labor becomes an object, an *external* existence, but that it exists *outside him*, independently, as something alien to him, and that it becomes a power on its own confronting him. It means that the life which he has conferred on the object confronts him as something hostile and alien.[75]

This analysis obviously presents the same structure as Feuerbach's critique of religious alienation, and, indeed, Marx himself constantly mentions the parallel between the two forms of alienation: "It is the same in religion. The more man puts into God, the less he retains in himself. The worker puts his life into the object; but now his life no longer belongs to him but to the object."[76] This parallelism even leads him to see in private property not the cause but the *consequence* of the alienation. "But analysis of this concept shows that though private property appears to be the reason, the cause of alienated labor, it is rather its consequence, just as the gods are *originally* not the cause but the effects of man's intellectual confusion. Later this relation becomes reciprocal."[77] This comparison is, of course, of limited validity, and Marx does not fall into the trap of regarding private property as an "effect of man's intel-

---

[74] "The more the worker produces, the less he has to consume; the more values he creates, the more valueless, the more unworthy he becomes; the better formed his product, the more deformed becomes the worker; the more civilized his object, the more barbarous becomes the worker; the more powerful labor becomes, the more powerless becomes the worker... It is true that labor produces wonderful things for the rich – but for the worker it produces privation. it produces palaces – but for the worker, hovels. It produces beauty – but for the worker, deformity. It replaces labor by machines, but it throws one section of the workers back to a barbarous type of labor, and it turns the other section into a machine." *CW*, III, 271–272, 273.
[75] *CW*, III, 272.
[76] *Ibid.*; cf. Feuerbach, in *The Essence of Christianity* (1854), p. 30."The more subjective God is, the more completely does man divest himself of his subjectivity, because God is, *per se*, his relinquished (*entäusserte*) self..."
[77] *CW*, III, 279–280.

lectual confusion": "Religious estrangement as such occurs only in the realm of *consciousness*, of man's inner life, but economic estrangement is that of real life; its transcendence therefore embraces both aspects."[78]

As for communism, before setting out his own conception of it, Marx settles accounts with the crude, utopian, or idealist forms that flourished in the 1840s.

Criticism of "crude" communism appeared already in his correspondence with Ruge, but, in the 1844 Manuscripts, Marx develops this criticism considerably. According to him, this communism is merely "a *generalization* and *consummation*" of the private-property relation.

> For it the sole purpose of life and existence is direct, physical *possession*. The category of the *worker* is not done away with, but extended to all men. The relationship of private property persists as the relationship of the community to the world of things. Finally, this movement of opposing universal private property to private property finds expression in the brutish form of opposing to *marriage* (certainly a *form of exclusive private property*) the *community of women*, in which a woman becomes a piece of *communal* and *common* property . . . This type of communism – since it neglects the *personality* of man in every sphere – is but the logical expression of private property, which is this negation. General *envy* constituting itself as a power is the disguise in which *greed* re-establishes itself and satisfies itself, only in *another* way. The thought of every piece of private property as such is at *least* turned against *wealthier* private property and the urge to reduce things to a common level . . . How little this annulment of private property is really an appropriation is in fact proved by the abstract negation of the entire world of culture and civilization, the regression to the *unnatural* simplicity of the *poor* and crude man who has few needs and who has not only failed to go beyond private property, but has not even reached it.[79]

This critique, which was most probably aimed at Babouvism, is to be found again in Marx's future writing: from *The Holy Family* to the *Manifesto*, Babeuf's communism would always be described as "crude." It needs to be emphasized, however, that, as compared with Marx's later works, the Manuscripts of 1844 give disproportionate space to this criticism of "crudeness," an attitude which can easily be compared with the reaction of the neo-Hegelians or the German émigrés to French communism. Feuerbach contrasted his "noble" communism with "vulgar" communism. Heine, despite his sympathy with the communists, regrets that "with their horny hands they will ruthlessly smash all the marble statues of beauty."[80] Marx, however, in *The German Ideology*, ridicules the criticism of "crude communism" by the "true socialists": "French communism is admittedly 'crude' because it is the theoretical

---

[78] CW, III, 297.
[79] CW, III, 294–295.
[80] Heine, *Lutèce* (preface), (Calmann-Lévy, 1893), p. xii.

expression of a *real* opposition . . . In fact, all these gentlemen [the "true socialists"] display a remarkable delicacy of feeling. Everything shocks them, especially matter; they complain everywhere of crudity."[81]

The criticism of the 1844 Manuscripts is also aimed at the opposite of crude communism, namely, "philosophical communism": "In order to abolish the *idea* of private property, the *idea* of communism is quite sufficient. It takes *actual* communist action to abolish actual private property." We even find in this text formulations that foreshadow the eleventh thesis on Feuerbach: "We see how the resolution of the *theoretical* antithesis is *only* possible in a *practical* way, by virtue of the practical energy of man. Their resolution is therefore by no means merely a problem of understanding, but a *real* problem of life, which *philosophy* could not solve precisely because it conceived this problem as *merely* a theoretical one."[82]

Finally, Marx comes out against the utopian communism of Cabet, Villegardelle, etc., which "seeks an *historical* proof for itself . . . among disconnected historical phenomena opposed to private property." For Marx, on the contrary, communism is based precisely upon the contradictions in the private-property system itself: "It is easy to see that the entire revolutionary movement necessarily finds both its empirical and its theoretical basis in the movement of *private property* – more precisely, in that of the economy."[83]

After having thus distinguished his communism from its crude, idealist, and utopian forms, Marx defines it, in a famous paragraph, as

> the real *appropriation* of the *human* essence by and for man: communism therefore as the complete return of man to himself as a social (i.e., human) being – a return accomplished consciously and embracing the entire wealth of previous development . . . It is the *genuine* resolution of the conflict between man and nature and between man and man – the true resolution of the strife between existence and essence, between objectification and self-confirmation, between freedom and necessity, between the individual and the species. Communism is the riddle of history solved, and it knows itself to be this solution.[84]

The parallel drawn between religious alienation and the alienation of labor, between God and private property, is now taken to the level of "disalienation" – a parallel between atheism and communism. Marx begins by assuming an historical continuity between the two movements: "Communism begins from the outset (*Owen*) with atheism."[85] He goes on to identify them by virtue of their "philanthropic" character – using the term probably in its etymological sense, as equivalent to "humanist." This "philanthropy" is abstract

---

[81] *CW*, V, 459–460.
[82] *CW*, III, 313, 302.
[83] *CW*, III, 297.
[84] *CW*, III, 296–297.
[85] *CW*, III, 297.

for atheism, practical for "communism": "The philanthropy of atheism is therefore at first only *philosophical*, abstract philanthropy, and that of communism is at once *real* and directly bent on *action*" (*Wirkung*).[86] Finally, he considers them as two forms of humanism which are realized by the negation of the negation, by a "mediation": "Atheism is humanism mediated with itself through the supersession of religion, whilst communism is humanism mediated with itself through the supersession of private property."[87]

Facing these "mediated" forms, Marx suggests a higher level, "positive humanism": "Only through the supersession of this mediation – which is itself, however, a necessary premise – does positively self-deriving humanism, *positive* humanism, come into being." This humanism thus appears as a "beyond" of communism, which still remains "as the negation of the negation, as the appropriation of the human essence through the intermediary of the negation of private property – as not yet the *true*, self-originating position but rather a position originating from private property."[88] These considerations are undoubtedly Feuerbachian in inspiration, and, indeed, Marx cites as one of Feuerbach's great merits "his opposing to the negation of the negation, which claims to be the absolute positive, the self-supporting positive, positively based on itself," and he emphasizes, for Feuerbach,

> the positive position as self-affirmation and self-confirmation contained in the negation of the negation is taken to be a position which is not yet sure of itself, which is therefore burdened with its opposite, which is doubtful of itself and therefore in need of proof, and which, therefore, is not in a position demonstrating itself by its existence – not an acknowledged position; hence it is directly and immediately confronted by the position of sense-certainty based on itself.[89]

Marx is here merely developing an idea of Feuerbach's, who wrote in *Principles of the Philosophy of the Future*:

> The self-mediated truth is the truth that is still attached to its opposite statement. One starts with the opposite statement which, however, is afterward sublated. If, however, the opposite statement is one that is to be sublated and negated, why should I begin with it and not immediately with its negation?[90]

---

[86] *CW*, III, 297, 341. Atheism is "the advent of theoretical humanism," while communism is "the vindication of real human life."
[87] *CW*, III, 341.
[88] *CW*, III, 341–342; 313.
[89] *CW*, III, 328, 329.
[90] Feuerbach, *Principles of the Philosophy of the Future* (Indianapolis: 1966), p. 54. In his remarkable 1926 study of Moses Hess, Lukács shows how Feuerbach's theory of "immediate knowledge" is "the epistemological justification of [the] ethical utopianism" of some of the Young Hegelians. Lukács, *Political Writings 1919–1929* (London: 1972), pp. 202, 206.

One has to start from this concept of "positive humanism" in order to understand a certain theme of the 1844 Manuscripts which has been passed over by most of their numerous interpreters: namely, the "limitations" of communism and its "transcendence" – a concept and theme that were to be flatly abandoned by Marx in his later writings. In these Manuscripts, Marx seems to see communism as merely the "revolutionary moment" beyond which lies "truly human society":

> Communism is the position as the negation of the negation and is hence the *actual* phase necessary for the next stage of historical development in the process of human emancipation and rehabilitation. *Communism* is the necessary forum and the dynamic principle of the immediate future, but communism as such is not the goal of human development, the form of human society.[91]

He speaks even of the "self-transcending" of communism and its "transcendence" by consciousness:

> It takes *actual* communist action to abolish actual private property. History will lead to it; and this movement, which in *theory* we already know to be a self-transcending movement, will constitute in actual fact a very rough and protracted process. But we must regard it as a real advance to have at the outset gained a consciousness of the limited character as well as the goal of this historical movement – and a consciousness which reaches out beyond it.[92]

Actually, the 1844 Manuscripts pay practically no attention to the problem of the relation between the workers and communism, or to that of the liberating revolution, except from the abstract angle of the relation between the proletariat as an alienated class and communism as a movement of disalienation.

Only once are *communist workers* mentioned – in the well-known paragraph about meetings of French workers:

> When communist *artisans* associate with one another, theory, propaganda, etc., is their first end. But at the same time, as result of this association, they acquire a new need – the need for society – and what appears as a means becomes an end. In this practical process the most splendid results are to be observed whenever French socialist workers [*ouvriers*] are seen together. Such things as smoking, drinking, eating, etc., are no longer means of contact or means that bring them together. Association, society and conversation, which again has association as its end, are enough for them; the brotherhood of man is no mere phrase with them, but a fact of life, and the nobility of man shines upon us from their work-hardened bodies.[93]

---

[91] *CW*, III, 306.
[92] *CW*, III, 313.
[93] *CW*, III, 313.

This remark is directly inspired by Hegel, who wrote in his *Philosophy of Law*: "Unification pure and simple is the true content and aim of the individual, and the individual's destiny is the living of a universal life."[94] But it shows also that, as a result of his first contacts with the communist movement in Paris, Marx saw in the proletariat the sphere which – in contrast to the bourgeoisie, dedicated to the atomistic individualism of its private interests – tends towards solidarity and association; in other words, the class which already provides, in embryo, the model of the future society.

b) *"The King of Prussia and Social Reform" (Vorwärts)*

The importance of the "critical marginal notes on the article 'The King of Prussia and Social Reform. By a Prussian,'" which Marx published in August 1844 in the Paris journal *Vorwärts*, has, in general, been singularly underestimated by the "Marxologists." Some of them (Nicolaievsky and Maenchen-Helfen, Mehring) even side with Ruge in his negative judgement of the Silesian workers' revolt. Yet, as regards the theory of revolution (and even Marx's overall ideological evolution), this article possesses crucial significance: it was the point of departure for the intellectual journey that led to the *Theses on Feuerbach* and *The German Ideology*. It opened, so to speak, a new phase in the movement of Marx's thought, the phase in which his theory of the revolutionary self-emancipation of the proletariat took shape.

The event which "unleashed" this process was, as already mentioned, the revolt of the Silesian weavers. In order to appreciate how important this revolt was for Marx we need to take account not only of the stir it caused in Germany – in the working class, in the bourgeoisie, and even where the King was concerned – but also the striking confirmation it gave to the theses of "permanent revolution" set out in the *Deutsch-Französische Jahrbücher*. In fact, a mere few months after Marx had forecast – on the basis of rather abstract reasoning and in contradiction to all appearances (absence of a labor movement in Germany) – that the proletariat was the only revolutionary class in Germany, a revolt had occurred which signalled the entry of the German working class on history's scene. What Georg Jung wrote to him from Cologne (June 26, 1844) corresponded basically to what Marx himself thought about this event: "The disturbances in Silesia have, no doubt, surprised you as much as they have surprised us. They bear striking witness to the correctness of the picture of Germany's present and future which you drew in the *Introduction to a Contribution to the Critique of Hegel's Philosophy of Law* in the *Jahrbücher* . . . What was with you, only a few months ago, still a bold and entirely new construction has become almost as obvious as a commonplace."[95]

---

[94] Hegel, *op. cit.*, p. 156.
[95] *Marx-Engels Archief*, International Institute of Social History, Amsterdam, shelf-mark D5. This letter is to be published by the Institute in a collection of the

92 • Chapter Two

We can now understand the enthusiasm with which Marx greeted the movement of the weavers, stressing its "theoretical and conscious character":

> First of all, recall the *song of the weavers*, that bold *call* to struggle, in which there is not even a mention of hearth and home, factory or district, but in which the proletariat at once, in a striking, sharp, unrestrained and powerful manner, proclaims its opposition to the society of private property. The Silesian uprising *begins* precisely with what the French and English workers' uprisings *end*, the consciousness of the nature of the proletariat. The action itself bears the stamp of this *superior* character. Not only machines, these rivals of the workers, are destroyed, but also *ledgers*, the titles to property. And while all other movements were aimed primarily only against the *owner of the industrial enterprise*, the visible enemy, this movement is at the same time directed against the banker, the hidden enemy. Finally, not a single English workers' uprising was carried out with such courage, thought and endurance.[96]

Whether or not this picture was correct or exaggerated – my brief survey of the events would seem to support Marx's view, except as regards the superiority of the movement to the French and English revolts, a point which is obviously open to discussion – what is essential is that, for Marx, the weavers' revolt meant total confirmation of the theses of the "Introduction," except for the schema "active thinking – passive proletariat." Consequently, the *Vorwärts* article reiterates those theses in the light of the disturbances in Silesia, *but abandons the Feuerbachian schema*.

First, Marx compares the revolutionary boldness of the proletariat with the *passivity* of the liberal bourgeoisie: the theme is the same as in the *Jahrbücher*, but with the adjective "passive" now reserved for the bourgeoisie. In reply to Ruge, for whom "because a few soldiers sufficed to cope with the feeble weavers, the destruction of factories and machinery . . . did not inspire any 'alarm' either in the King or the authorities,"[97] Marx asks:

> In a country where *not a single* soldier was needed to shatter the desires of the *entire* liberal bourgeoisie for freedom of the press and a constitution; in a country where passive obedience is the order of the day – can it be that in such a country the necessity to employ armed force against feeble weavers is *not an event*, and not an *alarming* event? Moreover, at the first encounter the feeble weavers were victorious. They were suppressed only by subsequent troop reinforcements."[98]

---

correspondence of the socialist circles connected with Marx. Part of it appears in French translation in Cornu, *op. cit.*, III, p. 83.

[96] *CW*, III, 201.
[97] Ruge, "Der König von Preussen und die Sozialreform," *Vorwärts*, July 27, 1844, p. 4; *CW*, III, 189.
[98] *CW*, III, 190.

The weavers' revolt even shows that the "tense and difficult relationship between [the bourgeoisie] and the proletariat" increases "the subversiveness and impotence" of the former.[99] Marx's conclusion clearly coincides with that of the "Introduction" – except, again, as regards the role of theory: "For just as the impotence of the German bourgeoisie is the *political* impotence of Germany, so also the capability of the German proletariat – even apart from German theory – represents the *social* capability of Germany."[100] And Marx himself refers his reader to his article in the *Deutsch-Französische Jahrbücher*: "He will find the first rudiments for an understanding of this phenomenon in my *Introduction to a Criticism of Hegel's Philosophy of Law (Deutsch-Französische Jahrbücher)*."[101]

For Ruge, the Silesian revolt failed because "the whole question has so far still not been vivified by the all-penetrating political soul"[102] – a strictly Hegelian position which had also been Marx's in 1842. Marx, however, explains the defeat of the first outbursts of the French proletariat by their political illusions, "their political understanding" (*Verstand*) which, in the case of the Lyons workers, for instance, "falsified their insight into their real aim, thus their *political understanding deceived* their *social instinct*."[103] In this way, another theme from the *Jahrbücher* enters the argument: the superiority of social over political revolution. Marx here shows, in opposition to Ruge, that there can be no political solution to social problems. He uses the example from history of the failure of all the "political" measures taken against pauperism by the Convention, by Napoleon, and by the English state.[104] Again, whereas, for Ruge, the weavers' riot was a local, partial event, in which there was "isolation of people from the community" and "separation of their thoughts from social principles,"[105] Marx, developing the premises already set out in "The Jewish Question" (the "human," universal character of social movements and the partial, limited character of political revolutions), here affirms that, "however *partial* the uprising of the *industrial workers* may be, it contains within itself a *universal* soul; however universal a *political* uprising may be, it conceals even in its *most grandiose* form a *narrow-minded* spirit."[106] Ruge concludes his article by proclaiming that "a social revolution without a political soul . . . is impossible" – to which Marx replies by describing the socialist revolution as "a political revolution with a social soul":

> *Revolution* in general – the *overthrow* of the existing power and *dissolution* of the old relationships – is a *political* act. But *socialism* cannot be realized

---

[99] *Ibid.*
[100] *CW*, III, 202.
[101] *Ibid.*
[102] Ruge, "Der König von Preussen," p. 4; *CW*, III, 203.
[103] *CW*, III, 204.
[104] *CW*, III, 194–197.
[105] Ruge, *op. cit.*; *CW*, III, 204.
[106] *CW*, III, 205.

without *revolution*. It needs this political act insofar as it needs *destruction* and *dissolution*. But where its *organizing* activity begins, where its *proper object*, its *soul* comes to the fore – there socialism throws off the *political* cloak.[107]

However, proceeding from his analysis of the Silesian revolt, Marx also comes to *a new conclusion*, an idea that was not in the *Jahrbücher*. He finds that "the excellent capabilities of the German proletariat for socialism"[108] can be manifested concretely "even apart from" philosophy, even without "the lightning of thought" from the philosophers. Finally, he discovers that the proletariat is not "the *passive* element" in the revolution, quite the contrary: "A philosophical people can find its corresponding practice [*Praxis*] only in socialism, hence it is only in the *proletariat* that it can find the dynamic element [*tätige Element*] of its emancipation." In this one sentence we perceive three themes that are new as compared with the "Introduction":

(a) the people and philosophy are no longer presented as two separate terms, with the second "penetrating" the first: the expression "a philosophical people" shows that this contrast has been transcended;
(b) socialism is no longer presented as pure theory, an idea "born in the philosopher's head," but as a *praxis*;
(c) the proletariat now plainly becomes the *active* element in emancipation.

These three elements already constitute the first waymarks of the theory of self-emancipation of the proletariat, and lead towards the category of *revolutionary praxis* in the *Theses on Feuerbach*.

It is also in the light of the weavers' revolt that Marx looks at "Weitling's brilliant writings," in which he now perceives "the educational level or capacity for education of the German workers in general," the "*vehement* and brilliant literary début of the German workers," "their gigantic *infant shoes*," and compares it with the "faint-hearted mediocrity" of the political literature of the German bourgeoisie."[109] The driving idea which emerges is, basically, that of the proletariat's potential tendency towards socialism. I have tried to demonstrate the mistake made by those who, like Rubel, have contrasted the themes of the "Introduction" with the theory of the party as "brain of the working class." I must now deal with a mistake in the opposite direction. Georg Mende, in his work on Marx's evolution from revolutionary democrat to communist, tries to ascribe to Marx – at the very moment when Marx is abandoning his schema of "thought which takes hold" of the proletariat – the conception held by Kautsky (and by Lenin before 1905) of the "introduction of socialism from without into the working class." Mende writes, in his analysis of the *Vorwärts*

---

[107] *CW*, III, 205–206.
[108] *CW*, III, 202.
[109] *CW*, III, 201–202.

article: "Another remark concerns the problem of spontaneity and consciousness, the problem of the need for a socialist consciousness to be brought into the proletariat from without." "That *social distress* produces *political* understanding is so incorrect that, on the contrary, what is correct is the opposite: *social well-being* produces *political* understanding. *Political* understanding is spiritualist, and is given to him who already has, to him who is already comfortably situated."[110] But what Marx wants to show by this observation is precisely the opposite, namely, that the bourgeoisie's social well-being produces political (i.e., bourgeois) understanding, whereas social distress can produce only *social understanding* (i.e., *socialism*). Moreover, he writes plainly, in the paragraph preceding the quotation: "Why does the anonymous author not couple social understanding with social distress, and political understanding with political distress, as the simplest logic requires?" And in the following paragraph he explains how, in Lyons, political understanding "falsified their [the workers'] insight into their real aim" and "deceived their social instinct."[111] In other words, the proletariat's "instinct" can lead it to socialism provided that "political understanding" does not enter from without to confuse the issue. The complementary mistakes of Rubel and Mende offer an almost "didactic" demonstration of the profound evolution, the veritable "qualitative leap" between the Marx of the "Introduction" and the Marx of the *Vorwärts* article.

This evolution can be understood only if we take account of what happened between February and August 1844: Marx's discovery of workers' communism in Paris, the weavers' revolt, etc.

Proceeding from these contacts with the labor movement and from his studies – economic, historical, political, and social – Marx begins, with the *Vorwärts* article, to escape from the equivocal world of "philosophical communism" and Feuerbachian "humanism" (the ideological prolongation of which was to be "true socialism"). He would make a radical and explicit criticism of that world in his subsequent writings, from *The Holy Family* to *The German Ideology*, but the "Critical Marginal Notes" of August 1844 already represent an implicit break. Based on an actual revolutionary event, they put in question not merely the Hegelian philosophy of the state (which had been done already in the *Jahrbücher* articles), but also Feuerbach's conception of the relations between philosophy and the world, theory and practice. In discovering in the proletariat the *active element* of emancipation, Marx, without saying a word about Feuerbach or philosophy, breaks with the schema to which he had still adhered in the "Introduction." By this *practical* stand taken on a revolutionary movement, the path is opened which leads to the *Theses on Feuerbach*.

---

[110] G. Mende, *Karl Marx: Entwicklung von revoluionären Demokraten zum Kommunisten* (Berlin: Dietz Verlag, 1960), p. 105. The Marx quotation is in *CW*, III, 203.
[111] *CW*, III, 203–204.

Ruge and several other neo-Hegelians failed to grasp the significance of this article. In a letter to Fröbel, December 6, 1844, Ruge shows his bafflement with Marx's article, which he can account for only by "the hatred and madness" of its author: "Marx, despite my efforts to keep our differences within proper limits, has everywhere carried them to extremes: he indulges in insults against me, in vulgar expressions, and has at least put into print his unscrupulous hatred and anger, and all this for what reason? ... For my part, I know of no motive other than my opponent's hatred and madness."[112] It was the same with Jung and other Young Hegelians in Cologne, who could not understand the ideological significance of the break between Marx and Ruge and put it down to personal factors. In a letter to Marx, November 19, 1844, Engels wrote:

> Jung, for instance, as well as many others, cannot be convinced that the difference between us and Ruge is one of principle, and still persists in believing that it is merely a personal squabble. When told that Ruge is no communist, they don't quite believe it and assert that in any case it would be a pity if such a 'literary authority' as Ruge were to be thoughtlessly discarded.[113]

The reason for this "general incomprehension" is probably to be sought in the "novelty" of the "Critical Marginal Notes," or, more precisely, in the fact that they already lay, implicitly, outside the "ideological field" of the Young Hegelians, without the theoretical implications of the break that was implied being developed.

c) *The Holy Family*

The Holy Family is the first work produced jointly by Marx and Engels. It followed immediately upon their historic encounter in Paris in August–September 1844, during which, as Engels was to write in 1885, "our complete agreement in all theoretical fields became evident."[114] However, despite this agreement on fundamentals, it would be absurd to deny that there were differences between them, nuances specific to each, if only owing to the "English" origin of Engels's socialism and the "French" origin of Marx's. For this reason (but without wishing to decide the inexhaustible argument about Marx's philosophy and Engels's dialectical materialism), I shall confine my attention here to writings by Marx himself, in so far as they can be clearly distinguished from those by Engels. This distinction is fairly easy to make in the case of *The Holy Family*, to which we know what part, a fairly small one, was contributed by Engels – a part, moreover, in which the frequent references to Chartism bear witness to the English background of his political evolution.

One of the central themes of *The Holy Family* is radical criticism of "critical criticism," the counterposing of "spirit" and "masses." The origin of this prob-

---

[112] Ruge, *Briefwechsel*, p. 382.
[113] *CW*, XXXVIII, 9–10.
[114] *CW*, XXXVI, 318.

lematic goes back to 1842–1843, to the downfall of the liberal and neo-Hegelian press, the event which revealed the gap between "German thought" and "German reality" (i.e., according to the Young Hegelians, between 'spirit" and "masses"). From that moment, three positions took shape:

(a) that of "Bruno Bauer and Co.," for whom the "masses" were the irreconcilable enemy of "critical thinking";
(b) that of Ruge, for whom "the education of the masses is the realization of theory" and it is necessary "to set the masses in motion in the direction indicated by theory";[115] a variant of this position was Marx's thesis in the "Introduction" – "the lightning of thought" has to strike "the ingenuous soil of the people," etc.;
(c) that of Marx from 1846: dialectical reciprocity between socialist theory and the revolutionary proletariat. In contrast to this position, the other two have in common one point which is decisive, namely, that the spirit alone is the *active* element which, for Bauer, has to operate above and outside the masses, whereas for Ruge (and the Marx of February 1844), it has to "take hold" of them and "set them in motion."

Marx's critique in *The Holy Family* is aimed not only at Bauer's thesis in the strict sense, but also at this presupposition which had been his own at the beginning of the year. In this sense, it continues and deepens the ideas outlined in the *Vorwärts* article, until it becomes a veritable "self-criticism" of the "Introduction." According to Bruno Bauer, "it is in the masses that must be sought the true enemy of the spirit. All the great actions in history up to now have been found wanting and have failed because the masses became interested in and enthusiastic about them."[116] Marx first shows that this ideology is nothing but *"a critically caricatured consummation of Hegel's conception of history*, which, in turn, is nothing but the *speculative* expression of the *Christian-Germanic* dogma of the antithesis between *Spirit* and *Matter*, between *God* and the world." It "presupposes an *Abstract* or *Absolute spirit* which develops in such a way that mankind is a mere *mass* that bears the spirit with a varying degree of consciousness or unconsciousness."[117] Having thus exposed what he calls "the *hidden* meaning" of Bauer's theories, Marx directs his criticism at the schema which logically follows from it – *and which is none other than his own schema of February 1844*: "On the one hand is the Mass as the passive, spiritless, unhistorical, *material* element of history. On the other is the Spirit, *Criticism*, Herr Bruno and co. as the active element from which all *historical* action proceeds."[118] This contrast is further expressed in another

---

[115] Ruge, *Gesammelte Schriften* (Mannheim, 1847), Bd. III, p. 220; Bd. VI, p. 134.
[116] Bauer, *Allgemeine Literatur Zeitung*, Heft I, 1843, p. 2, in D. Hertz-Eichenrode, "Massenpsychologie bei den Junghelianer," *International Review of Social History*, VII, 2 (1962), p. 243.
[117] *CW*, IV, 85. Cf. also *CW*, IV, 94, 141.
[118] *CW*, IV, 86. Cf. also *CW*, IV, 135: "The antithesis between spirit and mass is the

form: "A few well-chosen individuals as the active Spirit are counterposed to the rest of mankind, as the spiritless *Mass*, as *Matter*."[119] This ideology is that not only of the neo-Hegelians like Bauer but also of those, like the French "doctrinaires" (Guizot, Roger-Collard) who were "proclaiming the *sovereignty of reason* in opposition to the *sovereignty of the people*," a formula which Marx shows to be linked with bourgeois individualism: "If the activity of *real* mankind is nothing but the activity of a *mass* of human individuals, then *abstract generality, Reason, the Spirit,* on the contrary, must have an abstract expression restricted to a few individuals."[120] These observations show us that Marx's criticism of the views of "Bruno Bauer and co." is at the same time, implicitly, criticism of all political ideologies that counterpose an "enlightened minority" to the "ignorant masses." This enables us now to measure the distance that separates Marx's thinking from the Jacobin or Jacobino-Babouvist trends of the 19th century. In the same direction, when Marx writes that Bauer's "critical theology" amounts to "the annunciation of the Critical Savior and Redeemer of the world,"[121] he suggests that there is a connection between these ideologies and the myths of the "savior from on high," and he sets the theory of communism in fundamental opposition to this ideological structure. Finally, through his critique of Bauer's theories, Marx draws nearer to the idea of proletarian self-emancipation.

From his break with Young Hegelian idealism Marx goes over to the other extreme, basing his communism on the French materialism of the 18th century. The theme which serves as "hinge" in this transition is that of "the Critical gap which separates *mass-type* [*massenhaften*], profane communism and socialism from *absolute* socialism." For the latter, what is involved is only "emancipation in *mere theory*" whereas the former is that of "the Mass which considers material, practical upheavals necessary." For one school, men change themselves by "changing their '*abstract ego*' in consciousness," for the other, the change is brought about by "*real* change in their real existence."[122] Marx identifies his communism with that of the

> *mass-minded* communist workers employed, for instance, in the Manchester or Lyons workshops . . . [who] . . . do not believe that by "pure thinking" they will be able to argue away their industrial masters and their own practical debasement. They are most painfully aware of the *difference* between *being* and *thinking*, between *consciousness* and *life*. They know that property,

---

Critical 'organization of society,' in which *the* Spirit, or *Criticism*, represents the organising *work*, the mass – the *raw material*, and history – the *product*." Also, *CW*, IV, p. 66: "On one side is the '*divine element*' (Rudolph), . . . the only active principle – on the other side is the passive '*world system*' and the human beings belonging to it."

[119] *CW*, IV, 86.
[120] *CW*, IV, 85.
[121] *CW*, IV, 112.
[122] *CW*, IV, 94–95, 53.

capital, money, wage-labor and the like are no ideal figments of the brain but very practical, very objective products of their self-estrangement [*selbstentfremdung*] and that therefore they must be abolished in a practical, objective way...[123]

This key notion, that it is real, "external" conditions and not consciousness, the "ego," that has to be changed first, was not new. We find it already in the 18th century materialists, which at once explains why Marx, in *The Holy Family*, not only defends French materialism against the attacks of "Bruno Bauer and co.," but even maintains that one of the 18th century tendencies – the "non-Cartesian" branch of materialism – "leads directly to *socialism* and *communism*."[124]

> There is no need for any great penetration to see from the teaching of materialism on the original goodness and equal intellectual endowment of men, the omnipotence of experience, habit and education, and the influence of environment on man, the great significance of industry, the justification of enjoyment, etc., how necessarily materialism is connected with communism and socialism ... If man is shaped by environment, his environment must be made human.[125]

Marx sketches a schema of history in which this significant structure, which he finds in Condillac, for whom "the whole development of man ... depends on education and *external* circumstances," in Helvétius, who recognizes "the omnipotence of education," and, in general, in all the French materialists inspired by Locke,[126] leads directly to the communism of Fourier, Owen, Cabet, the Babouvists, and, above all, of "the more scientific French communists, *Dézamy, Gay* and others," who "developed the teaching of *materialism* as the teaching of *real humanism* and the *logical* basis of communism."[127] In other words, for him, the theoretical starting-point, the historical root, the philosophical foundation of communism are to be found in the materialist proposition that "circumstances shape men, and, in order to change men, circumstances have to be changed."

This fundamental choice leads Marx to appear once more – and for the last time – as a "Feuerbachian." After comparing Feuerbach with the French materialists, Marx concludes:

---

[123] *CW*, IV, 53.
[124] *CW*, IV, 130.
[125] *CW*, IV, 130–131.
[126] *CW*, IV, 129, 130.
[127] *CW*, IV, 131: "Fourier proceeds directly from the teaching of the French materialists. The Babouvists were crude, uncivilized materialists, but developed communism, too, derives *directly* from *French materialism* ... *Bentham* based his system of *correctly understood interest* on Helvétius's morality, and *Owen* proceeded from Bentham's system to found English communism."

> Just as Feuerbach is the representative of *materialism* coinciding with *humanism* in the *theoretical* domain, French and English *socialism* and *communism* represent *materialism* coinciding with *humanism* in the *practical* domain.[128]

There is no need to point out how paradoxical is the evolution from the "Introduction" to *The Holy Family*: the German idealist Marx of February and the French materialist Marx of the end of 1844 are both, implicitly or explicitly, "Feuerbachian"! This shows the futility of interpreting Marx exclusively in terms of Feuerbach's "influence." Here, as elsewhere, this "influence" is not a passive reception but a selection and reinterpretation by the writer who is "influenced." These intellectual operations can change radically in the course of the writer's ideological evolution.[129]

The origin of this paradox lies in the equivocal, ambiguous, torn nature of Feuerbach himself: both "German" and "French," partisan of the "head" and of the "heart," he sometimes declares himself in favor of their fusion in a new philosophy "of Gallo-Germanic blood,"[130] and sometimes for the "demarcation of activities,"[131] without managing to overcome this contradiction dialectically.

Marx remains imprisoned in this duality. In the "Introduction," he takes the side of the "German head" and the changing of men by "the lightning of thought," but, in *The Holy Family*, he is on the side of the "French heart" and the primacy of changing "circumstances."

The Holy Family is, in fact, the metaphysical-materialist moment in the development of Marx's thought, the moment wherein what is essential is negation of "the speculative *mystical identity* of *being* and *thinking*" and of "the equally mystical identity of *practice* and *theory*," negation of Bauer's tendency "not to recognize any *being* distinct from thought, any *natural energy* distinct from the *spontaneity of the spirit*, . . . any *heart* distinct from the *head*, any *object* distinct from the *subject*, any *practice* distinct from *theory*"[132] – negation which

---

[128] *CW*, IV, 125.
[129] Cf. Goldmann, *The Human Sciences, op. cit.* (London: 1969), Chapter III.
[130] Feuerbach, *Preliminary Theses*, in Ruge, *Anekdota, op. cit.*, p. 76.
[131] Feuerbach, *The Essence of Christianity* (London), pp. 291–292: "Therefore I dismiss the needs of the heart from the sphere of thought, that reason may not be clouded by desires. In the demarcation of activities consists the wisdom of life and thought . . . Necessarily, therefore the God of the rational thinker is another than the God of the heart, which in thought, in reason, only seeks its own satisfaction."
Engels confirms, in *Ludwig Feuerbach and the End of Classical German Philosophy* (1886) the Feuerbachian character of *The Holy Family*: "Then came Feuerbach's *Wesen des Christentums* . . . Enthusiasm was universal: we were all Feuerbachians for a moment. How enthusiastically Marx greeted the new conception and how much – in spite of all critical reservations – he was influenced by it one may read in *The Holy Family*." *CW*, XXVI, 364.
[132] *CW*, IV, 141.

greatly resembles Feuerbach's criticism of "the mystic," a "spiritual hermaphrodite," who "identifies immediately, without critical examination, the masculine principle of thought and the feminine principle of sensual contemplation."[133]

This "French materialist" moment, rejecting the "mystical identity," affirming the primacy of the "heart," meaning the material, the objective, practice, "circumstances," is a stage in Marx's theoretical evolution, a necessary stage, when he reacts radically against the previous neo-Hegelian stage, but it remains partial, "metaphysical," because still incapable of restabilizing the nonmystical unity of "heart" and "head."

This stage would be transcended by a "negation of the negation," by the *Theses on Feuerbach*, in which, through criticism of Feuerbach and the materialism of the 18th century. the unity of theory and practice was reconstituted. This time, however, it would be a non-speculative unity, a dialectical synthesis through *Aufhebung* (sublation) of the contraries. It would be the "monist," materialist and dialectical moment of *revolutionary praxis* as "coincidence of the changing of men with the changing of circumstances."

The materialist dimension of *The Holy Family* is also apparent at the level of the concept of "mass communism." *Massenhaft* means, primarily, material, concrete, practical, and as such, it is the opposite of Bauer's "spiritual." However, this structure also has another dimension no less important, namely the "proletarian mass" meaning of the term, in opposition to Bauer's theory which points to "a few well-chosen individuals" as the incarnation of the "critical spirit." In short, "mass communism" appears as the opposite of Bauer's "critical socialism," as a practical and material movement of the revolutionary proletarian masses.

The concrete historical process during which this communism is realized is that of the proletariat's self-emancipation through becoming conscious of its poverty, which leads it into revolutionary action. The proletarian condition is the complete loss of man, but through consciousness of this loss the way to reappropriation is opened: "The class of the proletariat . . . is, to use an expression of Hegel's, in its abasement the *indignation* at that abasement," it is "poverty which is conscious of its spiritual and physical poverty, dehumanization which is conscious of its dehumanization, and therefore self-abolishing," and so "the proletariat can and must emancipate itself" (*sich selbst befreien*).[134]

The decisive role assigned to consciousness as the basis for revolt,[135] as "mediation" between objective poverty and action, explains Marx's insistence on the

---

[133] Not in the English translation, which was made from the second, revised edition of Feuerbach's book. See *Das Wesen des Christentums*, Vol. 2 (Berlin: 1956), p. 455.
[134] *CW*, IV, 36, 37.
[135] True, certain formulations, inspired by the materialism of "the omnipotence of

"spiritual capacity" of the worker masses, even without intervention from on high: "Moreover prose and poetry emanating in England and France from the lower classes of the people would show ["Criticism"] that the lower classes of the people know how to raise themselves spiritually even without being directly *overshadowed* by the *Holy Ghost of Critical Criticism.*" Marx repeats, in almost the same words, the remark he made in his letter to Feuerbach in August 1844 (and in the Manuscripts of 1844), a remark inspired by his experience of workers' meetings in Paris: "One must know the studiousness, the craving for knowledge, the moral energy and the unceasing urge for development of the French and English workers to be able to form an idea of the *human* nobility of this movement."[136] Yet Marx was not unaware of the existence of different levels of proletarian consciousness. In the following remark, which inspired Lukács, who made it the epigraph for his chapter on class-consciousness in *History and Class Consciousness*, he draws a clear distinction between "class-consciousness" in the psychological sense and "consciousness of the historic task" of the proletariat:

> It is not a question of what this or that proletarian, or even the whole proletariat, at the moment *regards* as its aim. It is a question of *what the proletariat is*, and what, in accordance with this *being*, it will historically be compelled to do. Its aim and historical action is visibly and irrevocably foreshadowed in its own life-situation as well as in the whole organization of bourgeois society today. There is no need to explain here that a large part of the English and French proletariat is already *conscious* of its historic task and is constantly working to develop that consciousness into complete clarity.[137]

The materialism of "circumstances" shows through in the formulation – "its aim and historical action is visibly and irrevocably foreshadowed," but the conclusion of the paragraph suggests that this action is carried out not "automatically" but through the proletariat's becoming conscious of its role. Moreover, in recognizing that a part of the proletariat has already attained this consciousness, even if it has not yet "developed that consciousness into complete clarity" – which brings in a second distinction: between "primitive" and "clear" consciousness of the historic task – Marx reaffirms the historical tendency of the proletariat towards socialism. The theoretician's role is no longer to hurl "the lightning of thought" upon the passive mass, but to help

---

circumstances," suggest that revolt is provoked directly by material poverty, without the mediation of consciousness. "Marx has lost himself in the proletariat, yet at the same time has not only gained theoretical consciousness of that loss, but through urgent, no longer removable, no longer disguisable, imperative need (*Not*) – the practical expression of necessity [*Notwendigkeit*] – is driven to revolt against this inhumanity." *CW*, IV, 37. This "dualistic" formulation, in which coming to consciousness and revolt determined by poverty appear as two separate processes, would be transcended in *The German Ideology*.

[136] *CW*, IV, 135, 84.
[137] *CW*, IV, 37.

the proletariat in its intellectual labor, in the evolution of its consciousness, as yet vague and formless, towards complete clarity and coherence.

How does Marx situate his "communism of the masses" in relation to the other socialist and communist trends of the time? In *The Holy Family*, the line of demarcation is not drawn between utopian socialism and scientific socialism, but between materialist communism and "critical socialism," which fits with the general orientation of the work. Marx presents his conception of communism as the continuation, at the philosophical level, of the materialism of the 18th century. At the political level, it is in the "social" trends in the Revolution (particularly Babouvism) that he sees the first historical manifestation of the communist ideology: "The revolutionary movement which began in 1789 in the *Cercle social*, which in the middle of its course had as its chief representatives *Leclerc* and *Roux*, and which finally with *Babeuf's* conspiracy was temporarily defeated, gave rise to the *communist* idea which *Babeuf's* friend *Buonarroti* re-introduced in France after the revolution of 1830. This idea, consistently developed, is the *idea* of the *new world order*."[138] But even in Babouvism it is the "materialist" aspect that interests him above all: "The Babouvists were crude, uncivilized materialists, but developed communism, too, derives *directly* from *French materialism*."[139] Who were the representatives of "developed communism"? The end of the same paragraph suggests the answer: "Like Owen, the more scientific French Communists, *Dézamy, Gay*, and others, developed the teaching of *materialism* as the teaching of *real humanism* and the *logical* basis of *communism*."[140] This remark is extremely significant: it mixes together scientific and utopian communists and identifies, from their sole common feature – materialism as "the logical basis of communism" – two ideological worlds as radically different as those of Dézamy and Owen. Moreover, the choice of Owen as example also bears the same meaning. He was, among the utopian socialists, the most consistent supporter of the theory of "character formed by circumstances," and he based his socialist project on that assumption. In Marx's unpublished notebooks, there is a summary, in German, of a paragraph from Owen's *Book of the New Moral World*, in which the author defines socialism as "the suppression of the harmful influences which today surround mankind, through creating wholly new combinations of external circumstances."[141]

d) *The Theses on Feuerbach*

In his preface of 1888 to *Ludwig Feuerbach and the End of Classical German Philosophy*, Engels described the *Theses on Feuerbach* as "the first document in

---

[138] *CW*, IV, 119.
[139] *CW*, IV, 131.
[140] *Ibid.*
[141] *Marx-Engels Archief*, International Institute of Social History, shelf-mark B34, p. 13.

which is deposited the brilliant germ of the new world outlook."[142] Indeed, while the Marx of 1842–1844 was still operating within the "ideological field" of Young Hegelianism, and the Marx of *The Holy Family* rallied for a moment to the materialism of the 18th century, the *Theses on Feuerbach* set forth a *new Weltanschauung*. In this sense, they are, so to speak, the first of Marx's "Marxist" writings, the first text in which are outlined the foundations of his "definitive" philosophy, the thinking for which Gramsci, in his *Letters from Prison*, found the happy title of *"philosophy of praxis."*

There are at least three levels in the *Theses*, three closely intertwined themes, and each related to the others. The levels could be called, respectively, "epistemological," "anthropological," and "political," but to do so would be to misrepresent the problem, since what we have here is a radical break with traditional epistemology, anthropology, and politics. From a strictly "logical" standpoint, analysis of the *Theses* ought to proceed from the "abstract" to the "concrete," that is, from the general problem of the relations between theory and practice to the historical problem of revolutionary action. If I proceed in the opposite direction, this is because the evolution of Marx himself followed that path: his starting point was the political analyses in his *Vorwärts* article, which led him to revise his Feuerbachian assumptions at the abstract level.

From his contacts with the labor movement and the weavers' revolt, Marx concluded, in the *Vorwärts* article, that the proletariat was the *active* element in emancipation. What form of activity was meant? Obviously, the *revolutionary activity* of the workers struggling against "the existing state of affairs." Now, this "objective" activity, this *practice* – historically decisive, humanly essential – was in crying contradiction with Feuerbach's schema, which knew only two categories: the theoretical, spiritual activity of the "head" and the egoistic, "passive," crude, "Jewish" activity (the Jewish religion being for Feuerbach the finished expression of "practical egoism").[143] Marx thus finds in the *revolutionary* praxis of the proletariat the prototype of truly human activity, which is neither purely "theoretical" nor egoistically passive, but objective and practical-critical:

> Feuerbach wants sensuous objects, really distinct from conceptual objects, but he does not conceive human activity itself as *objective* activity. In *The Essence of Christianity* he therefore regards the theoretical attitude as the only genuinely human attitude, while practice [*Praxis*] is conceived and defined only in its dirty-Jewish form of appearance. Hence he does not grasp the significance of 'revolutionary,' of 'practical-critical' activity.[144]

---

[142] *CW*, XXVI, 520.
[143] Feuerbach, *The Essence of Christianity*, p. 113: "Their [the Jews'] principle, their God, is the most practical principle in the world, namely, egoism."
[144] *CW*, V, 3. I quote here Marx's original text, not the slightly modified version given by Engels in 1888.

This revolutionary praxis had for Marx, in the first place, a politico-social significance – overthrow of the social structure by the action of the masses – but if he put the term between inverted commas, that was because he was giving it a broader meaning, which includes the transformation of nature by a human activity: labor. Marx's use of the expression *revolutionäre Praxis* is, however, significant, bearing witness to the directly "political" origin of this category. Engels, unaware of this origin, or wishing to use a more explicit term, clearly embracing the two meanings, "revolution" and "labor," uses the expression *umwälzende Praxis* ("revolutionizing practice").[145]

This activity is *objective* (*gegenständlich*) because it "objectivizes itself" in the real world, unlike the purely subjective activity of the Feuerbachian spirit. It is *revolutionary* because it changes nature and society, and it is *practical-critical* in three senses: as practice guided by a critical theory, as criticism directed towards practice, and as practice which "criticizes" (denies) the existing state of affairs.

But the category of revolutionary praxis also destroys another schema, that of the French materialists who counterposed "the omnipotence of education" to the passivity of men who are "shaped by external circumstances": "The materialist doctrine concerning the changing of circumstances and upbringing forgets that circumstances are changed by men and that the educator must himself be educated. This doctrine must, therefore, divide society into two parts, one of which is superior to society. The coincidence of the changing of circumstances and of human activity or self-change can be conceived and rationally understood as *revolutionary practice*."[146] Revolutionary practice, which changes simultaneously circumstances and oneself – or the subject of the action (*Selbstveränderung*) – is, at bottom, *the transcendence, the sublation (Aufhebung) of the antithesis between 18th-century materialism (changing of circumstances) and Young Hegelianism (changing of consciousness)*. After having been, by turns, a German idealist and a French materialist, Marx formulates, in his third thesis on Feuerbach, nothing less than "the brilliant germ of the new world-outlook," which transcends, both "negating" and "conserving" them, the previous phases of his thought – and of the philosophical thought of the 18th and 19th centuries. The third thesis also makes it possible, at the political level, to overcome the dilemma of the communism of the 1840s, torn between a "Babouvist-materialist" trend which entrusted a group "raised above society," an élite of "wise and virtuous citizens," with the task of changing circumstances – by taking power through a sudden attack – and a "utopian-pacifist" trend which proposed to change "men first" and wished, by the

---

[145] CW, V, 4, 7.
[146] CW, V, 4. In Engels's version, Owen is given as the typical example of this doctrine. CW, V, 7. This choice is interesting, since Owen was presented in *The Holy Family* as the true "materialist" and "scientific" communist precisely because of his total support for the theory of circumstances.

power alone of propaganda and persuasion, to convince princes, bourgeois and proletarians alike of the merits of the communitarian way of life.

Finally, the category of revolutionary praxis is the *theoretical foundation* of the Marxist conception of self-emancipation of the proletariat by revolution. The coincidence of the changing of circumstances and of men means that, in the course of its struggle against the existing state of affairs, the proletariat transforms itself, develops its consciousness, and becomes capable of building a new society. This process reaches its culmination at the moment of the revolution, during which the broad masses "change" and become conscious of their role while changing circumstances through their action. Based upon the third thesis, the idea of self-liberation of the working class through communist revolution, self-education of the proletariat through its own revolutionary practice, constitutes the transcending of the various "political corollaries" of 18th-century materialism, the different ways of resorting to some entity "above society" – the Encyclopedists' hopes of "enlightened absolutism," the utopian socialists' appeal to monarchs, Jacobinism and Jacobino-Babouvism, etc. At the same time, Marx separates himself from all the trends of "idealist" socialism (such as German "true socialism") and the "pacifist," anti-revolutionary trends (such as the "Icarians").

All this is not, of course, to be found *in nuce* in the third thesis. But these were the themes that would be developed in *The German Ideology* in a rigorously coherent theory of *communist revolution by the masses*.

The eighth, ninth, and tenth theses are, so to speak, the "sociological" prolongation of the third. The old materialism confronted the contemplative (*anschauend*) individual with "social circumstances," meaning "bourgeois society" (*bürgerliche Gesellschaft*), as a set of social and economic laws that were "natural," independent of individuals' will or action: "The highest point reached by contemplative materialism, that is, materialism which does not comprehend sensuousness [*Sinnlichkeit*] as practical activity, is the contemplation [*Anschaung*] of single individuals and of civil society."[147] For the new materialism, which proceeds from active man, changing "circumstances," society, "all social life is essentially practical."[148] Its standpoint is "human society," that is, society as a "political," concrete network of social relations, as a structure created by men in the cause of their historical activity, their struggle against nature, etc.: "The standpoint of the old materialism is civil society: the standpoint of the new is human society, or social humanity."[149]

---

[147] CW, V, 5. (*Bürgerliche* is here translated as "civil" rather than "bourgeois" – Trans.)
[148] *Ibid.*
[149] *Ibid.*, see n. 147.

To understand this last thesis, we need to appreciate the ambiguity of the terms "bourgeois society" and "human society." *Bürgerliche Gesellschaft* is both the category of *civil* society, that is, an "individualist" way of perceiving social relations, and *bourgeois* society, that is, capitalist society, in which the bourgeoisie is, or tends to become, the ruling class. Similarly, "human society" means, on the one hand, a "practical" and "sociological" conception of (contemporary) social life, and, on the other, the socialist society of the future. The two meanings overlap, in so far as "civil society" is the ideology of bourgeois society and "human society" the theory of the revolutionaries who fight for a socialist society.

However, the more abstract and general developments of the category of revolutionary praxis lie at the level of the relations between theory and practice, knowledge and action.

The "gnoseology" of Feuerbach and of the old materialism, as these are presented in the *Theses*, envision social and natural reality as a pure *object*, the sensibility of the subject as passive *contemplation*, and theoretical knowledge as mere *interpretation* of reality. The two first assumptions are criticized by Marx at the beginning of the first and in the fifth thesis: "The chief defect of all previous materialism (that of Feuerbach included) is that things [*Gegenstand*], reality, sensuousness [*Sinnlichkeit*] are conceived only in the form of the *object* [*Objekts*] or of *contemplation*, but not as *sensuous human activity, practice*, not subjectively. Hence, in contradistinction to materialism, the *active* side was set forth abstractly by idealism – which, of course, does not know real, sensuous activity as such." (First thesis). "Feuerbach, not satisfied with *abstract thinking*, wants *contemplation* [*Anschauung*: in Engels's version, "sensuous contemplation"] – but he does not conceive sensuousness [*Sinnlichkeit*] as *practical*, human-sensuous activity." (Fifth thesis).[150]

The significance of these "aphorisms" becomes fully apparent, once again, only if we take account of the double meaning of *Sinnlichkeit* in Feuerbach and Marx: on the one hand "materiality," the material world, that which is concrete, but, on the other, "sensuousness," the activity (or passivity) of the senses, their "subjective faculty."[151] Most (French) translators keep to the first possibility – "*la matérialité*" for Molitor, "*la réalité concrète et sensible*" for Rubel, etc. – which results in obvious absurdities. Marx is made to accuse the old materialism of perceiving the material, concrete world only in the form of contemplation, "intuition." It is, of course, not *the material world* but the relation between the senses and this world, that is, *sensuousness*, which is, with the old materialists, pure contemplation.

---

[150] *CW*, V, 3, 4.
[151] Cf. Althusser, translator's note in Feuerbach, *Manifestes philosophiques* (Paris: P.U.F., 1960), p. 6.

Marx's thesis also needs to be divided into its two parts. "*Sinnlichkeit* is human-sensuous, practical activity" means:

(a) The concrete world, social and natural, is activity, practice, or the product of human praxis. This thematic would be developed in *The German Ideology*, where Marx shows that society is a set of production-relations and that even the natural milieu is profoundly changed by human labor;

(b) Sensuousness is not pure contemplation but human activity – on the one hand because it is exercised through labor and social praxis, on the other because sensuous perception is itself already *activity*.[152]

But the decisive break, at the level of the "problem of knowledge," between Marx and 18th-century philosophy (or all "earlier philosophy") comes with the eleventh thesis: "The philosophers have only *interpreted* the world in various ways: the point is to *change* it."[153] To grasp all the implications of this lapidary sentence, we need to go beyond the usual interpretations, which, in a way, remain on the surface. The meaning given to it by the more superficial popularizations counterposes theory and practice as mutually exclusive alternatives: "The philosophers have interpreted the world, Marx fights to change it: Marxism is revolutionary practice contrasted with abstract speculation, etc." This type of reasoning – against which Lenin came out with his well-known slogan: "no revolutionary practice without revolutionary theory" – is formally disproved not only by Marx's immense body of theoretical work but already by the *Theses on Feuerbach* themselves, in which it is clearly stated that the world must be "both understood in its contradictoriness and revolutionized in practice," "destroyed in theory and practice." The rational solution must be found "in human practice and the comprehension [*Begreifen*] of this practice."[154] The expression "practical-critical activity" itself suggests this active synthesis between thought and praxis, between "interpreting" and "changing."

Most of the "non-popular" interpreters of the eleventh thesis stay at that level. According to their more refined version, the thesis counterposes to "pure" interpretation, without practical consequences, revolutionary interpretation, accompanied by the corresponding activity. This version forgets that even allegedly "pure" contemplation has practical consequences: it contributes, directly or indirectly, consciously or unconsciously, to *conservation* of the *status quo*, by justifying it, ascribing to it a "natural" character, or sim-

---

[152] In this connection it is worthy of note that Goldmann relates the *Theses on Feuerbach* to the work of Piaget on "perceptive activity" (*Recherches dialectiques*, p. 126), while Naville compares them to the findings of experimental psychology: no stimulus without response, etc. *De l'aliénation à la jouissance* (Paris: Marcel Rivière, 1957), p. 188.

[153] CW, V, 5.

[154] CW, V, 4, 5.

ply by declining to call it in question. In other words, the counterposing suggested by the eleventh thesis is between an interpretation which contributes to perpetuation of the existing state of affairs and a *critical* interpretation linked with a revolutionary praxis.

At bottom, what we have here is not even an interpretation "linked with" or "accompanied by" a practice but a *total* human activity, *practical-critical* activity, in which theory *is already* revolutionary praxis, and practice is *loaded with theoretical significance*.[155] In *The Holy Family*, Marx was combating the mystical identity between theory and practice. He had to show, against "Bruno Bauer and Co.," that there is a practice which is different from pure philosophical speculation. In the *Theses*, the "French materialist" moment, purely negative, is transcended: Marx restores the unity of thought and action, a dialectical, "practical-critical," revolutionary unity.

Between the weavers' revolt (June 1844) and the *Theses on Feuerbach* (about March 1845), the process of formation of the Marxist *Weltanschauung* was completed. This was *the* great ideological turning point in the evolution of the young Marx. The Silesian rising, together with the communist movement he encountered in Paris, faced him concretely with the problem of the revolutionary praxis of the proletarian masses. In the *Vorwärts* article, Marx discovers the proletariat as the *active* element in emancipation, but he does not yet draw the philosophical conclusions from this discovery. A few weeks later, he sketches, in *The Holy Family*, a first attempt at a theoretical solution of the problem. He believes he can grasp revolutionary activity – which is evidently outside the Young Hegelians' world of thought – through the categories of the French materialism of the 18th century. Soon, however, he perceives that the revolutionary praxis of the *masses* cannot be fitted into the narrow framework of the "theory of circumstances": this is his break with "the old materialism," which at once spreads to all levels. The *Theses on Feuerbach* expose the "practical essence" of history and of social life, of "sensuousness" and of theory, of the relations of men with nature and among themselves, and, finally, outline a coherent set of ideas, a significant global structure: the *philosophy of praxis*, the general theoretical foundation for the idea of revolutionary self-emancipation of the proletariat.

e) *The German Ideology*

Written between September 1845 and May 1846, *The German Ideology* was a joint work by Marx and Engels, and the latter's contribution to it was probably greater than in the case of *The Holy Family*. Given that it is not possible to distinguish what was written by each of them, I regard the total work as expressing Marx's thinking, and this seems all the more justified because

---

[155] Cf. Goldmann, "L'idéologie allemande et les thèses sur Feuerbach," *L'Homme et la Societé*, No. 7 (1968), p. 54.

nearly all the manuscripts bear corrections or additions from his pen, and because Engels himself wrote that "When, in the spring of 1845, we met again in Brussels, Marx had already fully developed his materialist theory of history . . . This discovery, which revolutionized the science of history, and which, as we have seen, is essentially the work of Marx – a discovery in which I can claim for myself only a very small share – was . . . of immediate importance for the workers' movement . . . ."[156]

The German Ideology is, in a sense, the end point of the evolution since 1842 that I have traced and, in particular, is the completion of the turn inaugurated by the *Vorwärts* article of August 1844. That is why the work takes the form of a *self-criticism*: through his criticism of the "German ideologists," Marx is also aiming at the earlier phases of his own philosophical itinerary, and definitively transcending these. It is in this sense that we must interpret the well-known remark in the Preface to his *Contribution to the Critique of Political Economy* (1859):

> When, in the spring of 1845 he [Engels] too came to live in Brussels, we decided to set forth together our conception as opposed to the ideological one of German philosophy, *in fact to settle accounts with our former philosophical conscience*. The intention was carried out in the form of a critique of post-Hegelian philosophy . . . We abandoned the manuscript to the gnawing criticism of the mice all the more willingly since we had achieved our main purpose – self-clarification.[157]

This is especially clear in relation to the articles in the *Deutsch-Französische Jahrbücher*, in which, the authors of *The German Ideology* point out, "at the time," use was made of "philosophical phraseology," and the central theoretical categories of which – spirit, heart – were now rejected as "abstract thoughts."[158] On the other hand, there is no break between this manuscript and the *Theses on Feuerbach*, the essential themes of which it develops, by way of criticism of the "materialist" (Feuerbach) and idealist (Bauer, Stirner, Grün) trends in neo-Hegelianism, a criticism which leads on to a rigorous and precise structuring of the theory of communist revolution.

In the first place, the criticism by Marx and Engels is directed against the fundamental postulate of Young Hegelian idealism: "to change consciousness," "to interpret the existing world in a different way," without "in any way combating the real existing world." This postulate is present in Bruno Bauer, who "believes in the power of the philosophers and . . . shares their illusion that a modified consciousness, a new turn given to the interpretation of existing relations, could overturn the whole hitherto existing world," and in "Saint Max"

---

[156] *CW*, XXVI, 318.
[157] Marx, Preface to *A Contribution to the Critique of Political Economy* (London: 1971), p. 22 (My italics – M. L.)
[158] *CW*, V, 236, 172.

(Stirner), who thinks that one really destroys existing conditions "by getting out of [one's] head [one's] false opinion of them."[159] For the communist, however, what is needed is "revolutionizing the existing world, . . . practically coming to grips with it and changing the things found in existence."[160] This theme, a leitmotiv of *The German Ideology*, is there already in *The Holy Family*, but here it leads to a clear political conclusion, expressed in a sharply worded formulation: "communism is for us not a *state of affairs* which is to be established, an *ideal* to which reality [will] have to adjust itself. We call communism the *real* movement which abolishes the present state of things."[161] Against "true socialism," for which communism is a matter of "abstract theories" and "principles," and against Feuerbach, who "thinks that it is . . . possible to change the word 'communist' which in the real world means the follower of a definite revolutionary party, into a mere category,"[162] Marx emphasizes that "communism is a highly practical movement, pursuing practical aims by practical means."[163] To measure the full distance traveled since 1842, we need to compare these passages with the article on communism for *Rheinische Zeitung* – "the real *danger* lies not in *practical attempts* but in the *theoretical elaboration* of communist ideas" – with the articles in the *Deutsch-Französische Jahrbücher*, deeply impregnated with "philosophic communism" *à la* Moses Hess, and even with the *Manuscripts of 1844*, where what is discussed is the future communist society rather than the revolutionary workers' movement.

However, Marx does not remain at that level, which is the level of *The Holy Family*. As in the *Theses on Feuerbach*, he also criticizes 18th-century materialism, in particular the "theory of circumstances." He even calls "reactionary" the "so-called *objective* historiography," which treats "historical relations separately from activity," and he shows that, on the contrary, the conditions of activity "are produced by this self-activity."[164] Similarly, he ridicules those who completely separate "the transformation of existing conditions" from "people," forgetting that "existing conditions" have always been those of "people," and could never have been changed unless "people" changed them.[165] This identity between changing circumstances and changing oneself is true of all spheres of human life, starting with productive activity, labor: "Men, developing their material production and their material intercourse [*Verkehr*], alter along with this their actual world, also their thinking and the products of their thinking."[155]

---

[159] *CW*, V, 30, 100–101, 126. Cf. also *CW*, V, 431.
[160] *CW*, V, 38–39.
[161] *CW*, V, 49.
[162] *CW*, V, 458, 57.
[163] *CW*, V, 215.
[164] *CW*, V, 55, 82.
[165] *CW*, V, 379.
[166] *CW*, V, 37.

At the level of modern political history, this convergence is realized through the communist revolution, in which the changing of "existing [social] conditions" and that of the consciousness of the mass of humanity, that is, the proletariat, coincide. Here we arrive at the very heart of the Marxist theory of the revolutionary self-emancipation of the proletariat, which is based on two key ideas, each implying the other:

(1) Alienations can be recovered only in a non-alienated way. The character of the new society is determined by the very process of its creation:

> This appropriation is further determined by the manner in which it must be effected. It can only be effected through a union, which by the character of the proletariat itself can again only be a universal one, and through a revolution in which, on the one hand, the power of the earlier mode of production and intercourse and social organization is overthrown and, on the other hand, there develops the universal character and the energy of the proletariat, which are required to accomplish the appropriation, and the proletariat moreover rids itself of everything that still clings to it from its previous position in society.[167]

The last phrase introduces the second theme:

(2) The revolution is needed not only to destroy the old order, the "external" barriers, but also in order to enable the proletariat to overcome its "internal" barriers, change its consciousness and become capable of creating communist society:

> Both for the production on a mass scale [*massenhaften*] of this communist consciousness, and for the success of the cause itself, the alteration of men on a mass scale is necessary, an alteration which can only take place in a practical movement, a *revolution*: the revolution is necessary, therefore, not only because the *ruling* class cannot be overthrown in any other way, but also because the class *overthrowing* [*stürzende*] it can only in a revolution succeed in ridding itself of all the muck of ages and become fitted to found society anew . . . Stirner believes that the communist proletarians who revolutionize society and put the relations of production and the form of intercourse on a new basis – i.e., on themselves as new people, on their new mode of life – that these proletarians remain 'as of old.' The tireless propaganda carried on by these proletarians, their daily discussions among themselves, sufficiently prove how little they themselves want to remain 'as of old,' and how little they want people to remain 'as of old.' They would only remain 'as of old' if, with Saint Sancho [Stirner] they 'sought the blame in themselves' . . . but . . . they know too well that only under changed circumstances will they cease to be 'as of old,' and

---

[167] *CW*, V, 88.

therefore they are determined to change these circumstances at the first opportunity. *In revolutionary activity the changing of oneself coincides with the changing of circumstances.*"¹⁶⁸

There is no need to insist on the extraordinary importance of the theory of revolution outlined in these remarks and its radical opposition to the Jacobin, messianic, utopian, or reformist conceptions. I shall merely point out that this is an aspect of Marx's thought which is singularly overlooked by most of his interpreters.¹⁶⁹ This is all the more serious in that it is not an "accident" in Marx's work, but the result of a long ideological evolution (which I have traced step by step). This theory is, moreover, not just a marginal, isolated element artificially introduced into the *Theses on Feuerbach*, but, on the contrary, something closely imbricated in the central "philosophical" themes of his work.

Having thus established in general terms the nature of the communist revolution, Marx tries to answer the fundamental question: why and how does the proletariat become revolutionary?

To begin with, Marx reiterates one of the theses of his *Introduction to the Contribution to the Critique of Hegel's Philosophy of Law*, the one that bases the emancipating role of the proletariat on the *radical* and *universal* character of the suffering of this class, "which has to bear all the burdens of society without enjoying its advantages" and "which has no longer any particular class interest to assert against a ruling class."¹⁷⁰ In *The German Ideology*, though, this suffering has lost all passive significance. The term "passion" (*Leidenschaft*) is even used in a revolutionary and active sense. "'Worry' flourishes in its purest form among the German good burghers . . . whereas the poverty [*Not*] of the proletarian assumes an acute, sharp form, drives him into a life-and-death struggle, makes him revolutionary, and therefore engenders not 'worry' but passion."¹⁷¹

However, while it is true that the revolutionary character of the proletariat results from the concrete social condition of this class, that character appears rather as a tendency, a potentiality, which becomes actual only through the *historical practice* of the class itself. Marx here presents the thesis of the *Introduction* in the terms of the theory of praxis, for which "the being of men is their actual life-process," which means, at the socioeconomic level, that

---

¹⁶⁸ *CW*, V, 52–53, 214. (My italics – M. L.)
¹⁶⁹ An exception is the excellent introduction by Lelio Basso to the Italian edition of Rosa Luxemburg's works. Cf. Rosa Luxemburg, *Scritti Politici* (*Introduzione*) (Rome: E. Riuniti, 1967), p. 107. See also the thought-provoking introduction by Maximilien Rubel to his *Marx: Pages choisies pour une éthique socialiste* (Paris: M. Rivière, 1948).
¹⁷⁰ *CW*, V, 52, 77.
¹⁷¹ *CW*, V, 219. Marx even writes of "*revolutionäre Leidenschaft* ("revolutionary enthusiasm"). *CW*, V, 457.

"what they are . . . coincides with their production,"[172] and, at the level of the problem of revolution, that the proletariat becomes revolutionary only through its own revolutionary praxis. This apparent paradox becomes more comprehensible if one spaces it out into three stages:

(1) The proletariat becomes a class in the full sense of the term only through its fight against the bourgeoisie: "The separate individuals form a class only insofar as they have to carry on a common battle against another class";[173]

(2) In the course of this fight, the proletariat is obliged to use revolutionary methods, even if, at the start, its action does not challenge the regime itself: "Even a minority of workers who combine and go on strike very soon find themselves compelled to act in a revolutionary way – a fact he [Max Stirner] could have learned from the 1842 uprising in England and from the earlier Welsh uprising of 1839, in which year the revolutionary excitement among the workers first found expression in the 'sacred month,' which was proclaimed simultaneously with a general arming of the people";[174]

(3) Through this revolutionary practice, communist consciousness is born and develops among the worker masses. Still in line with the theory of praxis, Marx declares that consciousness cannot be "other than consciousness of existing practice," which means, in the case of the proletariat, that "for the production on a mass scale of this communist consciousness, and for the success of the cause itself, the alteration of men on a mass scale is necessary, an alteration which can only take place in a practical movement, a *revolution*."[175] Our "paradox" is therefore solved, in the last analysis, through the coincidence, in revolutionary praxis, of the "changing of circumstances" with the "changing of consciousness."

These remarks already show that Marx was now conceiving the problem of the relations between the proletariat and revolutionary ideas in terms that were quite different from those of the *Introduction*. In that article in the *Jahrbücher*, he had written that "revolution begins in the brain of the philosopher" – a theme typical of "philosophical communism" and which was to be revived by its theological heir, "true socialism" – whereas in *The German Ideology*, he stresses that "communism has by no means originated from paragraph 49 of Hegel's *Rechtsphilosophie*."[176] What, then, is the origin of communist ideas? Marx's reply is clear-cut: "the existence of revolutionary ideas

---

[172] CW, V, 36, 31.
[173] CW, V, 77.
[174] CW, V, 204–205.
[175] CW, V, 45, 52–53.
[176] CW, V, 208.

in a particular period presupposes the existence of a revolutionary class." In modern times, this class is obviously the proletariat, "a class ... which has to bear all the burdens of society without enjoying its advantages, which is ousted from society and forced into the sharpest contradiction to all other classes; a class which forms the majority of all members of society, *and from which emanates [ausgeht] the consciousness of the necessity of a fundamental [gründlichen] revolution, the communist consciousness*, which may, of course, arise among the other classes too through the contemplation of the situation of this class."[177] Obviously, this communist consciousness is not the outcome of abstract theoretical reflection by the workers, but of the concrete and practical process of the class struggle: it is the opposition between the bourgeoisie and the proletariat which has engendered communist and socialist ideas.[178]

It is from the standpoint of this new conception of the historical connection between communist theories and the proletariat that Marx criticizes the "true socialists" who "regard foreign communist literature not as the expression and the product of a real movement but as purely theoretical writings," and "detach the communist systems, critical and polemical writings from the real movement of which they are but the expression, and force them into an arbitrary connection with German philosophy."[179] This criticism is, once again, a self-criticism of the way in which Marx saw the problem, in the *Rheinische Zeitung* and the *Deutsch-Französische Jahrbücher*, along with the positions of Moses Hess, Engels, and all the "philosophical communists" of the years 1842–1844. One section of them evolved in the same direction as Marx, while the rest ended up with "true socialism": "It was just as inevitable that a number of German communists, proceeding from a philosophical standpoint, should have arrived, and still arrive, at communism by way of this transition, while others, unable to extricate themselves from this ideology, should go on preaching true socialism to the bitter end."[180]

But though Marx rejects fundamentally the idea that "revolution begins in the brain of the philosopher" – a view which he now describes as being that of the *idealist* for whom "every movement designed to transform the world exists only in the head of some chosen being"[181] – and while he proclaims plainly that communist consciousness *begins in the proletariat* (which at once shows us the incompatibility between Kautsky's ideas and those of *The German Ideology*), the possibility that communist ideas may be developed by members of other classes is not ruled out by him. On the contrary, he says that

---

[177] *CW*, V, 60, 52. (My italics – M. L.)
[178] *CW*, V, 419: "... when the contradiction between the bourgeoisie and the proletariat had given rise to communist and socialist views."
[179] *CW*, V, 455, 456.
[180] *CW*, V, 457.
[181] *CW*, V, 532.

communist consciousness "may, of course, arise among the other classes too through the contemplation of the situation of this class [the proletariat]."[182] Individuals who have attained that understanding may become *the theoretical representatives (theoretischen Vertreter) of the proletariat*, and they have a decisive role to play in the reinforcement and clarification of communist consciousness.

> In reality, the actual property-owners stand on one side and the propertyless communist proletarians on the other. This opposition becomes keener day by day and is rapidly driving to a crisis. If, then, the theoretical representatives of the proletariat wish their literary activity to have any practical effect, they must first and foremost insist that all phrases are dropped which tend to dim the realization of this opposition, all phrases which tend to conceal this opposition and may even give the bourgeois a chance to approach the communists for safety's sake on the strength of their philanthropic enthusiasms.[183]

The German Ideology is Marx's first work in which the term communist *party* is used. To be sure, no precise analysis of organizational problems is to be found there, but the word does bear a concrete meaning that distinguishes it from the literary or philosophical "party" of the Young Hegelians. In a paragraph of his chapter directed against "true socialism," Marx counterposes the genuine communist and workers' parties to the pseudo-parties of the German ideologists:

> Here we have, on the one hand, the actually existing communist party in France with its literature and, on the other, a few German pseudo-scholars who are trying to comprehend the ideas of this literature philosophically. The latter are treated just as much as the former as *"principal party* of this *age,"* as a party, that is to say, of infinite importance not only to its immediate antithesis, the French communists, but also to the English Chartists and communists, the American National Reformers and indeed to every other party "of this age" . . . But it has for a considerable time been the fashion among German ideologists for each literary faction, particularly the one that thinks itself "most advanced," to proclaim itself not merely "one of the principal parties," but actually "the principal party of the age." We have, among others, "the principal party" of critical criticism, "the principal party" of egoism in agreement with itself and now "the principal party" of the true socialists.[184]

This passage draws up a rather significant first list of the proletarian parties. We find in it groups or trends which were communist in the strict sense, both English and French, and also workers' parties which lacked a clear ideology

---

[182] *CW*, V, 52.
[183] *CW*, V, 469.
[184] *CW*, V, 466.

(Chartism, the National Reformers).[185] To this group was obviously to be added the German Communist Party that was now being formed: "It is obvious that since the appearance of a real communist party in Germany, the public of the true socialists will be more and more limited to the petty-bourgeoisie..."[186]

The historical development of the real communist parties was bound, in Marx's view, to progressively eliminate not only the literary factions of the "true socialist" type, but also the utopian sects and systems, which corresponded to the ideological level of the labor movement in its beginnings:

> As to the systems themselves, they nearly all appeared in the early days of the communist movement and had at that time propaganda value as popular novels, which corresponded perfectly to the still undeveloped consciousness of the proletarians, who were then just beginning to play an active part... As the party develops, these systems lose all importance and are at best retained purely nominally as catchwords. Who in France believes in Icarie, who in England believes in the plans of Owen...?[187]

The contrast with *The Holy Family* is striking: here "materialist communism" is no longer being counterposed to "critical socialism," Owen to Bauer, but the real proletarian party, communist or working-class, to the various literary, philosophical, and utopian sects, Owen's included.

---

[185] The National Reform Association was an organization created in October 1845 by an Industrial Congress, which brought together several workers' associations and the secret society called "Young America." The American section of the League of the Just, made up of German worker-émigrés, formed weeks later, a German-speaking branch under the title "Social Reform Association," a group influenced by the "true socialism" of H. Kruege. Cf. K. Obermann, "Die Amerikanische Arbeiterwegung vor dem Bürgerkrieg im Kampf für Demokratie und gegen die Herrschaft der Sklavenhalter," *Zeitschrift für Geschichtswissenschaft*, Heft 1, X. Jahrgang (1962).
[186] *CW*, V, 457.
[187] *CW*, V, 461.

Chapter Three
The Theory of the Party (1846–1848)

I. Marx and the Communist Party (1846–1848)

Why did the political activity of Marx and Engels in the workers' movement not begin, in systematic and organized fashion, until 1846? Some remarks by Engels in his sketch of the history of the League of Communists suggest the answer:

> When, in the spring of 1845, we met again in Brussels, Marx had already fully developed his materialist theory of history in its main features... and we now applied ourselves to the detailed elaboration of the newly-won outlook in the most varied directions... Now, we were by no means of the opinion that the new scientific results should be confided in large tomes exclusively to the "learned" world... It was our duty to provide a scientific substantiation for our view, but it was equally important for us to win over the European, and in the first place the German, proletariat to our conviction. As soon as we had become clear in our own minds, we set to work.[1]

It was, indeed, not accidental that their organic activity as a communist trend in the movement should have begun after the composition of the *Theses on Feuerbach* and the essentials of *The German Ideology*. Only then did they become "clear in their own minds," possessing a coherent general view, a revolutionary theory that both expressed and transcended the actual tendencies in the European workers' movement.

---

[1] CW, XXVI, 318–319.

Marx's activity during 1846–1848 was precisely the *practical-critical activity* preached by the *Theses on Feuerbach*: every practical decision, like every letter, circular, or speech was *theoretically significant*.

This activity had a definite aim: to form a communist vanguard freed from utopian socialism and the "true," conspiratorial, or "sentimental" varieties, and to create, on the international scale, but first of all in Germany, a revolutionary and "scientific" Communist Party which must be theoretically coherent, yet not become a sect cut off from the proletarian masses.

Marx's conception of the party, as this emerges from his activity at the head of the Correspondence Committee in Brussels and the League of Communists, as well as from his principal theoretical works of the period 1846–1848, was a new conception, both in relation to the previous phases of his political evolution – phases in which the problem of organization had not yet arisen – and to the existing workers' organizations. Here, too, Marx was working towards a synthesis which would incorporate, while transcending, the experience of the French secret societies and the English mass movement. It was no accident that the Communist League was the first embryo of such an organization: born in Paris, developed in London, made up of Germans, it was able to assemble the experience of the revolutionary vanguard in the principal European countries.

a) *The Communist Correspondence Committee*

The Communist Correspondence Committee formed in Brussels in February 1846 was the *first political organization* created by Marx and Engels. Why did they choose the name *Kommunistisches Korrespondenzkomitee*? According to Ryazanov, it was in memory of the Jacobin correspondence committees in the French Revolution, which were the means of communication between the Jacobin clubs in different towns, or of the Corresponding Societies, the English revolutionary societies of the late 18th century.[2] In my view, the "correspondence committee" character of the first "Marxist party" was due to a number of objective conditions:

(a) the international character of the project – to establish links between communists all over Europe;
(b) the dispersion of the German communists, both intellectuals and artisans, who were the immediate object of the ideological and organizational work of Marx and Engels;
(c) the simple fact that Brussels was away from the main centers of the labor and communist movement. The essential objectives of the

---

[2] Ryazanov, Introduction to Marx and Engels, *The Communist Manifesto*, op. cit., p. 19.

Committee were, on the one hand, to hasten the formation of an organized Communist Party in Germany, and even internationally, and, on the other, to win over the communist and workers' vanguard to Marx's new conceptions, through relentless theoretical struggle against "true socialism," utopian socialism, etc.

Already during 1845, Marx had established some international contacts. While in England with Engels (July 1845), he had entered into relations with the local section of the League of the Just and with the left wing of Chartism (G. J. Harvey), and from August 1845, he was in correspondence with Ewerbeck in Paris. However, it was only with the formation, in February 1846, of the Correspondence Committee that these connections were "institutionalized."

The driving center of the Committee was, of course, the Brussels group, led directly by Marx and Engels and composed basically of German refugees. These were mainly intellectuals – writers and journalists like L. Heilberg, F. Wolff, W. Wolff, S. Seiler, and G. Weerth – but there were also some artisans, such as the typographer S. Born, and some Belgians, such as P. Gigot. Also participating, though not for long, were E. von Westphalen (Marx's brother-in-law) and Wilhelm Weitling. Immediately after its creation, the Brussels Committee engaged in a ruthless intellectual and political struggle against the penetration of "true socialism" into, and the persistence of "artisanal communism" in, the German workers' movement. The break with Weitling and the circular against Kriege were the first phases in this struggle.

It was at the meeting of the Committee in Brussels in March 1846 that the split between Weitling and the "Marxists" took place. Present were Marx, Engels, Gigot, von Westphalen, Weydemeyer, Seiler, Heilberg, Annenkov, and Weitling himself, who was defended, to some extent, only by Heilberg and Seiler. The accounts we have of this stormy meeting are rather contradictory. Weitling's version, in a letter to Hess[3] of March 31, 1846, is particularly unreliable, though some of the statements he attributes to Marx are probable enough: for example, criticism of "artisanal," "philosophic," or "sentimental" communism and demand for a purge of the Communist Party.[4] It is in the memoirs of Annenkov, published in Russia in 1880, that we find the most detailed and probably the most accurate description of this historic confrontation. One of the passages in Marx's speech against Weitling, as reported by Annenkov, reveals at once the theoretical and practical significance of the break: "Especially in Germany, to appeal to the workers without a rigorous scientific idea and without a positive doctrine had the same value as an empty

---

[3] Ryazanov, "Introduction historique," *Manifeste communiste* (Paris: Costes, 1953), p. 23. [This is the French version of the work mentioned in note 2, but is fuller than the English one – Trans.]
[4] Ryazanov, "Introduction historique," *op. cit.*, p. 27.

and dishonest game at playing preacher, with someone supposed to be an inspired prophet on the one side and only asses listening to him with mouths agape allowed on the other."[5]

In order to appreciate the sharpness of these criticisms one must not forget that the Weitling of 1846 was no longer the Weitling of the *Guarantees of Harmony and Freedom* (1842). His theoretical positions were now (under the influence of "true socialists" like Kriege and neo-Christians like the "prophet" Albrecht) below the level of that work, and, furthermore, after his break with the League of the Just in London, he had put himself practically outside the German workers' movement.

The two accounts I have mentioned show that the break with Weitling was an episode in the ideological work of the Communist Correspondence Committee to rid German communism of utopian, artisanal, and neo-Christian tendencies, and also of false "prophets" and "new Messiahs," and to endow the proletarian struggle with a rigorous, scientific, and concrete doctrine.

This was also the background of the circular against Kriege in May 1846. Hermann Kriege was a German "true socialist," an émigré to New York, where he edited the periodical *Der Volks-Tribun*, organ of the Social Reform Association, the German branch of the National Reform Association. The latter, formed in October 1845 at an Industrial Congress organized by the secret society of workers and artisans called "Young America," gave expression to the nascent labor movement in the United States.

The content of the Brussels circular with regard to Kriege, on the one hand, and the National Reform Association, on the other, is extremely significant. It shows the radically uncompromising attitude of Marx (who wrote the circular) towards the German petty-bourgeois doctrinaires who claimed to be "communists" and, in contrast to that, his great tolerance and profound confidence where the genuine "mass" workers' movement was concerned.[6]

This attitude was expressed, in 1846–1848, in a very great regard for Chartism together with a pitiless critique of the petty-bourgeois ideologists, from the

---

[5] P. V. Annenkov, *The Extraordinary Decade: Literary Memoirs* (Ann Arbor: 1968), p. 169.

[6] Marx criticizes Kriege violently because he reduces communism, "a revolutionary movement of world-historical [*weltgeschichtlich*] importance, to the few words: love-hate, communism-selfishness," or to "the search for the Holy Spirit and Holy Communion," by "preaching *in the name of communism*, the old fantasy of religion and German philosophy." He criticizes him also because he baptizes as "communist" the National Reform Association's program for dividing up the land: "And what kind of 'wish' is this which the 1,400 million acres are to make a reality? None other than that *everybody* should be turned into a *private-property-owner*, a wish that is just as practicable and communist as that everybody should be turned into an emperor, king or pope."

"true socialists" to Proudhon. His position towards the League of the Just was half-way between those two: in the circular it is described as a "secret league of Essenes" (*CW*, VI, 50), but Marx's irony is turned more directly against Kriege than against the League itself.

Indeed, according to later statements by Marx and Engels, political work in the League was one of the chief purposes of the Communist Correspondence Committee.[7] Because the chief center of the League had been, since 1839, in England, relations between the "Just" and the Marxists were conducted chiefly through dialogue between London and Brussels.[8]

The attitude of a real communist towards this movement should have been quite different, namely, to show, while acknowledging the temporarily non-communist character of the Association, that it must, by virtue of its proletarian nature, evolve, sooner or later, towards communism: ' If Kriege had seen the free-land movement as a first, in certain circumstances necessary, form of the proletarian movement, as a movement which, because of the social position of the class from which it emanates, must necessarily develop into a communist movement, if he had shown how communist tendencies in America could, to begin with, only emerge in the agrarian form which appears to be a contradiction to all communism, then no objection could have been raised." This was, in fact, the attitude of Marx himself towards the movement, and he begins the second part of the circular with this preliminary statement:

> We fully recognize that the American National Reformers' movement is historically justified. We know that this movement has set its sights on a goal which, although for the moment it would further the industrialism of modern bourgeois society, nevertheless, as the product of a proletarian movement, as an attack on landed property in general and more particularly in the circumstances obtaining in America, will by its own inner logic inevitably press on to communism. *CW*, VI, 41, 45, 44, 41–42, 43.

[7] In *Herr Vogt* (1860), Marx defined thus the meaning of his activity in 1845–1846: "At the same time [in Brussels] we published a series of pamphlets, partly printed, partly lithographed, in which we mercilessly criticized the hotch-potch of Franco-English socialism or communism and German philosophy which formed the secret doctrine of the 'League' at the time. In its place we proposed the scientific study of the economic structure of bourgeois society as the only tenable theoretical foundation. Furthermore, we argued in popular form that it was not a matter of putting some utopian system into effect, but of conscious participation in the historical process revolutionizing society before our very eyes." Engels, in his note on the history of the League, wrote: "We influenced the theoretical views of the most important members of the League by word of mouth, by letter and through the press. For this purpose we also made use of various lithographed circulars, which we dispatched to our friends and correspondents throughout the world on particular occasions when we were concerned with the internal affairs of the Communist Party that was in the process of formation. In these the League itself was sometimes involved," and he quotes as an example the circular against Kriege. *CW*, XVII, 79, and XXVI, 319.

[8] It was the Marxists who opened negotiations. In May 1846, the Brussels Committee sent a letter to Schapper asking the League of the Just and the London Workers' Education Society – a "working-class" organization controlled by the League – to set up a Communist Correspondence Committee which would maintain regular contract

Marx's reservations shown during this dialogue were due not only to the League's ideological confusion, its kindly attitude to "sentimental communism" and its narrow artisanal character, but also to the close and "conspiratorial" structure of the *Bund der Gerechten*, which did not correspond at all to his conception of the Communist Party. I shall return to the problem of the conditions that Marx and Engels laid down, on the theoretical and organizational plane, for joining the League of the Just.

While the dialogue with London was going on, the Communist Correspondence Committee tried to win over to its views the Paris sections of the League, primarily through sustained correspondence with Ewerbeck. Given the latter's theoretical weakness and his constant political hesitations,[9] it was decided, however, to send to Paris in August 1846 none other than Friedrich Engels himself. Weitling's supporters having been ousted from the League by Ewerbeck, the essential struggle that Engels had to conduct was against the influence of the "true socialists" and Proudhon. Engels's letters show that what was at issue in the debate was, precisely, *the problem of revolution*.

> The main thing was to prove the necessity for revolution by force and in general to reject as anti-proletarian, petty-bourgeois and Straubingerian Grün's true socialism, which had drawn new strength from the Proudhonian panacea.[10]

---

with the Brussels committee. The reply came quickly. On June 6, 1846, Schapper wrote to Marx to tell him of the formation of a committee headed by Bauer, Moll, and himself. He also expressed approval of the break with Weitling, but condemned the "brusque tone" of the circular against Kriege. The Brussels Committee rejoined, on June 22, with a demand for firm struggle against "philosophic and sentimental communism," and proposing that they discuss a plan for a Communist Congress. The Londoners' reaction was ambiguous. In a letter to Marx dated July 17, Schapper complained of "the arrogance of men of learning" shown by the Brussels Committee and called again for moderating the criticism of Kriege, but agreed to the proposal for a congress and suggested that London be the venue. This mutual mistrust culminated in November 1846, when the League of the Just sent a circular to its members convening a congress in London for May 1847. This initiative, taken without consultation with the Brussels group, was very badly received by Marx and Engels and might have led to a break if Moll had not gone to Brussels in January 1847. Cf. *Marx, Chronik Seines Lebens, op. cit.*, pp. 33–37.

[9] Cf. B. Andreas, W. Mönke, "Neue Daten zur 'Deutschen Ideologie,'" in *Archiv für Sozialgeschichte*, Bd. VIII (1968), p. 74.

[10] This same problem figured prominently in the "draft definition of communism," which Engels put to the vote at a meeting of the League after interminable discussion with the "anti-revolutionary" disciples of Grün and Proudhon:

> I . . . defined the aim of communists as follows: (1) to ensure that the interests of the proletariat prevail, as opposed to those of the bourgeoisie; (2) to do so by abolishing private property and replacing same with community of goods; (3) *to recognize no means of attaining these aims other than democratic revolution by force*.

The activity of the Brussels Correspondence Committee aimed at forming a real German Communist Party was not confined, far from that, to political work directed towards the League of the Just and the German exiles. Several contacts were established in Germany itself with communist individuals and groups who organized, here and there, committees which kept regular contact with Brussels.[11]

Did this fluid and disjointed grouping already constitute a *party*? The frequent references to the "party" that appear in this correspondence between Germany and Brussels seem to suggest that this was the case. For example, Weydemeyer, in his letters of 1846 to Marx, writes of "the people of our party," "the interests of the party," "the party's money," "the party's aims," and so on.[12] And yet, in a letter of August 1846, Bernays, a former *Vörwarts* journalist, a friend and follower of Marx who had taken refuge in France, put an anxious question to him which shows how vague and indeterminate this "party" was: ". . . But who are we? Who constitute the nucleus of our party?"[13] Finally, Marx's letter of December 1846 to Annenkov indicates that, for him, the "party" was not yet something organized and precise, but merely the expression of German communism as a political trend that was highly heterogeneous and contradictory: "As for our own party, not only is it poor but there is a large faction in the German Communist Party which bears me a grudge because I am opposed to its utopias and its declaiming."[14]

One of the essential tasks facing Marx and the Brussels committee was, precisely, to help German communism advance beyond its formless state as a

---

After contributions by several workers who, according to Engels, "spoke quite nicely" and showed themselves to "have quite a sound intellect," the proposal was approved by a big majority: the Paris section of the League was "converted to Marxism" and would be represented at the June 1847 congress by Engels himself. CW, XXXVIII, 81, 82, 83. (My italics – M. L.)

[11] In Kiel, Georg Weber, a former journalist on *Vorwärts* (in which he had written articles much influenced by Marx), was appointed correspondent for North Germany. In Westphalia, Weydemeyer and his friends Mayer and Rempel corresponded regularly with Marx about the problems of the "party." In Cologne, Bürgers and Daniels kept contact with Brussels though they regarded the creation of a communist committee as premature. In Silesia, communist groups sent through Wilhelm Wolff regular reports on the situation of the workers, weavers, and peasants of their province. In Wuppertal, Köttgen tried to set up a correspondence committee and received a circular from Brussels with instructions on how to do it. Cf. *Chronik*, pp. 31–36. See for this period, 1846–1848, the excellent work by Herwig Förder, *Marx und Engels am Vorabend der Revolution*, Akademie Verlag (Berlin: 1960).

[12] *Marx-Engels Archief*, International Institute of Social History, shelf-mark D5. Cf. note 95 to Chapter 2.

[13] *Ibid.*, shelf-mark D1. Weydemeyer, too, complained of the "incoherent" (*Zerfahren*) character of the "party." (Letter to Marx, July 29, 1846, published in Andreas and Monke, *op. cit.*, p. 88).

[14] CW, XXXVIII, 105.

mere current of ideas, like the "party" of the "true socialists" and the other philosophic "parties," and become a structured and active organization. How was this to be achieved?

The circular of the Communist Correspondence Committee addressed to G. A. Köttgen, dated June 15, 1846, and signed by Marx, Engels, Gigot, and F. Wolff (Marx doubtless being the author), shows us, for the first time, how Marx conceived the process of constituting a communist party. The circular notes the absence in Germany of "a strong and organized Communist Party" and, replying to Köttgen's suggestion about the holding of a congress, puts forward this view: "We do not consider the time to be appropriate yet for a communist congress. Only when communist associations have been formed in the whole of Germany and means for action have been collected will delegates from the individual associations be able to gather for a congress with any prospect of success. And this will not be likely before next year."[15]

The significance of this plan is quite clear. Marx conceived the process of construction of a communist party as a movement *from below to above, from the base to the summit, from the periphery to the center*. True, this organizational program refers only to the situation in Germany in 1846, and one should guard against hasty generalizations. It remains the fact, nevertheless, that this passage is the first in which Marx envisions, in concrete and precise terms, the problems of organizing the German Communist Party, and the solutions he proposes do not contradict, quite the contrary, his general conceptions concerning revolution and communism.

Although the main aim of the Communist Correspondence Committee was indeed to provide a structure for German communism, it is no less true that, from the outset, it set itself a task on the international scale, namely, to establish regular communication and exchange of ideas between the socialist vanguard elements in France, Germany, and England.

In France, the "authorized negotiator" chosen was P. J. Proudhon, in whose work Marx had taken great interest since 1842. On May 5, 1846, a letter signed "Charles Marx" (with postscripts by Gigot and Engels) was sent to him, inviting him to become the French correspondent of the Committee. The letter stated that: "It will be the chief aim of our correspondence . . . to put the German Socialists in contact with the French and English Socialists." At this time, Marx thought he would be able to win Proudhon over to his positions, particularly to the fight against "true socialism." The postscript by Gigot, warning Proudhon against Grün's activities, testifies to this illusion.[16]

---

[15] *CW*, VI, 55.
[16] *Selected Correspondence of Marx and Engels* (Moscow and London: 1956), p. 32. The postscripts are in *Werke*, Vol. 27 (1965), p. 444.

Proudhon's reply reveals the abyss separating his new conceptions from those of Marx. He rejects *"revolutionary* action as a means of social reform" (a means which he admits he used to support) and proposes now to "burn Property gently (*à petit feu*)." He does not understand at all why Marx is combating "true socialism," and calls this struggle "the petty divisions within German socialism."[17]

Some "modern Proudhonists" enjoy themselves by contrasting the praise heaped on Proudhon by Marx in 1842–1844 with his virulent criticisms in 1846–1847.[18] They forget that not only Marx but Proudhon too had evolved profoundly between 1842 and 1847 – in opposite directions. The Proudhon of the *Deuxième mèmoire sur la propriété* (1841) wrote: "I urge revolution with all the means in my power," while the Proudhon of the May 1846 letter to Marx rejects revolutionary action as "an appeal to force, to the arbitrary: in short, a contradiction."[19]

While the attempt to work with Proudhon failed, the Committee's attempt to establish a link with the left wing of Chartism proved successful.

Marx's first direct contact with the Chartist leaders took place in August 1845, during a meeting in London of democrats and revolutionaries from various countries, which approved a proposal by Engels to form an international democratic association.[20] Engels had known the leader of the radical wing of the Chartists, George Julian Harvey, since 1843 and was to write, from September 1845, for *The Northern Star*, Harvey's paper.

What was the situation of Chartism in 1846? After a certain decline in 1843–1845, the movement seemed to have got its second wind. Two major events offered the opportunity for a decisive upturn. On the one hand, the abolition of the Corn Laws in June 1846 represented the victory of the liberal bourgeoisie over the rural aristocracy, and so brought to the forefront the conflict between proletariat and bourgeoisie. On the other, the victory of the Chartist leader O'Connor in elections "by show of hands," in July 1846, stood out as the first popular triumph in this new phase of the class struggle in England.

Given these circumstances, we can understand the interest shown by Marx in Chartism in 1846–1847 and his effort to establish contact with its revolutionary wing. Moreover, the positions of the most consistent leader of that wing, G. J. Harvey, were quite close to Marx's, so that some historians of Chartism have seen Harvey as a precursor of Marxism.[21]

---

[17] P. Proudhon, letter to Marx, May 17, 1846, in Ryazanov, "Introduction historique," *op. cit.*, pp. 31–34.
[18] P. Haubtmann, *Marx et Proudhon*, Economie et Humanisme (Paris: 1947), pp. 86–88.
[19] Proudhon, *Deuxième mémoire sur la propriété* (Paris: A. Lacroix, 1873), p. 349. Ryazanov, "Introduction historique," *op. cit.*, p. 32.
[20] CW, VI, 662, note 9.
[21] T. Rothstein, *From Chartism to Labourism* (London: 1929), p. 46. Harvey, deeply

The organization which served as base for the Chartist Left between 1837 and 1839 was the London Democratic Association, which recruited its members among the poorest workers and was the counterpart, within the Chartist movement, of W. Lovett's Working Men's Association, more moderate and made up of artisans and "superior" workers. In an article published in 1846 in the *Rheinische Jahrbücher* on the "Festival of Nations," held in London in September 1845, Engels wrote that "the most radical wing consisted of Chartists, proletarians as might be expected, but people who clearly grasped the aim of the Chartist movement and strove to speed it up," and that the members were "not only republicans but communists." Harvey is described by Engels as "a true proletarian" who is "perfectly clear about the aim of the European movement and completely *à la hauteur des principes*, although he knows nothing about the German theories of true socialism."[22]

Even after he joined the Communist League, Marx remained in contact with the revolutionary Chartists, Harvey and Ernest Jones, through the Fraternal Democrats, an association which enjoyed participation by the Chartist Left, the Communist League, and several groups of European exiles in London. Thus, during his stay in London, between November and December 1847, Marx appeared not only at the congress of the League, but also at meetings

---

affected by the French revolutionary tradition, had tried, from 1838 onward, to bring about an active synthesis between this tradition and that of the English workers' movement. In a letter of March 13, 1939, to *The Northern Star*, Harvey put forward some ideas which soon became the guiding principles of the most radical section of the Chartists:

(a) the working classes must rely on themselves and on themselves alone;
(b) the Owenite belief in the omnipotence of "education," the central idea of the reformist ("Moral Force") tendency among the Chartists, must be rejected;
(c) society is divided into classes which are opposed to each other in an implacable antagonism.

A year later, at the Chartist congress of 1839, Harvey was already the acknowledged leader of the group of revolutionaries who advocated "Physical Force." Cf. E. Dolléans, *Le Chartisme (1831–1848)* (Paris: Marcel Rivière, 1949), p. 93. See also W. Kunina, "George Julian Harvey," in *Marx, Engels und die ersten proletarischen Revolutionäre* (Berlin: Dietz Verlag, 1965).

[22] *CW*, VI, 6, 7, 8. Correspondence between the Brussels Committee and Harvey began in February 1846. He was one of the first persons to be invited to join the new organization. In his reply to Engels (March 30, 1846), Harvey lays down as the condition for his adhesion that Brussels must come to an agreement with the London League of the Just, with whom he had recently (March 15, 1846) formed the "Fraternal Democrats." On July 20, considering that this condition had been fulfilled, Harvey offered full support to the undertaking. It was in this very same period (July 17) that Marx and Engels sent to O'Connor, through Harvey, an address conveying the compliments of the "German democratic communists of Brussels" on his electoral victory. In this address, they said that, after the Free-Traders' victory, "the great struggle of capital and labor, of *bourgeois* and *proletarian*, must come to a decision." *CW*, VI, 58: *Chronik*, pp. 31, 35.

of the Fraternal Democrats. On November 29, he made a speech at a meeting to commemorate the Polish insurrection of 1830 which was organized by the Fraternal Democrats, and on that occasion proposed the holding of an international democratic congress.[23]

In order to understand the point of this "democratic" activity of theirs, we need to know the meaning that Marx, Engels, and Harvey gave to the term "democracy." In his article on the "Festival of Nations," Engels wrote that "democracy nowadays is communism. Democracy has become the proletarian principle, the principle of the masses."[24] In their address to O'Connor, Marx and Engels declared that, "nowadays," "democrats and workingmen . . . are almost the same."[25] Again, in his speech on Poland at the international meeting of the Fraternal Democrats in London, Marx spoke openly as a communist, saying that "the existing property relations must be done away with" and calling for "the victory of the proletariat over the bourgeoisie."[26] And the address of the Fraternal Democrats to the Brussels Democratic Association (December 1847), which was probably written by Harvey, amounts, behind the phrases about "democratic fraternity," to a call for international unity of the proletariat:

> But it is in the interest of the proletarians, everywhere oppressed by the same kind of taskmasters and defrauded of the fruits of their industry by the same description of plunderers, it is their interest to unite.[27]

From the organizational standpoint, it is notable that the Fraternal Democrats, whose vital center was the communist element among the Chartists, always hesitated to establish an organic structure, a "party." A statement by Harvey about the nature of the association defined this attitude of theirs: "Once for all we explicitly state that we repudiate all idea of forming any 'party' in addition to the parties already existing in England. We desire not to rival but to aid all men who are honestly combined to work out the emancipation of the people."[28] What were the reasons for this attitude? A speech by Jones, published in *The Northern Star* of February 5, 1848, provides the answer:

> There was at its formation a slight mistrust on the part of my Chartist brethren against the Fraternal Democrats – they feared it was an attempt to supersede the movement – to create a party within a party; they have now learned that every member of this society is a thorough Chartist and that Chartism is a test of admission for its members.[29]

---

[23] *CW*, VI, 619.
[24] *CW*, VI, 5.
[25] *CW*, VI, 59.
[26] *CW*, VI, 388.
[27] In G. D. H. Cole, *Chartist Portraits* (London: 1941), p. 286.
[28] Rothstein, *op. cit.*, p. 129.
[29] *Ibid.*, pp. 129–130.

This situation of the Fraternal Democrats within Chartism would seem to be the concrete basis for the conceptions we find in *The Communist Manifesto* regarding the relations between communists and workers' parties: the communists are not a special party in contrast to the other workers' parties, they are the most resolute section of the workers' parties in all countries – and so on.

b) *The Communist League*

The formal move of the leadership of the League of the Just to London did not take place until 1846 but, for practical purposes, after the defeat of the Paris insurrection of 1839, the English capital had become the organization's political center.

Having benefited from the experience of the French communists, the artisans of the League who emigrated to London would now also assimilate that of the English workers' movement, especially after the establishment, in 1844, of regular contacts with the Chartists, through the forming of the "Democratic Friends of All Nations." Under the influence of these contacts and of the social conditions of England, the League's London group underwent a profound evolution and began to look on communism and the struggles of the industrial proletariat in a way that was fundamentally opposite to that of Weitling, for instance, whose ideological world was on the scale of the little artisans' villages in Switzerland.[30] Some documents enable us to trace this change step by step: the circular of the German workers' association dated August 21, 1844, the second of the discussions between Weitling and the London leadership of the League (February 1845–January 1846), the circulars issued by the League's central committee between November 1846 and February 1847, and, finally, the *Kommunistische Zeitschrift* of September 1847.

The circular of the London workers' association, which was signed by Schapper and Moll among others, aimed at launching a subscription to help the Silesian workers. This text shows that the 1839 defeat had turned the communist artisans towards the utopian and "peaceable" socialism of Cabet, Owen, etc. The document rejected the Silesian revolt as a "partial rising," instead of which it advocates "the organization of labor" and an effort to emerge from poverty "not by violence, but by our own instruction and by a good education for our children."[31]

---

[30] Cf. Nicolaievsky and Maenchen-Helfen, *op. cit.*, p. 109; Fehling, *K. Schapper*, p. 64; Max Nettlau, "Londoner deutsche Kommunistische Diskussionen 1845," in *Archiv für die Geschichte des Sozialismus* . . . (Leipzig: C. L. Hirschfeld Verlag, 1921–1922), p. 363.

[31] In *Dokumente zur Geschichte des Bundes der Kommunisten* (Berlin: Dietz Verlag), pp. 65–66. On Cabet's influence on the Paris and London sections of the League after the 1839 defeat. Cf. Fehling, *K. Schapper*, p. 57.

The 1845–1846 discussions with Weitling show the League caught in the traditional dilemma of the workers' movement in the 1840s – whether to change "men" or "circumstances," whether to use violence or "education." Two positions stand out pretty clearly: on one side, Schapper, who rejects revolutions and talks only of *Aufklärung* and "enlightening propaganda," and, on the other, Weitling, for whom "preaching instruction to the hungry is absurd," since "no instruction is possible unless one has eaten and drunk." Weitling insisted on the need for revolutionary methods, but also on the need for "a dictator with authority over everything," and gives as his example Napoleon – which enables us to understand his future support for Napoleon III, in 1853–1855. However, some of the League's leaders, and the ones who seem to have been the most representative, tried to escape from the false dilemma. Thus, Bauer, after five months of discussion, suggested that "instruction [*Aufklärung*] always prepares the way for fresh revolutions" and, in reply to a remark by Weitling, for whom communism could be established by princes or rich men, exclaimed: "No! It's the workers who will do it."[32]

The circular of November 1846 indicates a certain advance already in comparison with 1844–1845, in so far as it condemns the "mania for systems" (*Systemkrämerei*) in general and that of Fourier in particular. But it is in the circular of February 1847 that Marx's influence becomes apparent – "sentimental" communism is vigorously condemned as "insipid amorous daydreaming" – as well as that of the Chartists, who are put forward as "an example to follow."[33]

Finally, the *Kommunistische Zeitschrift* of September 1847 is practically a "Marxist" organ, even if Marx did not write in it. Under the title a new slogan appears, replacing the old slogan of the League of the Just, "All men are brothers" – "Proletarians of all countries, unite!" And the chief article in the review, "The Prussian Diet and the proletariat in Prussia and in Germany generally," the author of which has not been identified with certainty (Engels or Wolff?) states clearly that "nobody wants or is able to emancipate us if we do not do it *ourselves*."[34]

When this evolution began, Marx and Engels had a reserved attitude towards the "league of the Essenes." They did not agree to join until Moll, the emissary sent to Brussels by the leaders of the Just, had assured them that they were "convinced of our views" and needed the help of the two friends in the fight against "backward and refractory elements" in the League.[35] Even after their talk with Moll, they still hesitated and this was shown in the long delay

---

[32] Nettlau, *op. cit.*, pp. 367–368, 373–374, 379–380.
[33] *Dokumente* . . ., *op. cit.*, pp. 78, 80, 88, 91.
[34] *Ibid.*, p. 104. Cf. W. Smirnowa, "Wilhelm Wolff," in *Marx und Engels und die ersten*, *op. cit.*, p. 515.
[35] *CW*, XXVI, 321. *CW*, XVII, 80.

between the formal agreement to join which they made with the emissary of the Central Committee (February 1847) and the formation by Marx of the Brussels group of the League (August). It was only after the positive results obtained by Engels at the first congress of the new Communist League (June 1847) that they began effectively to participate in the organization.

It was at this congress that the new rules of the organization were drawn up, on the basis of a draft by Engels. As I have already mentioned, the differences that Marx and Engels had with the League of the Just on organizational matters were at least as important as their theoretical differences. According to Engels, their agreement with Moll became possible only after the latter had recognized "the need to free the League from the old conspiratorial traditions and forms" and to replace "the obsolete League organization by one in keeping with the new times and aims."[36] Marx himself was to state, some years later, that "when Engels and I first joined the secret communist society we did so only on condition that anything conducive to a superstitious belief in authority be eliminated from the rules."[37]

We now perceive how important for them was the changing of the League's rules, and the light that can be thrown by an analysis of the new rules, finally adopted at the second congress, in Marx's presence, on their organizational conceptions, on the way they envisioned the internal structure of a communist party.

Comparison between the rules of the League of the Just, dating from about 1838, and those of the Communist League, November 1847, reveals some decisive differences which, taken together, enable us to reconstitute, more or less, the gist of these conceptions:

> (1) The organization's aim is no longer left vague (the rules of the Just spoke of "realizing the principles contained in the Rights of Man and the Citizen") but is affirmed in clear, sharp fashion: "The aim of the League is the overthrow of the bourgeoisie, the rule of the proletariat, the abolition of the old bourgeois society which rests on the antagonism of classes, and the foundation of a new society without classes and without private property" (Article 1). This represents a reflection in the Rules of the ideological changes undergone by the League rather than a strictly organizational change.
> (2) The organization is, implicitly at least, international in character. The article of the old rules according to which the League "is made up of Germans, i.e., of men of German language and customs," is cancelled.
> (3) All the strictly conspiratorial features of the organization of the Just are eliminated: the exaggerated importance given to secrecy (the article of

---

[36] CW, XXVI, 321.
[37] CW, XLV, 288.

the old rules which defined the League as "an essentially secret association" is cancelled, and public propaganda through manifestos is envisioned), together with the mystical admission rituals, typical of the secret sects inspired by the Carbonari, etc.

(4) The central committee is deprived of a number of discretionary powers which were also characteristic of the conspiratorial groups of the 1830s, such as the right to co-opt members and the right to issue ordinances "according to their conscience," without consulting the membership, privileges that had been given them in the statutes of the Just (articles 27 and 34).

(5) The old statutes failed to provide for any body in which decisions could be discussed democratically by representatives of the various local groups. These decisions had to be taken separately in each group, on the basis of suggestions from the Central Committee (or from members, communicated by the Central Committee) and a majority of the groups could legislate for the League (articles 33 and 34). In the rules of the Communist League, something essentially new is introduced: the legislative authority of the organization belongs to a congress elected by the method of proportional representation, to meet every year, and to which the Central Committee is responsible. The congress, too, is the final instance for disciplinary sanctions, and, last but not least, the congress has to issue, after every sitting, a manifesto in the name of the party (articles 21, 32, 36, 39).[38]

Engels describes this changing of the rules as the transition from an organization given to "hankering after conspiracy, which requires dictatorship" to one that is "thoroughly democratic, with elective and removable authorities," concentrating ("for ordinary peacetime at least") on propaganda.[39]

What was the nature of this Communist League born in 1847? What were the distinctive features of this first "draft" of a "Marxist party," as compared with the other organizations of the period that were communist, or regarded as such?

First, the League endeavored, without completely succeeding, to overcome the contradiction between the national limits of German communism and the international character of the proletarian struggle. Thus, despite the fact that the majority of the organization's members was German, it was already an "international association," not only through the dispersion of the German communist émigrés over Europe, but, above all, through the absence from its rules of any restrictive clauses regarding nationality, and through the

---

[38] *Dokumente* . . ., pp. 57–63 (rules of the League of the Just). *CW*, VI, 633–638 (rules of the Communist League).

[39] *CW*, XXVI, 322. Engels was wrong about the removability of the authorities, which was already provided for in the rules of the League of the Just (article 36).

internationalist character of the party's *Manifesto* and of its chief slogan: "Proletarians of all countries, unite!"

The Communist League tried also to overcome another contradiction that was typical of the workers' movement of the 1840s, that between the conspiratorial revolutionary societies and the organizations for "peaceable propaganda." The fight to transcend the ideological dilemma – Babouvism or Cabetism? – was now engaged on the organizational plane: to the new, Marxist theory of the revolution there must obviously correspond a new type of party.

Finally, the League sought to transcend the division in German socialism between the "philosophical parties" ("true socialism", etc.) and the narrow, limited artisans' sects, by bringing together in a single organization the communist vanguard of the intelligentsia and of the working class. Analysis of the social and occupational composition of the Communist League, between 1847 and 1852, suggests that this fusion was achieved, partially at least, and at the same time gives us indices on the first social basis of Marxism.

Among sixty-five members of the League (1847–1852) – not a sample, but *all* the members whose occupation I have succeeded in discovering,[40] there were thirty-three intellectuals and members of the liberal professions[41] and thirty-two artisans and workers.[42]

This calls for several observations:

> (a) The first group – intellectuals and liberal professions – is "over-represented," making up more than half of the total. True, this is partly due to the fact that the names and activities of writers and journalists have more chance of being known to posterity than those of the anonymous

---

[40] This information was compiled from the following works: *Karl Marx: Chronik seines Lebens*; Nicolaievsky and Maenchen-Helfen, *Karl und Jenny Marx* (Berlin: 1933); K. Obermann, *Die Arbeiter und die Revolution von 1848* (Berlin: Dietz Verlag, 1933); F. Mehring, *Geschichte der Deutschen Sozial-Demokratie*; Marx and Engels, *Werke*, Vols 4 and 5.

[41] Of these, 10 were writers, journalists, poets or publicists (H. Bürgers, E. Dronke, F. Engels, F. Freiligrath, L. Heilberg, K. Marx, W. Pieper, G. Weerth, F. Wolff); 6 were doctors (R. Daniels, H. Ewerbeck, K. d'Ester, A. Gottschalk, A. Jacoby, J. Klein); 5 were officers (F. Anneke, K. Bruhn, A. Hentze, J. Weydemeyer, A. Willich); 4 were lawyers (H. Becker, J. Miquel, S. Seiler, V. Tedesco); 2 were teachers (P. Imandt, W. Wolff); there was one engineer (A. Cluss), one civil servant (P. Gigot), one "surveyor in training" (J. Jansen), one chemist (K. Otto), one merchant (W. Reiff) and one student (W. Liebknecht).

[42] Of whom 7 were tailors (G. G. Eccarius, Haude, F. Lessmer, J. C. Lüchow, C. F. Mentel, Meyer, P. Nothjung); 5 were shoemakers (H. Bauer, Hatzel, Muller, Pierre, Wissig); 5 were joiners, cabinet-makers, etc. (Buhring, Hanse, G. Lochner, K. Schramm, J. Weiler); 3 printers (S. Born, K. Schapper, K. Wallau); 2 clerks (J. L. Erhard, W. Haupt); 2 painters (K. Pfänder, A. Steingens); 2 clockmakers (H. Jung, J. Moll); one brushmaker (J. P. Becker); one barber (Bedorf); one cigarette-maker (P. G. Roser); one goldsmith (Bisky); one lacemaker (R. Riedel) and one cooper (C. J. Esser).

"working-class base" of the League. But it is also true that this was a typical feature of some vanguard groups at the dawn of the working-class movement.

(b) The most numerous social and occupational section of the League is that of the writers and publicists. Besides the ten writers named, several other members of the organization were, at least temporarily, active in this way: F. Anneke, K. Bruhn, H. Becker, C. J. Esser, H. Ewerbeck, A. Gottschalk, K. Schramm, S. Seiler, W. Wolff, and others. The probable origin of the radicalism of this group has its roots in history – the collapse of the liberal and neo-Hegelian press as a result of the surrender of the bourgeoisie in 1842–1843. Marx's own political evolution is typical of this category.[43]

(c) The occupational categories that predominate in the workers' group seem to belong to the traditional artisan group: tailors, shoemakers, joiners. However, the development of manufacturing in Germany was already at this time causing a profound crisis among the artisans: masters and journeymen were on the way to becoming "propertyless artisan-proletarians" (*besitzlosen Handwerksproletarien*),[44] and the three categories mentioned were precisely those most affected by this crisis. The annual report of the Cologne Chamber of Commerce (I take this city as my example because it was the League's chief center in Germany) for 1847 refers to the "sharp fall in wages," to unemployment and the fate of many masters, who were obliged to become wage-workers, especially among the joiners, shoemakers, and tailors.[45] Why did the first communist vanguard in Germany arise from among these "proletarianized artisans" rather than the proletarians of large-scale industry? Probably because this social stratum had a level of culture and a tradition of organization

---

[43] The relatively large number of doctors is not peculiar to the League. All through the revolution of 1848, young doctors supplied cadres to the radical-democratic trend. The greatest representative of medical science in this period, Rudolf Virchow, wrote: "Who can be surprised that democracy found more supporters nowhere than among the doctors? That everywhere on the extreme Left, and to some extent at the head of the movement, doctors were to be found? Medicine is a social science and politics is nothing but medicine writ large." What were the reasons for this "medical radicalism"? On the one hand, the poor material situation of the medical profession in Germany in the 19th century and its oppression by the bureaucracy of the Prussian state. On the other, the obvious link between the illnesses of the masses, cholera epidemics, etc., and bad living conditions and working-class poverty. It is not accidental that documents on the health of the proletariat, official reports by doctors, provide an important share of the evidence against the capitalist regime in *The Condition of the Working Class in England* and even in *Capital*. Cf. P. Diepgen, *Geschichte der Medizin* (Berlin: Walter de Gruyter and Co., 1951), II: 1, pp. 221, 222, 224. Cf. also R. H. Shryock, *The Development of Modern Medicine* (New York: A. A. Knopf, 1947), p. 221.

[44] This expression was used in 1848 by the economist Bruno Hildebrand. Cf. K. Obermann, *Die Arbeiter, op. cit.*, p. 40.

[45] Obermann, *op. cit.*, p. 37.

and struggle that were higher than those of the factory workers, many of whom were of peasant origin and only recently come to live in towns. Furthermore, the proletarianized artisans had suffered a veritable process of "social degradation." From the labor "aristocracy," which the traditional artisans constituted, they had fallen, owing to unemployment and the crisis in the trades, lower even than the workers in the modern industries. It is quite obvious that the communism of this stratum was that of Weitling rather then that of Marx, and that the groups which were converted, more or less, to Marxism, were those that lived in the great industrial cities of Europe – London and Paris.

To sum up, the Communist League was, for Marx, a first practical attempt to overcome the contradiction between the national and international organization of the proletariat and to transcend the split in the communist movement between conspiracy and "peaceable propaganda," by creating a party which was neither a narrowly limited artisans' sect nor a pseudo-party of petty-bourgeois philosophers. This attempt was only a partial success, but it prepared the way for the appearance, twelve years after the dissolution of the League, of the International Workingmen's Association.

II. The Communists and the Proletarian Movement (1847–1848)

While it is the case that *The Poverty of Philosophy* and *The Communist Manifesto* open a new phase in Marx's work, qualitatively different from the one which culminated in *The German Ideology*, since their economic and historical themes continue the criticism of the neo-Hegelian philosophers, it is no less the case that "the theory of the Communist Party" developed in these two writings is coherent with the philosophico-political premises outlined in 1845–1846. In other words, one cannot fully comprehend the conceptions that Marx worked out in 1847–1848 concerning the relation between the communists and the workers' movement and between the Communist Party and the proletarian party unless these conceptions are fitted into the larger totality constituted by the theory of revolution to be found in the *Theses on Feuerbach* and *The German Ideology*.

It is because the communist revolution can only be the task of the working-class masses themselves that the relation between the communists and the proletariat cannot be that which was practiced by the utopian or Jacobino-Babouvist sects.

On the one hand, the role of the communists does not consist in remaining, like the "Icarians," outside the workers' movement, preaching the truth to the people by pure "peaceable propaganda," but in participating closely in the process of class struggle, helping the proletariat to find, through its own historical practice, the path of communist revolution. On the other, the Communist Party cannot, either, play the role of the Jacobin leader or the

Babouvist conspiratorial society – in other words, it cannot set itself above the masses and "make the revolution" in their place.

As I showed in my Introduction, the "general interest," the totality, is alienated by the Jacobins and Buonarroti in the person of an "incorruptible dictator" or an "enlightened minority," standing above the masses, who themselves are doomed to private interest and particularism. For Marx, on the contrary, the proletariat tends towards the totality through its practice of the class struggle, thanks to the role of *mediation*, which is played by its communist vanguard. The Communist Party as defined in the *Manifesto* is not the alienated crystallization of the totality; it is the theoretical and practical mediation between this totality (the ultimate aim of the workers' movement) and every partial moment in the historical process of the class struggle.

In short, Marx's Communist Party is not the heir of the bourgeois and utopian "savior from on high." It is the *vanguard* of the proletariat in its struggle to emancipate itself. It is the *instrument* of the masses for coming to consciousness and taking revolutionary action. Its role is not to act in place or "above" the working class but to *guide* the latter towards the path of its self-liberation, towards the communist "mass" revolution.

a) *The Poverty of Philosophy*[46]

We have seen the interest Marx took, in the period of the Communist Correspondence Committee (1846) in the new workers' parties that were being formed in England and the United States. In *The Poverty of Philosophy* (1847), we find a first analysis of the process of political organization of the proletariat, inspired above all by the example of the English workers' movement.

This analysis begins with the *combinations*, "the first attempts of workers to *associate* among themselves."[47] which were condemned not only by the bourgeois economists but also by the "socialists" (Marx probably means here the utopian socialists as well as Proudhon and the "true socialists") who "want the workers to leave the old society alone the better to be able to enter the new society which they have prepared for them with so much foresight." And Marx adds: "In spite of both of them, in spite of manuals and utopias, combination has not ceased for an instant to go forward and grow with the development and growth of modern industry."[48] In short, "When it is a question of making a precise study of strikes, combinations and other forms in

---

[46] I shall confine myself to studying the two main texts of this period, *The Poverty of Philosophy* and *The Manifesto*. Occasionally, I shall refer to some of Marx's articles written in 1847, to clarify points arising from these two central works.
[47] CW, VI, 210.
[48] *Ibid.*

which the proletarians carry out before our eyes their organization as a class, some (the bourgeois) are seized with real fear and others (the utopians) display a *transcendental* disdain."[49]

For Marx, the significant example of this process of "organizing the proletariat as a class" – an expression which means the same as Flora Tristan's "constitution of the proletariat as a class": centralized and permanent organization of the working class on the national scale – is the English workers' movement:

> In England they have not stopped at partial combinations which have no other objective than a passing strike, and which disappear with it. Permanent combinations have been formed, *trades unions*, which serve as bulwarks for the workers in their struggles with the employers. And at the present time all these local *trades unions* find a rallying point in the *National Association of United Trades*, the central committee of which is in London, and which already numbers 80,000 members. The organization of these strikes, combinations and *trades unions* went on simultaneously with the political struggles of the workers, who now constitute a large political party, under the name of *Chartists*.[50]

The general conclusion which Marx draws from this historical experience is that *there is not necessarily any break in continuity* between local resistance to an individual capitalist and political struggle, between the combination and the proletarian party. The process of class struggle constantly lifts forms of organization to higher levels and wider groupings.[51]

In other words, "the domination of capital has created for this mass [of workers] a common situation, common interests. This mass is thus already a class as against capital, but not yet for itself. In the struggle, of which we have pointed out only a few phases, this mass becomes united, and constitutes itself as a class for itself."[52]

The expression "in the struggle" is the key to this famous passage, which brings us back to the themes of *The German Ideology*: that it is through its own practice, in the course of its historical struggle against the bourgeoisie, that the proletariat becomes conscious and organized, and transforms itself into a mass which is united by a common situation, *a class for itself*.

---

[49] *CW*, VI, 211.
[50] *CW*, VI, 210.
[51] "If the first aim of resistance was merely the maintenance of wages, combinations, at first isolated, constitute themselves into groups as the capitalists in their turn unite for the purpose of repression, and in face of always united capital, the maintenance of the association becomes more necessary to them than that of wages ... In this struggle – a veritable civil war – all the elements necessary for a coming battle unite and develop. Once it has reached this point, association takes on a political character." *CW*, VI, 210–211.
[52] *CW*, VI, 211.

The big mistake made by the utopians, and especially by their followers, in 1847, was their ignorance of or "transcendental disdain" for this independent praxis by the proletariat. These utopian socialists who, "to meet the wants of the oppressed classes, improvise systems and go in search of a regenerating science," "see in poverty nothing but poverty, without seeing in it the revolutionary, subversive side, which will overthrow the old society."[53] This error is understandable "so long as the very struggle of the proletariat with the bourgeoisie has not yet assumed a political character," but "in the measure that history moves forward, and with it the struggle of the proletariat assumes clearer outlines, they no longer need to seek science in their minds; they have only to take note of what is happening before their eyes and to become its mouthpiece." In this way, a new science comes into being which, being "produced by the historical movement and associating itself consciously with it, has ceased to be doctrinaire and has become revolutionary."[54]

These passages show that, for Marx, the role of the communist theoretician is to be "the mouthpiece of what is happening." In an article in the *Deutsche Brüsseler Zeitung* (October 28, 1847), against Karl Heinzen, Marx repeats this idea, in a lapidary formulation: "The writer may very well serve a movement of history as its mouthpiece, but he cannot, of course, create it."[55] For this reason, the *revolutionary science* of this theoretician differs fundamentally both from the doctrinaire science of the utopians, developed outside the workers' movement, and from the "revolutionary philosophy" preached in the *Introduction to a Contribution to the Critique of Hegel's Philosophy of Law*. It is a *practical-critical activity* in the sense of the *Theses on Feuerbach*: produced on the basis of an historical practice it makes itself the critical, coherent and consistent expression of this practice and consciously associates itself therewith, as instrument and guide for revolutionary action.

b) *The Manifesto of the Communist Party*

The two themes of *The Poverty of Philosophy* which I have analyzed – the formation of the proletarian party and the role of the communist writers – were taken up again and developed in the *Manifesto*.

The well-known historical outline of the process which led from Luddism to political organization,[56] inspired above all by the experience of the English

---

[53] *CW*, VI, 177, 178.
[54] *Ibid*.
[55] *CW*, VI, 337.
[56] "At first the contest is carried on by individual laborers, then by the workpeople of a factory, then by the operatives of one trade, in one locality, against the individual bourgeois who directly exploits them They direct their attacks not against the bourgeois conditions of production, but against the instruments of production themselves; they destroy imported wares that compete with their labor, they smash to

workers' movement (and perhaps that of Flora Tristan), shows the decisive importance that Marx attributed to the powers of *self-organization* of the proletariat and the role of the class struggle in the formation of the workers' political party, a process and a role which were ignored or disdained by the utopian and conspiratorial sects.

The new communist theory, which proceeds from this actual proletarian praxis, is qualitatively different from the dogmatic doctrines of "critical-utopian" socialism:

> The theoretical conclusions of the Communists are in no way based on ideas or principles that have been invented or discovered by this or that would-be universal reformer.
>
> They merely express, in general terms, actual relations springing from an existing class struggle, from a historical movement going on under our very eyes.[57]

As for the communist writers of bourgeois origin, Marx presents the problem not in terms of an *alliance between two groups* – those who think and those who suffer – as he did in 1843, but in terms of *some individuals joining the revolutionary class*:

> Finally, in times when the class struggle nears the decisive hour ... a small section of the ruling class cuts itself adrift and joins the revolutionary class, the class that holds the future in its hands. Just as, therefore, at an earlier period, a section of the nobility went over to the bourgeoisie, so now a portion of the bourgeoisie goes over to the proletariat, and in particular a

---

pieces machinery, they set factories ablaze, they seek to restore by force the vanished status of the workman of the Middle Ages ...

"But with the development of industry the proletariat not only increases in number; it becomes concentrated in greater masses, its strength grows, and it feels it strength more ... The collisions between individual workmen and individual bourgeois take more and more the character of collisions between two classes. Thereupon the workers begin to form combinations (trades unions) against the bourgeois; they club together in order to keep up the rate of wages; they found permanent associations in order to make provision beforehand for these occasional revolts. Here and there the contest breaks out in riots ...

"Now and then the workers are victorious, but only for a time. The real fruit of their battles lies not in the immediate result but in the ever-expanding union of the workers."

How is this union to be brought about? By the centralization of "numerous local struggles" into "one national struggle between classes," which means a political struggle, since "every class struggle is a political struggle." This centralization results in the "organization of the proletarians into a class, and consequently into a political party." CW, VI, 492–493.

[57] CW, VI, 498.

portion of the bourgeois ideologists, who have raised themselves to the level of comprehending theoretically the historical movement as a whole.[58]

But the *Manifesto* does not confine itself to developing the themes of *The Poverty of Philosophy*: it contributes fundamental explanations where a new problem is concerned, namely, the *communist party* and its relations with the proletarian movement.[59]

The starting point of a Marxist concept of a communist party is fundamental criticism of the utopian socialists, of their attitude to the independent workers' movement and to the proletariat's political organizations.

1) The inventors of the critical-utopian systems, and their followers, see the proletariat as "a class without any historical initiative [*Selbsttätigkeit*] or any independent political movement." "Only from the point of view of being the most suffering class does the proletariat exist for them"[60] – as for Marx in 1842–1843.
2) Instead of "the gradual class organization of the proletariat," they put forward "an organization of society specially contrived by these inventors."[61]
3) "They habitually appeal to society at large, without distinction of class; nay, by preference to the ruling class."[62]

---

[58] *CW*, VI, 494.

[59] I here pass over the problem of relations between the Communist Party and the bourgeois parties: this involves the theme of "permanent revolution" in Germany, which deserves a special study. I merely observe that, while the *Manifesto*'s tactical positions are not the same as those in the *Introduction* (1844) where the German revolution is concerned, since it calls for the communists to "fight with the bourgeoisie whenever it acts in a revolutionary way" (*CW*, VI, 519), it nevertheless retains the same strategic conception, i.e., it continues to believe in the possibility that a backward country like Germany may "leap over" the bourgeois stage of history that France and England went through.

As in 1844, Marx emphasizes in the *Manifesto* the historical backwardness of the German bourgeoisie and draws the conclusion not, as in the 1844 *Introduction*, that a bourgeois revolution is impossible in Germany but that such a revolution would be ephemeral – "but the prelude to an immediately following proletarian revolution."

> The communists turn their attention chiefly to Germany, because that country is on the eve of a bourgeois revolution that is bound to be carried out under much more advanced conditions of European civilization, and with a much more developed proletariat, than that of England was in the seventeenth and of France in the eighteenth century, and because the bourgeois revolution in Germany will be but the prelude to an immediately following proletarian revolution. *CW*, VI, 519.

[60] *CW*, VI, 515.
[61] *Ibid.*
[62] *Ibid.*

4) "Hence, they reject all political, and *especially all revolutionary, action*; they wish to attain their ends by peaceful means and endeavor by small experiments, necessarily doomed to failure, and by the force of example, to pave the way for the new social Gospel."[63]

5) The consequence in the field of organization that follows from this sectarian tendency is that the utopians "violently oppose all political action on the part of the working class; such action, according to them, can only result from blind unbelief in the new Gospel"; thus, for example, in England the Owenites reject Chartism.[64]

Behind this criticism we perceive, clearly showing through, Marx's own conception, which is exactly the opposite of the utopians' sectarianism. For him the activity of the Communist Party must be based precisely upon the historical *Selbsttätigkeit* of the proletariat, upon its gradual organization as a class. It has to integrate itself in the workers' political movement in order to guide that movement towards revolutionary action.

It is on the basis of these premises that we need to interpret the two enigmatic phrases in the *Manifesto* which define the organizational relation between the communists and the proletarian party:

> The Communists do not form a separate [*besondere*] party opposed to other working-class parties.[65]

> The Communists, therefore, are, on the one hand, practically, the most advanced and resolute section [*Teil*] of the working-class parties of every country, that section which pushes forward all the others; on the other hand, theoretically, they have over the great mass of the proletariat the advantage of clearly understanding the line of march, the conditions, and the ultimate general results of the proletarian movement.[66]

Does this mean that the communists do not constitute a party? Evidently not, since:

(a) the work is entitled *Manifesto of the Communist Party* and, in the introduction, its purpose is said to be to "meet this nursery tale of the Spectre of Communism with a Manifesto of the *party* itself."[67]

(b) in the same chapter we find this expression: "The communists are distinguished from the other [*übrigen*] working-class parties by" [two points only].[68] So, then, the Communist Party is a proletarian party among other proletarian parties.

---

[63] Ibid.
[64] CW, VI, 517.
[65] CW, VI, 497.
[66] Ibid.
[67] CW, VI, 481.
[68] CW, VI, 497. Cf. also, p. 498: "The immediate aim of the Communists is the same as that of all the other proletarian parties."

(c) the Communist League, of which Marx was a member and for which the *Manifesto* was written, did indeed constitute a Communist *Party*.

How is this contradiction to be resolved? Rubel, who is one of the few authors to examine the problem frankly, puts forward the following hypothesis: the communists are not a *workers' party* but an *intellectual élite*. "According to Karl Marx, the communists are a sort of intellectual élite: 'Theoretically, they have over the great mass of the proletariat the advantage of clearly understanding the line of march, the conditions, and the ultimate general results of the proletarian movement'" (*Communist Manifesto*).[69]

But this conception is incompatible not only with *Theses on Feuerbach* and the "philosophy of praxis" – and it is not accidental that Rubel quotes in support of his hypothesis a phrase of Marx's from the *Introduction* ("theory ... becomes a material force as soon as it has gripped the masses")[70] – but with the *Manifesto* itself. In his quotation from the *Manifesto*, he omits the preceding words: "The Communists ... are ..., practically, the most advanced and resolute section of the working-class parties of every country, that section which pushes forward all the others."[71] If we read the paragraph as a whole we see plainly that, for Marx, the communists are a vanguard *both theoretical and practical*, the two things being, moreover, from his point of view inseparable.

It seems to me that the problem can be solved only though a concrete analysis of the relation between the communists who were close to Marx and the workers' movement in 1847–1848. The "Communist Party" of which the *Manifesto* speaks was an international party, the embryos of which were the Communist League and the Fraternal Democrats: that is, on the one hand, an organization made up mainly of Germans, but dispersed all over Europe, and, on the other, an organization concentrated in London but made up of exiled representatives of workers' and communist groups from several European countries. Since there was no workers' party in Germany, the problem arose principally in England, in the following practical form: what should be the connections between the Fraternal Democrats, a communist organization to which the London organization of the League belonged, and the great proletarian party of Chartism? We know that on December 13, 1847 – that is, at just the time when Marx was in London – the Fraternal Democrats had decided, after almost two years of hesitation, to organize themselves formally, by adopting rules and electing a secretariat composed of Harvey (England), Schapper (Germany), Jean Michelet (France), Peter Holm

---

[69] Rubel, "Remarques sur le concept de parti prolétarien chez Marx," *Revue française de sociologie*, 2nd year, No. 3, July-September 1961, p. 176.
[70] *Ibid.*, p. 169.
[71] CW, VI, 497.

(Scandinavia), Nemet (Hungary), A. Schabelitz (Switzerland), and Oborski (Poland).[72] From that moment the Fraternal Democrats became, for practical purposes, a "party within the [Chartist] party."

The same conclusion emerges from an analysis of the statements by Harvey and Jones I quoted earlier. Harvey, writing for the Fraternal Democrats, declared that "we repudiate all idea of forming any 'party' *in addition to* the parties already existing in England." Jones, the other "Marxist" leader of Chartism, wrote in February 1848: "There was... a slight mistrust on the part of my Chartist brethren against the Fraternal Democrats – they feared it was an attempt *to supersede the movement – to create a party within a party*."[73] It is clear that "to supersede the movement" and "to create a party within a party" are two policies which are not only different but fundamentally contrary to one another. Besides, the description that Jones gives, in the same passage, of the Fraternal Democrats is clearly that of a "party within the [Chartist] party." "They have now learned that every member of this society is a thorough Chartist and that Chartism is a test of admission for its members."[74]

Let us now repeat the passages in the *Manifesto*: "The Communists do not form a separate party opposed to other working-class parties." "Practically, [the Communists] are the most advanced and resolute section of the working-class parties," etc. We can see now that these phrases encapsulate the organizational tactic which Marx had worked out together with the London section of the League and with the "Marxist" wing of the Chartists. The Communist Party must not organize itself *alongside* or *in place of* the proletarian party, but *within* it, as its most resolute and conscious "section." In other words, the communists must constitute a party within the workers' party – which enables us to understand why the *Manifesto* speaks of a communist *party* while denying that this forms "a separate party opposed to other working-class parties."

This situation was not only that of the Fraternal Democrats within Chartism but also that of the German communist émigrés in America in the National Reform Association, the second organization considered by the *Manifesto* to be a "proletarian party." Indeed, by forming a Social Reform Association affiliated to the National Reform Association, the German communists of New York had likewise formed nothing other than "a party within a party."[75]

In proposing to organize the vanguard within the mass movement, to form the Communist Party inside the workers' party, Marx wished to avoid both the rocks of utopian sectarianism, isolated and outside the workers' strug-

---

[72] Rothstein, *From Chartism, op. cit.*, pp. 130–131.
[73] *Ibid.*, pp. 129–130. (My italics – M. L.)
[74] *Ibid.*
[75] Cf. Obermann, "Die Amerikanische Arbeiterbewegung," *op. cit.*, p. 113.

gles, and those of pure and simple dissolution of the communists in the proletarian mass.

When we analyze these formulations in the *Manifesto*, we need, therefore, to distinguish the essential idea, which is to organize the communist vanguard in such a way as to avoid both sterile sectarianism and opportunist "entryism," in a form appropriate to the historical conditions of 1848: structuring the Communist Party as a faction within the proletarian mass party.

A comparable situation existed in the 20th century in some countries, during the years before and after the formation of the Third International: in Germany between 1917 and 1919, the Spartacus League, which was communist, remained inside the Independent Social-Democratic Party, which was "centrist," and in Britain in 1919–1920, Lenin advocated affiliation of the Communist Party to the Labour Party.

We must now see what, according to Marx in 1848, the Communist Party had in common with the workers' party and what marked it off from that party.

The *Manifesto* defines thus the ground common to both parties: "The immediate aim of the Communists is the same as that of all the other proletarian parties: formation of the proletariat into a class, overthrow of the bourgeois supremacy, conquest of political power by the proletariat."[76] The two parties which alone are treated in the *Manifesto* as "proletarian" are the Chartists and the National Reformers.[77] "Just as in England the workers form a political party under the name of the *Chartists*, so do the workers in *North America* under the name of the National Reformers, and their battle-cry is not at all *rule of the princes* or the *republic*, but *rule of the working class* or the *rule of the bourgeois* class."[78] Marx's judgment did not err: both the Chartists and the National Reformers fought openly to conquer power for the proletariat. We have already seen this in the case of the Chartists. As for the National Reform Association, its foundation congress (October 1845) set itself the task of "directing the organization of the masses so that the workers may at last confront capital and themselves make the laws."[79]

Yet Marx was fully aware of the ideological limitations of these two movements, the most striking symbol of this being their "agrarian program," which looked forward to the workers' return to the soil through the purchase of small-holdings.[80] Moreover, it was only the left wing of these parties that

---

[76] *CW*, VI, 498.
[77] "Section II has made clear the relations of the Communists to the existing working-class parties, such as the Chartists in England and the Agrarian Reformers in America." *CW*, VI, 518.
[78] *CW*, VI, 324.
[79] Obermann, *op. cit.*, p. 113.
[80] For Feargus O'Connor's land scheme, cf. E. Dolléans, *Le Chartisme*, p. 233. For

understood the importance of international unity of the proletariat. Consequently, differentiation of the communist vanguard within the workers' party was just as necessary as this vanguard's participation in the political organization of the proletariat.

What distinguishes the Communist Party from the workers' parties? Marx answers this question in a decisive passage of the *Manifesto* which was to be repeated, almost word for word, in the program of the Third International:

> [The Communists] have no interests separate and apart from those of the proletariat as a whole.
>
> They do not set up any separate principles of their own by which to shape and mold the proletarian movement.
>
> The Communists are distinguished from the other working-class parties by this only: (1) In the national struggles of the proletarians of the different countries, they point out and bring to the front the common interests of the entire proletariat, independently of all nationality; (2) In the various stages of development which the struggle of the working class against the bourgeoisie has to pass through, they always and everywhere represent the interests of the movement as a whole.[81]

From this passage, it is clearly apparent that the distinction between the communist party and the proletarian party is not at all of the same order as that which opposes the utopian sects to the workers' movement. It is to such sects that Marx is referring when he speaks of shaping the proletarian movement by "separate principles," and Engels, in the 1888 edition of the *Manifesto*, actually replaced the word "separate" by "sectarian."[82] The communists place themselves, in relation to the mass movement, at the opposite pole to the sects. They represent, in this movement, not a *separate* principle but the movement's most general and *universal* aims. The structure of this passage in the *Manifesto* is the same as that of the passage in the *Introduction* where the proletariat is defined as being not a *particular* class of bourgeois society, demanding its *particular* rights, but a sphere which possesses a *universal* character through its suffering, etc.

The communist party is thus the representative of the historic interests of the international proletariat, that is, of the *totality*: in relation to every *partial* movement – merely local or national, ideologically confused, narrowly demand-making, unconscious of the ultimate aims of the class struggle – it plays the decisive role of *mediation of this totality*.

---

the "agrarian reform" preached by the American group, cf. Marx's circular against Kriege. *CW*, VI, 41–44.

[81] *CW*, VI, 497.

[82] *CW*, VI, 497, note a (*"sektierischen"* for *"besonderen"*); *CW*, VI, 495. (My italics –M. L.)

The 10 is the vanguard of the workers' movement, that section of the proletariat which is conscious of its historic mission. But it is not an "enlightened minority" bearing the responsibility to carry out that mission on behalf of the proletarian masses: "All previous historical movements were movements of minorities or in the interest of minorities. *The proletarian movement is the self-conscious, independent movement of the immense majority, in the interest of the immense majority.*"[83]

---

[83] CW, VI, 495. (My italics – M. L.)

Chapter Four
Party, Masses, and Revolution, from Marx's Time to Ours

I. Marx after 1848

The theory of revolutionary self-emancipation by the proletariat was not a "youthful episode," a transitory moment, abandoned by the "mature" Marx. It remained, for the entire period between 1848 and his death, one of the fundamental assumptions of his political activity. It lights up and helps to endow with their true meaning his great political and politico-ideological battles – the German revolution of 1848–1850, the fights against Lassalle and against Bakunin, the Paris Commune, the critique of opportunism in German Social-Democracy.

I am not, of course, going to undertake here a detailed and exact study of the period 1848–1883, but only to indicate the program for such a study, drawing attention to certain crucial passages in which the theory of the self-emancipatory revolution is clearly implicit.

a) *The address of the Central Council to the League (March 1850)*

I have already pointed out (in Chapter 1) the amazing parallelism between Marx's evolution from the *Rheinische Zeitung* (1842–1843) to the *Introduction to a Contribution to the Critique of Hegel's Philosophy of Law* (1844) and the evolution which took him from the *Neue Rheinische Zeitung* (1848–1849) to the "Address of the Central Council to the League" (1850). In both cases, the surrender of the liberal bourgeoisie to the feudal state led Marx to the idea of the permanent revolution, which, still abstract and "philosophical" in 1844, became rigorous and concrete in 1850 – and in 1850, as in 1844, Marx believed that the signal for the proletarian revolutions would be given by "the crowing of the Gallic cock," that is, by the French working class.[1]

The central idea of the "Address" is to "make the revolution permanent" until the proletariat has taken power after ousting, one after the other, the possessing classes.[2] This theme is not in contradiction with the *Manifesto*, which also suggests continuity in the revolutionary process, with the bourgeois revolution as "immediate prelude to a socialist one." The essential difference in comparison with 1848 is that, now, Marx no longer speaks of "fighting with the bourgeoisie whenever it acts in a revolutionary way," for the good reason that he no longer believes the bourgeoisie capable of taking up a "revolutionary attitude."

The "Address" is, undoubtedly, a brilliant forecast of the socialist revolutions of the 20th century, starting with that of 1917, and it refutes absolutely the long-established myth that Marx never contemplated a proletarian revolution happening in a capitalist country that was backward and semi-feudal.

One of Marxism's bourgeois critics, George Lichtheim, has suggested that this schema of "uninterrupted revolution" put forward by Marx was inspired by the way the French Revolution developed between 1789 and 1794 and was, therefore, essentially *Jacobin*. Lichtheim calls the "Address" of March 1850 a "Jacobin-Blanquist aberration" on Marx's part.[3]

While it is true that the theory of the revolution outlined in the "Address" draws, among other sources, from the experience of the French Revolution, it is quite wrong to call it "Jacobin" or "Jacobin-Blanquist," and this for two basic reasons:

1. The aim of the revolutionary process advocated by the "Address," namely, the taking of power by the proletariat, lies *beyond* "petty-bourgeois democracy," Jacobinism;
2. The character of this process is neither Jacobin nor Jacobin-Blanquist, but essentially *self-emancipatory*.

It is, in fact, enough to read the "Address" with attention to realize that, at every moment, the *subject* of revolutionary action is not the Communist League or a Jacobin-style minority, but *the workers*. This does not mean, of course, that the League has no role to play, as the communist vanguard, nor that the

---

[1] "They [the German workers] at least know for a certainty this time that the first act of this approaching revolutionary drama will coincide with the direct victory of their own class in France and will be very much accelerated by it." *CW*, X, 286–287.
[2] "While the democratic petty bourgeois wish to bring the revolution to a conclusion as quickly as possible, and with the achievement, at most of the above demands, it is our interest and our task to make the revolution permanent, until all more or less possessing classes have been forced out of their position of dominance, the proletariat has conquered state power . . ." *CW*, X, 281.
[3] G. Lichtheim, *Marxism: An Historical and Critical Study* (New York: F. Praeger, 1962), p. 125.

proletariat does not need to organize itself in a party: the League's role is, precisely, to fight for the organization of a mass workers' party, within which it will be the most conscious and most active section, in accordance with the organizational conceptions of the *Manifesto*:

> Instead of once again stooping to serve as the applauding chorus of the bourgeois democrats, the workers, and above all the League, must exert themselves to establish an independent, secret and public organization of the workers' party alongside the official democrats and make each community the central point and nucleus of workers' associations in which the attitude and interests of the proletariat will be discussed independently of bourgeois influences.[4]

What forms should the revolutionary and self-liberating struggle of the proletarian masses assume? According to the "Address," the proletarians must establish their own authority over against the bourgeois authority, by forming workers' councils:

> Alongside the new official governments they must immediately establish their own revolutionary workers' governments, whether in the form of municipal committees and municipal councils or in the form of workers' clubs or workers' committees, so that the bourgeois-democratic governments not only immediately lose the support of the workers but from the outset see themselves supervised and threatened by authorities backed by the whole mass of the workers."[5]

Let me point out, in passing, the extraordinary resemblance between this program and the events of 1917 in Russia – organization of soviets, dual power, etc. The authority of these councils cannot, of course, be exercised without arming the workers, without forming "Red Guards." Consequently

> the arming of the whole proletariat with rifles, muskets, cannon and ammunition must be carried out at once, the revival of the old civic militia directed against the workers must be resisted. However, where the latter is not feasible the workers must try to organize themselves independently as a proletarian guard with commanders elected by themselves and with a general staff of their own choosing, and to put themselves under the command not of the state authority, but of the revolutionary municipal councils set up by the workers."[6]

In conclusion, the German workers

> must do the utmost for their final victory by making it clear to themselves what their class interests are, by taking up their position as an independent party as soon as possible and by not allowing themselves to be misled for a single moment by the hypocritical phrases of the democratic petty-bour-

---

[4] *CW*, X, 281–282. Cf. R. Schlesinger, *Marx, his Time and Ours* (London: Routledge and Kegan Paul, 1951), p. 270.
[5] *CW*, X, 283. (On page 284 it is said that the workers must be "centralized in clubs.")
[6] *Ibid.*

geois into refraining from the independent organization of the party of the proletariat. Their battle-cry must be: The Revolution in Permanence.[7]

Basically, the "Address" reiterates, in *practical, precise*, and *concrete* form, the main revolutionary themes of Marx's youthful writings: the 1844 theory of permanent revolution, the 1845–1846 theory of proletarian communist revolution, the 1847–1848 theory of the workers' party. It reiterates them in the light of an actual historical experience – the German revolution of 1848–1850 – and, taken together, along with their strategical and tactical developments, they constitute a most extraordinary prefiguration of the socialist revolutions of the 20th century.

b) *Against Lassalle's "state socialism"*

Bourgeois and Social-Democratic historians often present the conflict between Marx and Lassalle as a personal quarrel or a mere difference on tactics. A more thorough analysis of the problem shows, however, that the divergence between them was fundamental and concerned the essential assumptions behind their respective political activities.[8]

The structure of Lassalle's political thought was that of "socialism from above," by the grace of a Savior, and was therefore radically opposed to Marx's theory of the self-emancipatory revolution.[9]

The starting point of this thought was Hegel's philosophy, which young Lassalle had studied in Berlin, and from which he was to retain, above all, the conception of the state and of the decisive role played by *welthistorische Individuen*. One of his first works, the historical play *Franz von Sickingen*, looked at the great political and religious struggles of the Reformation from the angle of the actions of "great men."

It was during his political agitation in 1862–1864 that Lassalle's ideas on liberation of the workers by the intervention of the state or an "historic individual" entered the realm of practice. Called to lead the General Association

---

[7] CW, X, 287.

[8] After Lassalle's visit to London in July–December 1862 Marx became more fully aware of his plans and said, in a letter to Engels (August 7, 1862) that "all we had in common politically were a few remote objectives." CW, XLI, 400.

[9] It is not accidental that those tendencies which have, explicitly or implicitly, abandoned the Marxist theory of revolutionary self-emancipation by the proletariat, go back to Lassalle's position, whether consciously or not. On the "Lassallism" of present-day German Social-Democracy, see the article by Carlo Schmid (member of the executive committee of the SPD) on the party's centenary, in *Le Monde* of May 28, 1963. For the parallelism between Lassalle and Stalin, see Goldmann, "Pour une approche marxiste des études sur le marxisme," *Annales*, January–February 1963, p. 116.

of German Workers, Lassalle launched the slogan of "formation of producers' co-operatives with help from the state." This was, for him, the process that could lead to the establishment of socialism. At the same time he "flirted" publicly with the Prussian King's government and carried on secret talks with Bismarck, to whom he promised support from the Workers' Association in exchange for "social" intervention by the Prussian state.

Furthermore, being convinced of his messianic role as "great liberator" of the workers, Lassalle concentrated in his own hands all the powers of the Association. He gave it an organizational structure that was ultra-centralist, authoritarian, anti-democratic, even dictatorial, which deprived the members and the local sections of all initiative and autonomous activity.[10]

The intimate connection between Lassalle's messianism, the authoritarian organization of the General Association of the German Workers, and his appeal to Bismarck – three elements which fit together in a coherent structure of "socialism from above" – is clearly revealed in his letter of June 8, 1863, to the "Iron Chancellor." Lassalle enclosed with this letter the rules of the General Association, which he called "the constitution of my realm," and which he presented to Bismarck as a proof of the "instinctive tendency of the working class towards dictatorship" and of the possibility for the workers to accept the monarchy as "the natural bearer of the social dictatorship."[11]

The criticism of Lassalle by Marx, whose essential conceptions were absolutely opposite to Lassalle's, was aimed not only at his tactics but also at the very foundations of his political activity.

Their first polemic seems to have taken place in 1859, in connection with Lassalle's play *Franz von Sickingen*. In a letter of April 19, 1859, Marx accuses Lassalle of having identified himself with his hero and of "regarding the Lutheran-knightly opposition as superior to the plebeian-Münzerian."[12] A few years later Marx compared the role of Lassalle, who wanted to "compel" Bismarck to annex Schleswig-Holstein, with that of "his own Sickingen," who wants to compel Charles V to assume the leadership of the movement."[13]

In a letter to Kugelmann, February 23, 1865, Marx also compares Lassalle to the Marquis Posa, a character in Schiller's *Don Carlos*, who "defends the people" against His Majesty Philip II: "Lassalle wanted to play the Marquis Posa

---

[10] A. K. Worobjowa [Vorobeva], "Aus der Geschichte der Arbeiterbewegung in Deutschland und des Kampfes von Karl Marx und Friedrich Engels gegen Lassalle und das Lassalleanentum 1862–1864," in *Aus der Geschichte des Kampfes von Marx und Engels für die Proletarische Partei* (Berlin: Dietz Verlag), pp. 264–265.
[11] Ibid., p. 268.
[12] CW, XL, 420.
[13] CW, XLII, 66 (letter from Marx to Engels, January 25, 1865). Cf. Worobjowa, *op. cit.*, p. 339.

of the proletariat to the Philip II of the Uckermark [the King of Russia], with Bismarck as intermediary between himself and the Prussian monarchy."[14] Lassalle and Bismarck, von Sickingen and Charles V, Marquis Posa and Philip II – the "great leader" who wants to persuade the King to free the people, this is the attitude condemned by Marx's acidic irony.

For Marx, it was not the "socialist" intervention of the Prussian monarchy, nor "state aid," that would emancipate the workers, but the independent and revolutionary action of the workers' movement. In a letter to Schweitzer (a follower of Lassalle's and leader of his Association), Marx noted that "the central point of [Lassalle's] agitation" was "state aid versus self-help," which was "the slogan circulated in 1843 sqq. by *Buchez*, the leader of *Catholic* socialism, against the genuine workers' movement in France."[15]

In his *Critique of the Gotha Program* (1875), Marx wrote "Instead of arising from the revolutionary process of the transformation of society, the 'socialist organization of the total labor' 'arises' from the 'state aid' that the state gives to the producers' co-operative societies which the *state*, not the worker, *calls into being*. It is worthy of Lassalle's imagination that with state loans one can build a new society just as well as a new railway!"[16] These passages reveal what was really at issue in the conflict between Marx and Lassallism: on one side, state aid, intervention by the Prussian monarchy, and on the other, independent action by the actual workers' movement and revolutionary transformation of society.

In the above-mentioned letter to Kugelmann, Marx compares Lassalle's maneuverings to the *Realpolitik* of Miquel and the other leaders of the National Verein, a bourgeois party which supported the Prussian monarchy. At the same time, however, he shows that, while this sort of compromise was normal for the bourgeoisie, it had no sense for the working class, which "must in the nature of things be genuinely 'revolutionary.'"[17]

We find the same theme in a letter of February 13, 1865, to Schweitzer. Here Marx notes that "the bourgeois party in Prussia discredited itself . . . by seriously believing that with the 'New Era' [of Bismarck] the government had fallen into its lap by the grace of the Prince Regent." But, he added, "the workers' party will discredit itself *even more* if it imagines that the Bismarck era or any other Prussian era will make the golden apples just drop into its mouth, by grace of the King," because, unlike the bourgeoisie, "the working class is revolutionary or it is nothing."[18]

---

[14] *CW*, XLII, 103.
[15] *CW*, XLIII, 132 (letter from Marx to Schweitzer, October 13, 1868).
[16] *CW*, XXIV, 93.
[17] *CW*, XLII, 103.
[18] *CW*, XLII, 96. (My italics – M. L.)

These views of Marx's were not expressed in correspondence only. In two public statements of February 1865, which appeared in the *Sozialdemokrat*, the organ of Lassalle's Association, over the names of Marx and Engels, the maneuverings of Lassalle's followers who led the Association were denounced. In the first of these statements, the criticism is still indirect: Marx speaks of the Paris proletariat being "as opposed as ever to Bonapartism" and as refusing to sell for a mess of pottage "its historical birthright as bearer of revolution," and adds: "We recommend this example to the German workers."[19] The second statement defined the formal break between Marx and Engels and the editors of the *Sozialdemokrat*. It rejected "Royal-Prussian governmental socialism." Marx's article in the *Deutsche Brüsseler Zeitung* on the communism of the *Rheinischen Beobachter* (September 12, 1847) was quoted as expressing "the opinion of the undersigned" regarding alliance between the proletariat and the government.[20] In that article, Marx had declared that "the government cannot unite with the Communists, nor the Communists with the government, for the simple reason that of all the revolutionary parties in Germany the Communists are by far the most revolutionary . . . ," and added: "They delude themselves that the proletariat wishes to be helped, they do not conceive that it expects help from nobody but itself."[21]

Finally, Marx also criticizes two aspects of Lassalle's activity which brought him close to pre-Marxist utopian socialism, namely, messianism and sectarianism. In his letter to Kugelmann, Marx wrote that Lassalle offered himself to the workers as "a mountebank of a savior who was promising to help them reach the promised land with one bound,"[22] and in a letter to Schweitzer (October 13, 1868) he declared that "like everyone who claims to have in his pocket a panacea for the suffering of the masses, he [Lassalle] gave his agitation, from the very start, a religious, sectarian character . . . He fell into Proudhon's mistake of not seeking the real basis of his agitation in the actual elements of the class movement, but of wishing, instead, to prescribe for that movement a course determined by a certain doctrinaire recipe."[23]

c) *The First International*

Marx defined what he saw as the meaning of the International in the first point of the preamble to its rules: "The emancipation of the working classes

---

[19] *CW*, XX, 36.
[20] *CW*, XLII, 97.
[21] *CW*, VI, 220, 225.
[22] *CW*, XLII, 103.
[23] *CW*, XLIII, 133. In his 1925 study of Lassalle, Lukács showed (a) that the relation between "leader" and "masses' envisioned by Lassalle was exactly what Marx had criticized in relation to Bruno Bauer, and (b) that the dualism as between science and the workers' movement which is found in Lassalle is rooted, methodologically, in his "Fichtean neo-Hegelianism." Cf. Lukács, *Political Writings 1919–1929* (London: 1972), pp. 161, 172.

must be conquered by the working classes themselves." It was in the name of that principle that he opposed uncompromisingly all the tendencies within the International Workingmen's Association which sought to create utopian, dogmatic or conspiratorial sects outside of the actual workers' movement.

In a letter of November 23, 1871, to Bolte, Marx discussed the meaning of the internal struggles in the First International:

> The International was founded in order to replace the socialist or semi-socialist sects by a real organization of the working class for struggle. The original Rules and the Inaugural Address show this at a glance. On the other hand, the International could not have asserted itself if the course of history had not already smashed sectarianism. The development of socialist sectarianism and that of the real labor movement always stand in indirect proportion to each other. So long as the sects are justified (historically) the working class is not yet ripe for an independent historical movement. As soon as it has attained this maturity all sects are essentially reactionary. For all that, what history exhibits everywhere was repeated in the history of the International. What is antiquated tries to reconstitute and assert itself within the newly acquired form. And the history of the International was *a continual struggle of the General Council* against the sects and attempts to assert themselves within the International itself against the real movement of the working class.

As examples of these "reactionary sects," Marx cites the Proudhonist "mutualists" in France, the Lassalleans in Germany, and Bakunin's Alliance for Socialist Democracy.[24]

The same theme recurs in the circular against Bakunin issued by the General Council of the International, "The Fictitious Splits in the International" (1872), in which Marx stresses the difference between the "sectarian movement" which Bakunin wanted to re-establish through his numerous secret associations, and "the genuine and militant organization of the proletariat":

> The first phase of the proletariat's struggle against the bourgeoisie is marked by a sectarian movement. That is logical at a time when the proletariat has not yet developed sufficiently to act as a class. Certain thinkers criticize social antagonisms and suggest fantastic solutions thereof, which the mass of workers is left to accept, preach and put into practice. The sects formed by these initiators are abstentionist by their very nature, i.e., alien to all real action, politics, strikes, coalitions, or, in a word, to any united movement. The mass of the proletariat always remains indifferent or even hostile to their propaganda . . . Contrary to the sectarian organizations with their vagaries and rivalries, the International is a genuine and militant organi-

---

[24] *CW*, XLIV, 252, 255.

zation of the proletarian class of all countries united in their common struggle against the capitalists and the landowners, against their class power organized in the state.[25]

For Marx, self-emancipation and revolution were two inseparable features of the proletarian struggle. And while he fought the sectarian tendencies which forgot the former, he also broke with the opportunist tendencies which rejected the latter: for example, the English trade-unionists Lucraft and Odger, who would not declare solidarity with the Paris Commune.

Bourgeois writers who, like Lichtheim, want to contrast Marx's "realistic outlook" in 1864 with his "utopianism" in 1871,[26] have not understood the true meaning of Marx's political activity. What they call an "ambiguity" is, precisely, the indissoluble unity – the philosophical foundations of which, in the writings of his youth, I have shown – between communist revolution and the self-emancipation of the workers, in Marx's theory and practice alike.

d) *The Paris Commune*

For Marx the Paris Commune was nothing less than the first historical and concrete manifestation of that communist revolution "of the masses" that he had defined in his youthful writings as the first moment of that process in which the changing of men coincides with the changing of circumstances:

> The working class did not expect miracles from the Commune. They have no ready-made utopias to introduce *par décret du peuple*. They know that in order to work out their own emancipation, and along with it that higher form to which present society is irresistibly tending by its own economical agencies, they will have to pass through long struggles, through a series of historic processes, transforming circumstances and men.[27]

The Commune had indeed been the work not of an "enlightened" minority or a secret sect, but of the working-class masses of Paris: "no longer allowing the defense men to limit it to the insulated efforts of the most conscious and revolutionary portions of the Paris working class."[28] Replying to the calumnies of the reaction, which presented the Commune as a conspiracy got up by the International, Marx wrote:

> The police-tinged bourgeois mind naturally figures to itself the International Workingmen's Association as acting in the manner of a secret conspiracy, its central body ordering, from time to time, explosions in different countries. Our Association is, in fact, nothing but the international bond between the most advanced working men in the various countries of the civilized

---

[25] CW, XXIII, 106–107.
[26] Lichtheim, *op. cit.*, p. 105.
[27] CW, XXII, 335.
[28] CW, XXII, 482.

world. Wherever, in whatever shape, and under whatever conditions the class struggle obtains any consistency, it is but natural that members of our association should stand in the foreground.[29]

The Commune was neither a conspiracy nor a putsch, it was "the people acting for itself by itself."[30] The Paris correspondent of the *Daily News* found no leader wielding "supreme authority" – on which Marx comments ironically that "this shocks the bourgeois who wants political idols and 'great men' immensely."[31]

The authority installed by this self-emancipatory revolution could not, indeed, be an authority of the Jacobin type. It was and could not but be "a working-class government," "a government of the people by the people,"[32] "a resumption by the people for the people of its own social life."[33] And this was clear from its first decree, abolishing the standing army and replacing it with the people in arms.

Moreover, whereas the Jacobino-Blanquists conceived the taking of power as a simple conquest of the machinery of state, Marx showed, from the experience of the Commune, that the communist revolution, the task of the workers themselves, had to *smash* this machinery, which was adapted to parasitic domination *over* the people, and replace it with institutions adapted to popular self-government. This emerges clearly from Marx's well-known letter to Kugelmann (April 12, 1871), where he speaks of destruction of "the bureaucratic-military machine" as something "essential for every real people's revolution on the continent,"[34] as well as from the first draft of *The Civil War in France*, where Marx writes of the Commune "doing away with the state hierarchy altogether and replacing the haughty masters of the people by its always removable servants."[35] The final text of the circular speaks, too, of "this new Commune, which breaks the modern state power" and of the "plain workingmen" who "for the first time dared to infringe upon the governmental privilege of their 'natural superiors.'"[36]

If Marx supported, helped, and defended the Commune, despite his conviction that it was doomed to defeat, despite his ideological differences with the trends which predominated in it (Proudhonists, Blanquists, etc.), and despite the opposition of the English trade-unionists who were members of the International, it was because he saw in it the first real manifestation of that

---

[29] *CW*, XXII, 354–355.
[30] *CW*, XXII, 464.
[31] *CW*, XXII, 478.
[32] *CW*, XXII, 334, 339.
[33] *CW*, XXII, 486.
[34] *CW*, XLIV, 131.
[35] *CW*, XXII, 488.
[36] *CW*, XXII, 333, 336.

revolutionary and communist self-emancipation of the proletariat, the form of which he had forecast already in 1846.[37]

e) *Marx and Engels and German Social-Democracy*

The commonly accepted view which sees Marx and Engels as the leaders of the German Social-Democratic Party in 1875–1883 does not stand up to any serious analysis of the actual events of that period.

From the Party's foundation in 1875, through the fusion of the Eisenach group (Liebknecht, Bebel, etc.) with the Lassalleans, Marx and Engels waged together

---

[37] In his brilliant (but sometimes neo-Kautskian!) work on Marx's political thought, Shlomo Avineri puts up a bizarre hypothesis according to which "the various drafts of *The Civil War in France* offer clear evidence that Marx considered the Commune not a working-class affair, but a petty-bourgeois, democratic-radical *émeute*," a view which he had not expressed in the final, published version because, "after all, a eulogy is not the right moment for an autopsy." S. Avineri, *The Social and Political Thought of Karl Marx* (Cambridge University Press, 1969), p. 247.

Yet the drafts of *The Civil War in France* show that, for Marx, the Commune was no "petty-bourgeois riot" but, on the contrary, "the greatest revolution of the century," whose character he explicitly affirms:

> The red flag hoisted by the Paris Commune crowns in reality only the government of workmen for Paris! They have clearly, consciously, proclaimed the Emancipation of Labor and the transformation of Society as their goal! But the actual "social" character of their republic consists only in this, that workmen govern the Paris Commune! *CW*, XXII, 499.

According to Avineri:

> Actually, there is nothing proletarian in the social legislation of the Commune except its abolition of night baking. In the section of the draft dealing with legislation affecting the working class Marx cannot show more than a few laws against prostitution and the abolition of some payments which were remnants of feudal legislation. On the other hand, he devotes much more space to the sub-chapter called "Measures for the working class but mostly for the middle classes." Avineri, *op. cit.*, p. 248.

This calls for some observations:

(a) The space devoted to sub-chapters can hardly serve as a conclusive argument, but, in any case, the sub-chapter entitled "Measures for the working class" takes up fifty-one lines in the *Werke*, whereas the one entitled "Measures for the working class but mainly for the middle classes" takes up only thirty-one.
(b) One of the measures mentioned by Marx in the section on legislation affecting the working class (a measure much more significant than the decrees on the bakers and others mentioned by Avineri) is the setting-up by the Commune of a committee to look into the best ways of "handing over the deserted workshops and manufactures to co-operative workmen societies." *CW*, XXII, 472.
(c) Marx stressed on several occasions that it was not so much its social legislation that gave the Commune its class character as the working-class nature of the authority it established.

a vigorous and uncompromising political struggle against the opportunist, reformist and petty-bourgeois tendencies that showed themselves in German Social-Democracy, tendencies to which their closest collaborators (Liebknecht and Bebel) themselves made weighty concessions.

If we leave aside the affair of the Gotha Program, which was still connected with the fight against Lassallism, the most representative of the divergences between Marx and Engels and the reformist sections of the Party was the battle waged in 1877–1880 against the "counter-revolutionary" intellectuals (the Zürich group) and the right wing of the Parliamentary group, a battle which almost resulted in a formal and public break with the leadership of the SPD.

In a letter of October 19, 1877, to F. A. Sorge, Marx complains that "a corrupt spirit is asserting itself in our party, not so much among the masses as among the leaders." He particularly criticizes the compromise made by the "leaders" with "a whole swarm of immature undergraduates and over-wise graduates who want to give socialism a 'higher, idealistic' orientation." The typical representative of this "swarm," according to Marx, was one Dr. Höchberg, who edited in Zürich the periodical *Zukunft* – which Marx describes as "pitiful."[38]

This same Höchberg published in 1879, in the *Jahrbuch für Sozialwissenschaft und Sozialpolitik*, which he edited under the pseudonym "Dr. Ludwig Richter," an article composed by himself, C. A. Schramm, and (already . . .) E. Bernstein, in which he advocated a "revision" of the Party's policy, abandonment of its "narrowly working-class" character, and of its excessively revolutionary tendencies, etc.

About the same time, a Social-Democratic deputy, Max Kayser, made a speech in the Reichstag approving Bismarck's protectionist measures. When this speech was severely criticized by a friend of Marx and Engels, Hirsch, in his periodical *Die Laterne*, the parliamentary group and the Party leadership sided with Kayser.

Confronted with these two serious symptoms of the "corrupt spirit" among the Party's leaders, Marx and Engels decided that it was high time to make a pronouncement. They called on the Leipzig group (Bebel, Liebknecht, Bracke, etc.) to condemn the reformist tendencies, particularly Höchberg's *Jahrbuch*, or, if necessary, to repudiate publicly the leaders of the Party. In a letter to Engels, September 10, 1879, Marx wrote:

> I altogether agree with your view that no further time should be lost in stating our views, *forcibly*, and *ruthlessly*, as to the *Jahrbuch* bunkum, i.e., *pro nunc* "presenting" it to the Leipzigers in black and white. Should they proceed to go ahead with their "party organ" in this way, we shall

---

[38] *CW*, XLV, 283.

have to disavow them publicly. In such matters the line has to be drawn somewhere.³⁹

One week later, Marx and Engels sent to Bebel and the other leaders in Leipzig a circular letter which set out their opinion "in black and white." This text, which is one of the forgotten documents of Marxism,⁴⁰ is of considerable interest: the tendencies subjected to criticism in it were precisely those which are typical of 20th-century reformist social-democracy – and, as it happened, Bernstein, the pioneer of revisionism, was attacked in it by name.

As I see it, the circular of September 1879 is of decisive importance: here we find Marx, in one of the last political battles of his life, defending with clarity and determination, the same principles which I have singled out in his youthful writings: socialist revolution and self-emancipation by the proletariat.

The circular begins by tackling the Kayser affair. After expressing their agreement with Hirsch's criticisms, Marx and Engels state that these criticisms have lost none of their force, quite the contrary, because the Parliamentary group has sided with Kayser. They ask their friends in Leipzig:

> Has German Social-Democracy indeed been infected with the parliamentary disease, believing that, with the popular vote, the Holy Ghost is poured upon those elected, that meetings of the factions are transformed into infallible councils and factional resolutions into sacrosanct dogma . . . ?⁴¹

Undoubtedly, though, the most significant part of the document is that which deals with the Höchberg-Bernstein-Schramm affair. Paraphrasing ironically the theses of the *Jahrbuch* article, Marx and Engels write:

> In the view of these gentlemen the Social-Democratic Party ought *not* to be a one-sided workers' party but a many-sided party of "all men imbued with a true love of mankind." This it is to prove, above all, by divesting itself of crude proletarian passions and applying itself, under the direction of educated philanthropic bourgeois, "to the formation of good taste" and "the acquisition of good manners . . ."

> German socialism has laid too much stress on "winning over the masses, thus omitting to prosecute vigorous (!) propaganda amongst the so-called upper strata of society." For "the party still lacks men who are fit to represent it in the Reichstag." It is, however, "desirable and necessary to entrust the mandates to men who have had the time and the opportunity to become thoroughly conversant with the relevant material. Only rarely and in

---

³⁹ CW, XLV, 389.
⁴⁰ It was published for the first time in 1931, in the journal *Die Kommunistische Internationale*.
⁴¹ CW, XLV, 400.

exceptional cases do . . . the simple working man and small master craftsman have sufficient leisure for the purpose."

Therefore, elect bourgeois! In short, the working class is incapable of emancipating itself by its own efforts. In order to do so it must place itself under the direction of "educated and propertied" bourgeois who alone have "the time and the opportunity" to become conversant with what is good for the workers. And, secondly, the bourgeoisie are not to be combated – not on your life – but *won over* by vigorous propaganda.

If, however, you wish to win over the upper strata of society, or at least their well-intentioned elements, you mustn't frighten them – not on your life. And here the Zürich trio believe they have made a reassuring discovery: "Now, at the very time it is oppressed by the Anti-Socialist Law, the Party is showing that it *does not* wish to pursue the path of forcible, bloody revolution, but rather is determined . . . to tread the path of legality, i.e., of *reform* . . ." Should Berlin ever be so uneducated as to stage another March 18 (1848), it would behoove the Social-Democrats not to take part in the fighting as "louts besotted with barricades". . . but rather to "tread the path of legality," to placate, to clear away the barricades and, if necessary, march with the glorious army against the one-sided, crude, uneducated masses. Or, if the gentlemen insist that that's not what they meant, then what did they mean? . . .

. . . The program is not to be *relinquished* but merely *postponed* – for some unspecified period. They accept it – not for themselves in their own lifetimes but posthumously, as an heirloom for their children and their children's children. Meanwhile they devote their "whole strength and energies" to all sorts of trifles, tinkering away at the capitalist social order so that at least something should appear to be done without at the same time alarming the bourgeoisie.[42]

The circular ends with a veritable profession of faith by Marx and Engels and an unconcealed threat to break with the Party:

As for ourselves, there is, considering all our antecedents, only one course open to us. For almost 40 years we have emphasized that the class struggle is the immediate motive force of history and, in particular, that the class struggle between bourgeoisie and proletariat is the great lever of modern social revolution: hence we cannot possibly co-operate with men who seek to eliminate that class struggle from the movement. At the founding of the International we expressly formulated the battle-cry: The emancipation of the working class must be achieved by the working class itself. Hence we cannot co-operate with men who say openly that the workers are too un-

---

[42] *CW*, XLV, 403, 403–404, 405.

educated to emancipate themselves, and must first be emancipated from above by philanthropic members of the upper and lower middle classes. If the new party organ is to adopt a policy that corresponds to the opinions of these gentlemen [Höchberg and Co.], if it is bourgeois and not proletarian, then all we could do – much though we might regret it – would be publicly to declare ourselves opposed to it and abandon the solidarity with which we have hitherto represented the German party abroad. But we hope it won't come to that.[43]

Be it noted, in passing, that the reformist parliamentarism of Höchberg and Bernstein, though apparently the exact opposite of Jacobino-Babouvism, shares with it one decisive feature: emancipation of the workers not by themselves but "from on high," thanks to an enlightened minority. For Buonarrot_'s followers, this minority was the conspiratorial sect and the "social dictators," for the proto-revisionists of _879, it was "educated bourgeois" and the Social-Democratic deputies to the Reichstag.

Against the Höchbergs and Bernsteins, Marx and Engels proclaimed themselves, in their 1879 circular, resolutely revolutionary (they did not ever leave out the traditional barricades) and irreducibly loyal to the motto of the International, which they plainly define as their "battle-cry" – the principle of proletarian self-emancipation. This resolution and this loyalty are expressed "roughly and without respect," even at the risk of breaking with their best friends and followers in Germany.

In a letter to Sorge written two days after the circular, Marx repeated its essential ideas. Regarding the Party leadership's attitude in the Kayser affair he wrote:

> To what depths they have already been brought by parliamentarism will be evident to you from the fact that they impute it a dire crime in Hirsch to have – what? – handled that scoundrel Kayser somewhat roughly in the *Laterne*, on account of his disgraceful speech regarding Bismarck's customs legislation . . . Be that as it may; they are so far infected with parliamentary criticism as to believe themselves *above criticism* and to denounce criticism as a *crime de lèse majesté!*[44]

As for the Zürich group (Höchberg, Bernstein, Schramm, Viereck, Singer) he defined them as persons who, "nonentities in theory and nincompoops in practice, are seeking to draw the teeth of socialism (which they have rehashed in accordance with academic formulae) and of the Social-Democratic *Party* in particular, to enlighten the workers, or, as they put it, to provide them [the workers], out of their confused and superficial knowledge, with 'educative

---

[43] *CW*, XLV, 408.
[44] *CW*, XLV, 414.

elements' and, above all, to make the party 'respectable' in the eyes of the philistines. They are poor *counter-revolutionary* windbags."[45]

The leader of the group, Höchberg, is presented by Marx as "a partisan of 'peaceable development'" who "expects proletarian emancipation to be achieved solely by 'educated bourgeois', i.e., people like himself." As for his article in the *Jahrbuch*, Marx considered that "Never has anything more discreditable to the party appeared in print."[46]

In conclusion, "things might well come to such a pass that Engels and I would feel compelled to issue a 'public statement' against the Leipzigers and their allies in Zürich."[47]

The conflict went on until 1880, with Marx and Engels refusing to write for the Party's new central organ, the *Sozialdemocrat*, because opportunist tendencies were represented therein, and this despite repeated and insistent appeals from Bebel and Liebknecht. In November 1880, Marx wrote to Sorge to lament "how wretchedly" the "so-called Party organ, the Zürich *Sozialdemokrat*" had been conducted.[48]

II. After Marx: from Lenin to Che Guevara

I am not, of course, going to undertake here a general review of 20th-century Marxist theories about revolutionary self-emancipation and the relation between the proletarian masses and the Communist Party. The picture I shall draw will be very partial, leaving out, among others, the principal thinkers of pre-1914 Social-Democracy (Plekhanov, Kautsky, etc.) as well as Stalin and his followers. There will also be no analysis of the rich and complex thought of Mao Tse-tung, which I think should be studied in a different context.

I shall outline some hypotheses and suggestions, in very summary form, about the social settings of the various theories. As for the theories themselves, I shall analyze them in relation to three essential, closely interconnected themes: (1) levels of class-consciousness; (2) relation between Party and masses, especially during the revolution; (3) internal structure of the Party.

It seems to me that the thinkers I have chosen (Lenin, Rosa Luxemburg, Gramsci, Lukács, Trotsky, Guevara) belong to one and the same "current" in Marxism, that which applies, in the light of 20th-century conditions, Marx's

---

[45] *CW*, XLV, 413.
[46] *Ibid.*
[47] *CW*, XLV, 412.
[48] *CW*, XLVI, 42.

theses on the proletariat's self-emancipation. It is a contradictory and varying current, within which Lenin and Luxemburg represent two poles that are partly opposite, partly complementary, but are fundamentally *homogeneous*.

a) *Lenin's centralism*

Lenin's writings on the organizational problems of the Russian Social-Democratic Party in 1900–1904, particularly *What Is To Be Done?* (1902) and *One Step Forward, Two Steps Back* (1904), form a coherent set expressing a typically "centralist" conception of the socialist movement.

This tendency is usually explained by reference to "the Russian sources of Bolshevism": the Machiavellianism and omniscience of leaders in Nechaev, the "subjectivism" of Lavrov and Mikhailovsky, the Jacobino-Blanquism of Tkachev, etc.[49] It is indeed undeniable that the traditions of 19th-century Russia – especially the conspiratorial structure of the terrorist group *Narodnaya Volya* – were among the socio-cultural settings of the theories developed in *What Is To Be Done?* Lenin himself acknowledged this, in so far as he did not conceal his admiration for the *Zemlya i Volya* group, the precursor of *Narodnaya Volya* formed in 1876 by the Populists and Plekhanov, which he considered a "magnificent organization . . . that should serve us as a model."[50]

And the direct heirs of the *Narodniki*, the Socialist Revolutionaries, future mortal foes of Bolshevism, warmly approved of Lenin's centralism before 1905.[51]

However, we need to be on guard against caricatures of the "Lenin equals Nechaev" type, and, above all, we must not forget that the "sources" do not explain much, but, on the contrary, themselves need explaining. In other words, we have to show why Lenin was inspired, precisely in the period 1901–1904, by the centralist schemas of the Russian "Blanquists" of the 19th century.

It seems to me that it is in the particular conditions of the Russian Social-Democratic movement of before 1905 that the social bases of Lenin's theories must be sought:

(a) The isolated, closed character of the Social-Democratic Party, very much in a minority and at its very beginning, consisting of a few small groups

---

[49] Cf. M. Collinet, *Du Bolchèvisme*, Ed. Le livre contemporain (Paris: Amion-Dumont, 1957); N. Berdyaev, *The Origins of Russian Communism* (London: 1937); D. Shub, *Lenin* (New York: Mentor Books, 1951); G. Lichtheim, *Marxism, op. cit.*
[50] *CWL*, V, 474.
[51] I. Deutscher, *Trotsky: I, The Prophet Armed*, p. 94, n. 1. One of them wrote about *What Is To Be Done?*: "Here the line of demarcation between the *Narodovoltsy* and the Social-Democrats is erased." Cf. *Que faire?*, Ed. du Seuil (1966), p. 248: "*Que faire? et les socialistes-révolutionnaires.*"

of "professional revolutionaries," relatively cut off from a mass movement which was then more "economist" than political in tendency;
(b) The dispersed, divided and disorganized situation of the Social-Democratic nuclei;
(c) The strictly clandestine character of the movement, owing to police repression by the Tsarist regime, and, consequent on this, the limited, "professional," non-democratic character of the organization. Lenin himself gave the requirements of underground struggle as one of the chief justifications of his centralist views;[52]
(d) The struggle waged by the Social-Democratic leaders gathered round the old, pre-1903 *Iskra*, and by Lenin in particular, against the "economist" tendency (Martynov, Akimov, the journals *Rabochaya Mysl* and *Rabochaya Delo*) which tended to reduce the working-class movement to trade unionism and the fight for reforms, refusing to put revolutionary political struggle on the order of the day. The "economists" worshipped the trade-unionist spontaneity of the unpoliticized masses of the workers and consequently denied the need for a centralized secret organization. Later, Lenin was to emphasize more than once that *What Is To Be Done?* could not be understood except in the specific context of the polemic against "economism."

The more general theoretical foundation for the organizational conceptions of *What Is To Be Done?* and *One Step Forward, Two Steps Back*, is the distinction made by Lenin between two forms of proletarian class consciousness, which differ in their nature and in their historical origin:

(1) The "spontaneous" forms of this consciousness which arise organically from the first struggles of the proletariat, emotional to start with – "outbursts of desperation and vengeance" – but attaining later their full development as "trade-union consciousness," meaning the conviction that the workers must get together in unions, fight the bosses, demand from the government laws that the workers need, and so on.[53] These reactions constitute the highest level of consciousness that the working class can attain by itself, when left to its own resources, within the limited sphere of economic struggles and relations between workers and employers. Even when this consciousness assumes a political character, it remains wholly alien to socialist politics, being confined to the fight for juridico-economic reforms (right to strike, labor protection laws, etc.)
(2) Social-democratic consciousness, which does not arise spontaneously in the workers' movement but is introduced into it "from without" by socialist intellectuals from the possessing classes. It triumphs only through

---

[52] *CWL*, V, 451–472, *passim*.
[53] *CWL*, V, 375.

an ideological battle waged against spontaneity and the "trade-union-ist" tendencies of the proletariat, which enslave the class to bourgeois ideology.[54] Socialist consciousness is, essentially, consciousness of the fundamental antagonism between the interests of the proletariat and the existing social and political regime. It does not focus the workers' attention solely upon themselves but upon the relations between all the classes and on class society as a whole, fitting every separate event into the general picture of capitalist exploitation.[55]

It was on the basis of this analysis of the structure of the proletariat's class consciousness that Lenin built his theory of the Party, which offers institutionalization of the different levels of consciousness in organizational terms.

Lenin begins by drawing a sharp line of demarcation between the Party and the class, the vanguard organization and the mass movement, the conscious minority and the hesitant majority within the proletariat, and, at the same time, tries to create links between these two compartments. In *One Step Forward, Two Steps Back*, he suggests five hierarchical levels, in accordance with degree or organization and consciousness.

In the Party:

(1) the organizations of (professional) revolutionaries;
(2) the organizations of (revolutionary) workers.

Outside the Party:

(1) workers' organizations associated with the Party;
(2) workers' organizations not associated with the Party but actually under its control and direction;

---

[54] CWL, V, 375, 383. Originally, the thesis about the introduction of socialism "from without" was not Lenin's but Kautsky's. In *What Is To Be Done?* Lenin quotes approvingly the following passage from Kautsky (whom at that time he saw as *the* great orthodox Marxist):

> The vehicle of science is not the proletariat but the *bourgeois intelligentsia*: it was in the minds of individual members of this stratum that modern socialism originated, and it was they who communicated it to more intellectually developed proletarians who, in their turn, introduce it into the proletarian class struggle where conditions allow that to be done. Thus, socialist consciousness is something introduced into the proletarian class struggle from without (*von Aussen Hineingetragenes*) and not something that arose within it spontaneously (*urwüchsig*). Accordingly, the old Hainfeld program quite rightly stated that the task of Social-Democracy is to imbue the proletariat [literally: saturate the proletariat] with the *consciousness* of its position and the consciousness of its task. CWL, V, 383–384.

[55] CWL, V, 400, 439.

(3) unorganized elements of the working class who in part also come under the direction of the Social-Democratic Party, at any rate during major manifestations of the class struggle.[56]

The principles which constitute the schema of relations between the Party and the masses are also applied to the internal structure of the revolutionary organization, through the following rules:

(a) the political content of the Social-Democrats' struggle and the obligatory clandestinity of its activity require that the organization of revolutionaries shall "consist chiefly of people professionally engaged in revolutionary activity," unlike the organizations adopted to the needs of the economic struggle, which should be as broad as possible;[57]

(b) for the same reasons, it is impossible for the Party to be "democratic," with elections, control of leaders, etc. The Party's structure must be "bureaucratic" and centralistic, based on the principles of building the Party "from the top down" and "from above to below." Democracy, autonomy of units, and the principle of organization "from below to above" are typical of opportunism in the Social-Democratic movement;[58]

(c) consequently, the leadership of the party must be in the hands of "tried and tested leaders . . . professionally trained, schooled by long experience." The worst enemies of the working class are demagogues who spread distrust of leaders and stir up the "bad and ambitious instincts" of the crowd;[59]

(d) finally, an iron discipline must govern the Party's inner life, a discipline for which the workers have naturally been prepared by the "school" of factory life, but from which petty-bourgeois, inclined to anarchism by their conditions of existence, try to escape.[60]

To his opponents among the Social-Democrats who accused him of "Jacobinism" on the organizational plane, Lenin replied that the revolutionary Social-Democrat was none other than "a Jacobin who wholly identifies himself with the *organization* of the proletariat."[61]

Lenin's writings in the period 1902–1904 undoubtedly form a coherent whole which has to be studied as such. However, does this whole constitute "the essence of Bolshevism" or "the finished expression of Leninism," as is claimed by many among his supporters as well as among his opponents?

During the Stalin period, *What Is To Be Done?* was translated and circulated throughout the international communist movement as Lenin's last word on

---

[56] *CWL*, VII, 266.
[57] *CWL*, V, 464.
[58] *CWL*, VII, 205–207, 383–396, 396–397.
[59] *CWL*, V, 461.
[60] *CWL*, VII, 391–392.
[61] *CWL*, VII, 383.

problems of organization.⁶² Yet Lenin himself, in 1921, considered the translation of this work "not desirable" and demanded that, if it were to be published in non-Russian languages, it should at least be accompanied by "good commentaries," "in order to avoid false applications"!⁶³

Already in 1907, in a new preface to the book, Lenin made reservations concerning it, acknowledging that it contained some expressions that were somewhat clumsy or imprecise, and saying that it must not be separated from "its connection with the concrete historical situation of a definite, and now long past, period in the development of our Party": it was "a controversial correction of Economist distortions and it would be wrong to regard the pamphlet in any other light." Moreover, Lenin made it clear that he never had "any intention of elevating my own formulations, as given in *What Is To Be Done?* to 'programmatic' level, constituting special principles."

He suggested that these formulations corresponded to the period when the Social-Democrats were shut up in the narrow setting of the "circles," and added:

> Only the broadening of the Party by enlisting *proletarian* elements can, in conjunction with open mass activity, eradicate all the residue of the circle spirit which has been inherited from the past and is unsuited to our present tasks. And the transition to a democratically organized workers' party, proclaimed by the Bolsheviks in *Novaya Zhizn* in November 1905, i.e., as soon as the conditions appeared for legal activity – this transition was virtually an irrevocable break with the old circle ways that had outlived their day.⁶⁴

It would seem that this profound change, between 1904 and 1907, in Lenin's theses was closely connected with an historic event which occurred between these two dates and which showed the tremendous political initiative possessed by the Russian worker masses – the revolution of 1905–1906. To be convinced of this, one need only read Lenin's writings during 1905, which set forth a whole new overall vision of the working-class and Social-Democratic movement, a conception sometimes not far from Rosa Luxemburg's.

Lenin no longer speaks of consciousness "introduced from without," but of the masses attaining consciousness through their own practice, through their concrete revolutionary experience:

---

⁶² In the history of the Communist Party of the Soviet Union written under Stalin's direct inspiration, it was said that "The theoretical theses expounded in *What Is To Be Done?* later became the foundation of the ideology of the Bolshevik Party." *History of the Communist Party of the Soviet Union: A Short Course* (Moscow: 1939), p. 38.
⁶³ T. Cliff, *Rosa Luxemburg* (London: International Socialism, 1959), p. 48.
⁶⁴ *CWL*, XIII, 101, 108, 105, 107.

> The masses . . . enter the political arena as active combatants. These masses are learning in practice, and before the eyes of the world are taking their first tentative steps, feeling their way, defining their objectives, testing themselves and the theories of all their ideologists . . . Nothing will ever compare in importance with this direct training that the masses and the classes receive in the course of the revolutionary struggle itself.[65]

In his well-known article of January 1905, "The Beginning of Revolution in Russia," he writes, regarding Bloody Sunday (January 9) in St Petersburg, that "The revolutionary education of the proletariat made more progress in one day than it could have made in months and years of drab, humdrum, wretched existence."[66] He goes so far as to affirm, towards the end of 1905, that "The working class is *instinctively, spontaneously Social-Democratic* and more than ten years of work put in by Social Democracy has done a great deal to transform this spontaneity into consciousness."[67]

He now sees the relation between leaders and class in a new light, and points out, in a commentary in 1906 on the Moscow insurrection of December 1905, that "the proletariat sensed sooner than its leaders the change in the objective conditions of the struggle and the need for a transition from the strike to an uprising. As is always the case, practice marched ahead of theory."[68]

Consequently, a new conception of the relation between the Party and the masses appears in Lenin's thinking. He now emphasizes *the initiative of the workers themselves*:

> The initiative of the workers themselves will now display itself on a scale that we, the underground and circle workers of yesterday, did not even dare dream of.[69]

---

[65] *CWL*, VIII, 104.

[66] *CWL*, VIII, 97.

[67] *CWL*, X, 32. (My italics – M. L.) Cf. also his article of November 1905, "The Socialist Party and Non-Party Revolutionism": "As a result of the special position which the proletariat occupies in capitalist society, the striving of the workers towards socialism and their alliance with the Socialist Party assert themselves with elemental force at the very earliest stages of the movement." *CWL*, X, 77.

[68] In an essay of 1907 Lenin compares the attitude of Marx towards the Commune with that of the Social-Democrats towards the revolution of 1905 and exclaims:

> The *historical initiative* of the masses was what Marx prized above everything else. Ah, if only our Russian Social-Democrats would learn from Marx how to appreciate the *historical initiative* of the Russian workers and peasants in October and December 1905! (Italics in the original.) *CWL*, XII, 109.

[69] *CWL*, X, 36. *CWL*, XI, 173.

It is for this reason that he proposes, in opposition to the Party's "committee men," that the soviet of workers' deputies be transformed into the political center of the revolution, a provisional revolutionary government. He even drafts a public proclamation by this future government, around the following central theme:

> We do not shut ourselves off from the revolutionary people but submit to their judgement every step and every direction we take. We rely fully and solely on the free initiative of the working masses themselves.[70]

Finally, the "new course" finds expression also in the internal organization of the Party, which is being joined by masses of revolutionary workers. A Fourth Congress of the Party is convened, and Lenin demands that delegates from the new members be admitted, along with the representatives of the established "committees." And he sees in the decision to convene the Fourth Congress "a decisive step towards the full application of the democratic principle in Party organization."[71]

It is instructive to compare Lenin's attitude to the outbreak of the revolution in January 1905 with that of Stalin, which is typical of the Party's "committee-men." In a leaflet addressed to "the workers of the Caucasus," Stalin wrote: "Let us stretch out our hands to one another and *rally round the Party Committees*! We must not forget for a moment that *only the Party Committees can worthily lead us, only they* will light up our road to the 'promised land' called the socialist world!"[72] At this same time Lenin was calling for the formation of *revolutionary committees* – that is, committees that would bring together all revolutionaries, Social-Democrats or not – "at every factory, in every city district, in every large village."[73]

b) *"Spontaneity-ism" in Rosa Luxemburg*

Rosa Luxemburg's views on Party organization, as set forth in her articles published in 1903–1904 in *Die Neue Zeit*, the theoretical organ of the Social-Democrats, and in her pamphlet *General Strike, Party and Trade Unions* (1906),

---

[70] CWL, X, 27.
[71] CWL, X, 33–34.
[72] Stalin, Works, I, p. 80.
[73] CWL, VIII, 99. See also on this subject Lenin's writings in 1917. Immediately after his arrival in April, Lenin issued (to the great scandal of most of the Bolshevik Party's leaders), the slogan: "All power to the Soviets!" – a power which he defined thus: "It is a revolutionary dictatorship, i.e., a power directly based on revolutionary seizure, on the direct initiative of the people from below, and *not on a law* enacted by a centralized state power." CWL, XXIV, 38. Again a few weeks before the October revolution, he wrote: "Don't be afraid of the people's initiative and independence. Put your faith in their revolutionary organizations ... Lack of faith in the people, fear of their initiative and independence, trepidation before their revolutionary energy, instead of all-round and unqualified support for it – this is where the S. R. and Menshevik leaders have sinned most of all." CWL, XXV, 370.

were fundamentally opposed to Lenin's pre-1905 centralism in their emphasis on the revolutionary initiative of the masses themselves and the reservations they expressed regarding concentration of power in the hands of he Party's leading group.

It appears to me, once more, that it is in the situation of the German workers' movement in general, and particularly, in that of its revolutionary wing, that we must seek the roots of Rosa Luxemburg's theses:

(a) The German Social-Democratic Party was a *mass* organization, legal and highly organized;

(b) Opportunist and "revisionist" tendencies were being revealed already at that time (1903–1906) in the Party's leadership, especially in the Parliamentary group. The radical wing of the SPD placed its hopes in the revolutionary potentialities of the masses and not in the capacity for initiative possessed by the bureaucratic leaders, who were seen as an essentially timid and conservative element. In the trade unions (which were linked with the SPD), the left-wing minority had long been waging a hard fight against the anti-democratic and *centralist* tendencies of the reformist trade-union bureaucracy.[74] Moreover, some revisionist intellectuals (Georg Bernhard, Maximilian Harden) were pleased to point out in their politico-literary essays the superiority of the "educated leaders" over the "blind mass," which brought down upon them vigorous criticism from Rosa Luxemburg.[75]

(c) Rosa Luxemburg, like the entire Marxist tendency in the SPD, envisioned the "collapse" of capitalism in Germany essentially in *economic* terms, unlike Tsarist Russia, where the only imaginable limits to capitalism were *political*. This enables us to understand better not only the differences between Luxemburg and Lenin on the accumulation of capital,[76] but also their disagreement on matters of organization. For Rosa Luxemburg, the "catastrophic" crisis of the capitalist economy would bring the broad masses to a revolutionary position independently of the "conscious" action of its leaders, and even against them, should they prove to be an obstacle.

(d) The tradition which inspired the Marxist Left of the German Party was that of the "Social-Democratic Workers' Party" founded at Eisenach in 1869 with the support of Marx and Engels. In this party, the democratic

---

[74] Cf. C.E. Schorske, *German Social-Democracy 1905–1917* (New York: J. Wiley, 1965), pp. 10–11, 133, 249.

[75] "Geknickte Hoffnungen" ("Hopes dashed") in *Neue-Zeit*, 1903–1904, Bd. I, No. 2, in French as "Masse et chefs," in Rosa Luxemburg, *Marxisme contre dictature* (Paris: Spartacus, 1947), pp. 39–42.

[76] Cf. Goldmann, *Human Sciences, op. cit.*, pp. 79–80.

and "autonomist" tendency was the opposite of the dictatorial centralism of the General Association of German Workers founded by Lassalle.[77]

Rosa Luxemburg's theses did not change between 1903 and 1906, since the Russian Revolution of 1905 merely confirmed her hopes regarding the revolutionary capacity of the proletarian masses. Her two articles on organization which appeared in *Die Neue Zeit*, together with her pamphlet on the general strike, expound the same theory, by way of three characteristic themes: class consciousness, relations between the Party and the masses, and the Party's internal organization.

For Rosa Luxemburg, the process whereby the worker masses become conscious results less from the propaganda contained in the party's pamphlets and leaflets than from their experience of the revolutionary struggle, of the direct and independent action of the proletariat:

> The sudden general rising of the proletariat in January, under the powerful impetus of the St Petersburg events, was outwardly a political act of the revolutionary declaration of war on absolutism. But this first general direct action reacted inwardly all the more powerfully as it for the first time awoke class feeling and class-consciousness in millions upon millions as if by an electric shock . . . Absolutism in Russia must be overthrown by the proletariat. But in order to be able to overthrow it the proletariat requires a high degree of political education, of class-consciousness and organization. All these conditions cannot be fulfilled by pamphlets and leaflets but only by the living political school, by the fight and in the fight, in the continuous course of the revolution.[78]

Here Rosa Luxemburg shows herself to be a faithful disciple of Marx's theory of revolution: it is in the revolutionary praxis of the masses that both the "outside," the circumstances, and the "inside," the class-consciousness, are changed. Revolutionary consciousness can become general only through a "practical" movement, the "mass-scale" changing of men can be effected only in the revolution itself.[79] The category of praxis – which is for her as with

---

[77] R. Luxemburg, *Selected Political Writings* (London: 1971), p. 301. According to Cliff (*op. cit.*, p. 42), one of the possible sources of Rosa Luxemburg's conceptions was her struggle against the Polish Socialist Party (PPS), which was, on the one hand, "social-patriotic," and, on the other, conspiratorial and terrorist.
[78] Luxemburg, *The Mass Strike, the Political Party and the Trade Unions* (Colombo, 1964), p. 27.
[79] This applies also, in Rosa Luxemburg's view, to the building of socialism. The new communist morality has no better guarantee than the active and democratic participation of the masses in the building of the future society:

> The highest idealism in the interest of the collectivity, the strictest self-discipline, the truest public spirit of the masses are the moral foundations

Marx the dialectical unity of the objective and the subjective, the *mediation* by which the class *in itself* becomes the class *for itself* – enables her to transcend the rigid and metaphysical dilemma of German Social-Democracy, between the abstract moralism of Bernstein and the mechanical economism of Kautsky (whereas, for the former, a "subjective," moral, and spiritual change in the people is the pre-condition for the advent of "social justice," for the second it is objective economic evolution that leads "inevitably" to socialism). This allows us to understand better why Rosa Luxemburg set herself against not only the neo-Kantian revisionists but also (from 1905) the strategy of passive waiting advocated by the "orthodox center." And it was the dialectic of praxis that enabled her to transcend the traditional dualism embodied in the Erfurt Program between reforms, the "minimum program," and revolution, "the ultimate aim." In the strategy of the mass strike which she advocated in 1906 (against the trade-union bureaucracy) and in 1910 (against Kautsky), Rosa Luxemburg found a way to transform economic struggles or the fight for universal suffrage into a general revolutionary movement.[80]

Rosa Luxemburg considered that during a radical uprising of the worker masses the separation that a "pedantic schema" sought to maintain between the economic (trade-union) struggle and the political (social-democratic) struggle would disappear, becoming two intermingled aspects of the class struggle, with the artificial line drawn between trade union and socialist party "washed away."[81] Rejecting the contrast between "trade-unionist consciousness" and "Social-Democratic consciousness" (Lenin), she suggests a distinction between the "theoretical and latent" consciousness which is characteristic of the workers' movement during the period when bourgeois parliamentarism is dominant and the "practical and active" consciousness which arises during the revolutionary process, when the mass itself (and not just the Party's deputies and leaders) appears on the political scene, crystallizing its "ideological education" directly in *praxis*. It is through this practical and active consciousness that the backward and unorganized strata will

---

of socialist society, just as stupidity, egotism and corruption are the moral foundations of capitalist society. All these socialist civic virtues, together with the knowledge and skills necessary to direct socialist enterprises, can be won by the mass of the workers only through their own activity, their own experience. "What Does the Spartacus League Want?" in *Selected Political Writings, op. cit.*, p. 369.

[80] In his 1931 article "On Some Problems of the History of Bolshevism," Stalin compared Rosa Luxemburg with Lenin and criticized her for not having broken with Kautsky before 1914. The fact is that she had attacked Kautsky long before Lenin did, as Lenin himself generously acknowledged in a letter of October 27, 1914, to Shliapnikov: "Rosa Luxemburg was right when she wrote, long ago, that Kautsky has the 'subservience of a theoretician' – servility, in plainer language, servility to the majority of the party, to opportunism." *CWL*, XXXV, 167–168. Cf. L. D. Trotsky, "Hands off Rosa Luxemburg!" in *Writings of L. D. Trotsky, 1932* (1973), p. 131 sq.

[81] Luxemburg, *Selected Political Writings, op. cit.*, pp. 241, 252.

show themselves, in a period of revolutionary struggle, to be the most radical element and not the element that lags behind.[82]

This theory of class-consciousness obviously leads to a conception of the relations between the party and the masses which is very different from the one set out in *What Is To Be Done?* and *One Step Forward, Two Steps Back*. While opposing opportunist parliamentarism, which claims to wipe out any distinction between the party and the unorganized strata of the people, so that "the active kernel of the proletariat is . . . dissolved in the amorphous mass of voters," Rosa Luxemburg insists that "an absolute dividing wall cannot be erected between the class-conscious kernel of the proletariat, already organized as party cadre, and the immediate popular environment which is gripped by the class struggle and finds itself in the process of class enlightenment."[83]

For this reason, she criticizes those who base their political strategy on what she considers an overestimation of the role of organization in the class struggle – which is usually complemented by an underestimation of the political maturity of the still unorganized proletariat, forgetting the educative effect of "the storm of great unsettling class struggles," during which the influence of socialist ideas spreads far beyond the limits suggested by the membership lists of organizations or even the electoral statistics of calm periods. This does not mean, of course, that the conscious vanguard has to remain with folded arms waiting for the "spontaneous" arrival of a revolutionary movement. On the contrary, its role is, precisely, to "hasten the development of things and endeavor to accelerate events."[84]

Finally, summing up her views on organization and replying to Lenin's famous image which compares the Social-Democrat to "a Jacobin indissolubly associated with the organization of the proletariat," Rosa Luxemburg proclaims that "the fact is . . . that Social-Democracy is not bound up with the organization of the working classes; rather, it is the very movement of the working class."[85] Moreover, according to Rosa Luxemburg, it is the task of Social-Democracy to do away with the antithesis between "the leaders" and "the mass they lead," between the "heads" of the Party, consummate statesmen, and the soft human clay of the "blind herd," the antithesis which constitutes the historical foundation of all class rule.[86] The clear consciousness that the masses have of themselves is, "for socialist action, a condition just as indispensable as the mass's lack of consciousness was in former times for the

---

[82] Luxemburg, *Mass Strike, op. cit.*, p. 53.
[83] Luxemburg, *Selected Political Writings, op. cit.*, pp. 299, 289–290.
[84] Luxemburg, *Mass Strike, op. cit.*, pp. 55, 57.
[85] Luxemburg, *Selected Political Writings, op. cit.*, p. 290.
[86] "Masse et chefs," *op. cit.* (cf. n. 75), pp. 37–39. These remarks were aimed not at Lenin but at the German, French (Jaurès), and Italian (Turati) revisionists. She quotes, as an historic example of this attitude, Bruno Bauer, who saw in the "mass" the worst enemy of the "spirit."

actions of the ruling classes."[87] Consequently, the role of the leaders must be, precisely, to deprive themselves of their position as "heads," "in so far as they made the mass the leader and themselves the executive organs of the mass's conscious action."[88] In short, the only "subject" entitled to the role of leader is the "collective ego" of the revolutionary working class, whose mistakes "are infinitely more fruitful than the infallibility of the best of all possible 'central committees.'"[89]

Starting from these assumptions, Rosa Luxemburg rejects what she calls Lenin's "ultra-centralism" in *One Step Forward* . . . In her view, this centralism of his has a clearly "Jacobino-Blanquist" character which tends to make the Central Committee the sole active nucleus of the Party.

In "sterile and domineering" fashion, the leading nucleus will be more concerned to supervise and regulate the movement than to develop it. To this sort of centralism, appropriate to an organization of conspirators, she opposes socialist centralism, which can only be a "self-centralism"; reign of the majority in the party, imperious concentration of the will of the vanguard, against all particularisms, national, religious, or occupational.[90] The discipline which the proletariat acquires in "the school of factory life," and which, according to Lenin, makes it naturally take to party discipline, is for Rosa Luxemburg, "the corpse-like obedience of a dominated class." It has nothing to do with the freely accepted self-discipline of Social-Democracy, which the working class can acquire only by thoroughly rooting out the habits of obedience and slavery imposed by capitalist society.[91]

In conclusion, while it is true that Rosa Luxemburg underestimated the role of organization in the revolutionary struggle, it needs to be stressed that she did not (unlike some "Luxemburgists") set up the spontaneity of the masses as an absolute and abstract principle. Even in her most "spontaneity-ist" work, *Mass Strike, Party and Trade Unions* (1906), she recognizes that the socialist party must take the *"political* leadership" of the mass strike, which means "to give the slogans, the direction of the struggle; to organize the *tactics* of the political struggle, etc." She even recognizes that the socialist organization is "the most important vanguard of the entire body of the workers" and that "the political clarity, the strength and the unity of the labor movement flow from this organization."[92] It should be added that the Polish organization led

---

[87] Ibid., p. 37.
[88] Ibid.
[89] Selected Political Writings, op. cit., p. 306.
[90] Ibid., pp. 290, 295.
[91] Ibid., p. 291.
[92] Selected Political Writings, op. cit., p. 247; Mass Strike, p. 55.

by Rosa Luxemburg (SDKPiL), which was clandestine and revolutionary, was much more like the Bolshevik Party than the SPD.[93]

Finally, a neglected aspect which has to be taken into account is Rosa Luxemburg's attitude (especially after 1914) to the International, which she conceived as being *a centralized and disciplined world party*. It is not the least of ironies that Karl Liebknecht, in a letter to her, criticizes her conception of the International as being "too mechanically centralist," with "too much 'discipline' and too little spontaneity," treating the masses "too much as instruments of action, not as bearers of the will – as instruments of action willed and decided by the International, not as willing and deciding for themselves."[94]

The defeat suffered in January 1919 showed clearly the limits of spontaneity-ism and the vital role to be played by a strong revolutionary vanguard. Perhaps Rosa Luxemburg recognized that more than ever in her last articles in 1919, since there she emphasized that "the masses ... need clear guidance and ruthless, determined leadership."[95]

---

[93] Cf. Trotsky, "Luxemburg and the Fourth International" (1935), in *Writings ... 1935–1936* (1977), p. 30:

> Rosa herself never confined herself to the mere theory of spontaneity, like Parvus, for example, who later bartered his fatalism about the social revolution for the most revolting opportunism. In contrast to Parvus, Rosa Luxemburg exerted herself to educate the revolutionary wing of the proletariat in advance and to bring it together organizationally as far as possible. In Poland she built up a very rigid independent organization ... She was much too realistic in the revolutionary sense to develop the elements of the theory of spontaneity into a consummate metaphysics.

[94] Cf. K. Liebknecht, "A Rosa Luxemburg: Remarques à propos de son projet de thèses pour le groupe 'Internationale,'" in *Partisans*, No. 45, January 1969, p. 113. Rosa Luxemburg's theses were written in prison in 1915 and published in 1916 as an appendix to the "Junius Pamphlet." The paragraphs aimed at in Liebknecht's criticism are these:

> 3. The center of gravity of the proletariat's class organization is the International. The International decides the tactics of the national sections in time of peace on questions of militarism, colonial policy, trade policy, and the celebration of May Day, and, in addition, the entire policy to be applied in wartime.
> 4. The duty to carry out the International's decisions takes precedence over all other organizational obligations. National sections that violate these decisions place themselves outside the International.
> 5. Only the mobilized masses of the proletariat in all countries can exert decisive power in the struggle against imperialism and against war. Thus the policy of the national sections aims above all to prepare the masses for political action and resolute initiative ... so that the will of the International takes shape in actions by the broadest masses of workers of all countries. J. Riddell, ed., *Lenin's Struggle for a Revolutionary International* (New York: 1984), pp. 417–418.

[95] In J. P. Nettl, *Rosa Luxemburg* (London: OUP, 1966), Vol. II, p. 765.

c) *Gramsci: from workers' councils to Machiavelli*

Antonio Gramsci's ideas on problems of organization underwent between 1919 and 1934 so profound and radical an evolution that one might almost speak of an "ideological break." Whereas his articles published during the years preceding the foundation of the Italian Communist Party (1921) in the Piedmont edition of *Avanti* (the official organ of the Italian Socialist Party) and in the weekly *Ordine Nuovo* (the periodical of the communist wing of the PSI) dealt with questions of organization in terms that were very close to "Luxemburgism," the notebooks he compiled in prison in 1933–1934 (published by Einaudi after the war under the title *Note sul Machiavelli*) go even beyond "Jacobino-Blanquism" and relate closely to Machiavelli's *Prince*.

There are good reasons to believe that this ideological evolution resulted from the deep-going changes that the workers' and communist movement underwent in those fifteen years, in the world generally and in Italy in particular.

In order, first, to understand the "spontaneity-ism" implicit in Gramsci's writings of 1919–1920 we have to place those writings in their historico-social context:

(a) Throughout continental Europe, after the War and under the influence of the Soviet revolution, the workers' movement was in a period of "mass upsurge," with uninterrupted outbreaks of strikes, social revolutions and even communist risings (Germany and Hungary in 1919).

(b) In Italy, specifically, the proletarian masses showed much more initiative and fighting spirit than the leadership of the trade unions or the socialist party.[96] In Turin, in the course of an historic movement which Gramsci witnessed and took part in, the rebellious workers went so far as to occupy the factories and to organize workers' councils spontaneously.

(c) The Party leadership, dominated by "centrist" elements, lagged far behind the revolutionary level attained by the masses, to the point that, during the general strike in Turin, it refused to give its full support to the movement, which it sharply criticized as an "anarchist deviation." Like Rosa Luxemburg in 1904 Gramsci was facing a party which, though formally revolutionary (the PSI called itself a "section of the Third International") was inwardly sapped by parliamentarism and reformism.

---

[96] Gramsci points out "the historical paradox that, in Italy, it is the masses who propel and 'educate' the party of the working class and not the Party which guides and educates the masses." And he adds: "This Socialist Party, which proclaims itself to be the guide and educator of the masses, is in fact nothing more than a wretched clerk, recording the way in which the masses are operating of their own accord." *Pre-Prison Writings* (Cambridge: 1994), pp. 195, 196.

It is therefore not surprising that, in his articles of 1919–1920, Gramsci uses formulations similar to those of the program of the Spartacus League[97] and that he mentions Rosa Luxemburg along with Marx and Lenin as the inspirer of his fundamental belief: "Only the masses can achieve the communist revolution, and ... neither a party secretary nor a president of the republic can achieve it by issuing decrees."[98]

For Gramsci, as for Rosa Luxemburg, it is the spontaneous and uncoercible movements of the working masses that indicate the actual direction in which history is developing. These movements are prepared subterraneanly, in the obscurity of the factories and the consciousness of the masses, wherein the spiritual independence and historical initiative of the masses are gradually forged.[99]

In Italy, the great historic manifestation of the revolutionary spontaneity of the proletariat took concrete form in the workers' councils of 1919–1920, in which the workers trained themselves for management and prepared for self-government in a workers' state.[100] Consequently, the political power of the masses, the power to guide the movement, had to be in the hands of the organisms representing the masses themselves – the council and the system of councils – whereas the technicians of the organization (who, as technicians, as specialists, were not removable) had to be restricted to purely administrative functions, without any political power.[101]

What should be the Party's role in this situation? According to Gramsci, the Party must never try to confine the movement mechanically within the narrow framework of its organization. By doing that, it would become, unconsciously, an organ of conservation and would see the revolutionary process escape from its control and influence. In the concrete case of the factory councils, the Party and the trade unions must not set themselves up as tutors or as ready-made superstructures for these new institutions.[102] On the contrary, the Party must serve as "the instrument, the historical form of the process of inner liberation through which the worker is transformed form *executor* to *initiator*, from *mass* to *leader* and *guide*, from pure brawn to a brain and a will."[103]

---

[97] Gramsci, *Selections from Political Writings (1910–1920)* (1977), p. 188. "Communist society cannot be built by fiat, through laws and decrees: it arises spontaneously from the historical activity of the working class ..." Luxemburg, *Selected Political Writings*, p. 368.
[98] *Selections from Political Writings*, p. 351.
[99] *Selections*, p. 173; *Pre-Prison Writings*, pp. 163, 169.
[100] *Selections*, p. 171.
[101] *Selections*, p. 177.
[102] *Pre-Prison Writings*, p. 167; *Selections*, p. 144.
[103] *Pre-Prison Writings*, p. 191.

In short, the Communist Party must not be a company of doctrinaires, of "would-be Machiavellis," nor "a party that makes use of the masses for its heroic imitations of the French Jacobins," but "a party . . . that will represent the masses who want to free themselves autonomously, by their own efforts, from political and industrial servitude."[104]

This structure of relations between the Party and the masses is to be reflected in the Party's internal organization, which, according to Gramsci, must be constructed "from below to above":

> There is a permanent and autonomous communist grouping within every one of these [factory] organizations. The individual groupings are combined, by area, into ward groupings, which in turn are represented in a steering committee within the Party section.[105]

In the period between 1927 and 1935, the workers' movement in Europe suffered from the impact of some fundamental changes, both in the relation of forces with its adversary and in its own structure:

(a) A general retreat of the revolutionary movement, political stagnation of the masses, repeated defeats of Communism – all of which provoked a tendency among the leaders of the movement to assign extreme importance to the Party and the "heads."[106]

(b) The defeat of the workers' parties coincided, in Italy and Germany, with the accession to power of Fascism, backed by wide strata of the politically backward people in town and country: events which produced, among sections of the Social-Democratic intelligentsia (Karl Mannheim, Erich Fromm) profound bitterness and great mistrust of the "irrational tendencies" and "fear of freedom" allegedly characteristic of the broad masses, and, parallel with this, among leading communists a "falling back" upon the Party apparatus and reinforcement of the authority of the "heads" over the "mass" of the membership.

(c) Finally, in this period (1927–1935), there began crystallizing the process of internal bureaucratization of the communist movement – "Stalin-ism" – which reached one of its climaxes in 1935 with the beginning of the "Moscow Trials" and the liquidation of the old Bolshevik leaders.

These three events: the retreat of the masses, the victory of Fascism, and the development of Stalinism constitute, in my view, the key to understanding the metamorphosis of Gramsci's political ideas.

One of the clearest symptoms of this metamorphosis is his attitude to Rosa Luxemburg's views, which, though explicitly approved by him in 1919, were

---

[104] *Pre-Prison Writings*, p. 172.
[105] *Selections*, p. 312.
[106] Cf. C. Lefort, "Le marxisme et Sartre," *Les Temps Modernes* No. 89, April 1953, p. 1566.

now treated as theories "hastily and even superficially" developed on the basis of the 1905 experience. He particularly blames Rosa Luxemburg for having underestimated the "voluntary" and organizational factors in the revolutionary struggle, through being carried away by her "economist" and spontaneity-ist prejudices, which brought her to a sort of rigid economic determinism, aggravated by a veritable "historical mysticism."[107] According to the *Note sul Machiavelli*, written by Gramsci in prison, spontaneity-ism, which is based on mechanistic assumptions, overlooks the resistance of "civil society" to the irruptions of the directly economic factor (crises, etc.) and forgets that objective premises do not produce revolutionary consequences unless they are "activated" politically by capable parties and persons.[108]

For the Gramsci of 1933, the Party has to play the role of a "modern prince," as the legitimate heir of the tradition of Machiavelli and the Jacobins. As such, it "takes the place, in men's consciousness, of the deity or the categorical imperative" and becomes the point of reference for defining what is either useful or harmful, what is right and what is wrong. It has "a progressive police function."[109] In other words, "given the principle that there are leaders and led, governors and governed, the truth is that 'parties' have proved, up to now, the most adequate means for developing leaders."[110]

The internal organization of the revolutionary party, in its turn, has to conform to the principle of democratic centralism, defined as "the continual insertion of elements arising from among the masses into the firm structure of the apparatus of leadership."[111] This necessarily implies a well-delimited internal hierarchy: at the base, a diffuse element of "ordinary people, whose participation is marked by discipline and loyalty, not by the creative spirit": at the top, the leading group, "endowed with power which is extremely coherent, centralizing and disciplinary, and, perhaps, on that account, inventive": between the two, an intermediate element which links together these extremes.[112] It must be added, however, that Gramsci was not unaware of the dangers of this sort of organizational program: his criticisms of "bureaucratic centralism," of the conservative habits of leading bureaucracies, and of the alienating fetishism of the Party[113] suggest, in spite of the foregoing, a certain continuity between the author of the *Note sul Machiavelli* and the author of the leading articles in *Ordine Nuovo*.

---

[107] Gramsci, *Note sul Machiavelli, sulla Politica e sullo Stato Moderno*, 4th edition (Turin: Einaudi, 1955), p. 65.
[108] *Ibid.*, pp. 5, 66, 78.
[109] *Ibid.*, pp. 6–8, 28.
[110] *Ibid.*, p. 18.
[111] *Ibid.*, p. 76.
[112] *Ibid.*, p. 53.
[113] *Ibid.*, pp. 51, 76, 157.

d) *Lukács's theoretical synthesis*

The idea of effecting a synthesis that would dialectically overcome spontaneity-ism and sectarianism was probably suggested to Georg Lukács by his own experience as a "People's Commissar" in Béla Kun's ephemeral Republic of Workers' Councils in Hungary (March–July 1919). In that revolutionary experience, "the spontaneous revolutionary energy of the working class represented an immense force," but its rapid defeat showed that, "while the revolutionary spontaneity of the working class is at the basis of the proletarian revolution, it is not possible to found the dictatorship of the proletariat on that force alone."[114]

Furthermore, after the victory of the Bolsheviks' October Revolution and the defeat of the Spartacist rising of January 1919, it was necessary to draw up an ideological balance-sheet of the organizational theses which had been subjected to a decisive test in the revolutionary process. In that historical situation, this balance-sheet could not but be unfavorable to "Luxemburgism." However, Lukács's book *History and Class Consciousness* was written in a transitional period (1919–1922) when the situation in Germany was still potentially revolutionary and "Luxemburgism" still a strong trend in the European communist movement. Additionally, the author was living at that time in Germany, where this trend was especially influential. All of which enables us to understand why, despite its reservations, this book remained deeply "impregnated" by Rosa Luxemburg's conceptions.

For Lukács, the basic errors of Luxemburgist spontaneity-ism are, on the one hand, belief that the proletariat's coming to consciousness is the mere actualization of a latent content and, on the other, forgetting the ideological influence of the bourgeoisie, thanks to which, even during the worst economic crises, some strata of the working class remain politically backward. Spontaneous mass actions are the psychological expression of economic laws, but real class-consciousness is not the automatic product of objective crises.[115]

In this way, he introduces a distinction, which forms one of the central themes of his book, between the "psychological consciousness" of the workers, meaning the actual empirical thoughts of the masses, which can be described and explained psychologically, and the real "class-consciousness of the proletariat," which is "the sense, become conscious, of the historical role of the class." This true class consciousness is not the sum or the average of what the member of the class think, but an "objective possibility": the most appropriate rational reaction that one could "impute" (*zurechnen*) to this class, that

---

[114] E. Molnar, "The historical role of the Hungarian Councils Republic," *Acta Historica*, Review of the Hungarian Academy of Sciences, Vol. 61, 1959, pp. 234–235.

[115] Lukács, *History and Class Consciousness* (London: 1971), pp. 303–311.

is, the consciousness that the class would have if it were capable of grasping the totality of the historical situation.[116]

However, this "imputed" class consciousness is not a transcendental entity, an "absolute value" floating in the world of ideas: on the contrary, it assumes an historical, concrete, and revolutionary shape – the Communist Party. For Lukács, in fact, the Communist Party is the organizational form of class consciousness which, as bearer of the highest objective possibility of consciousness and revolutionary action, plays a mediating role between theory and practice, between man and history.[117] In the debate on relations between this party and the broad unorganized masses, one must above all avoid the tendency which is typical of the bourgeois view of history, namely, considering the real process of history separately from the evolution of the masses. Both Party sectarianism and spontaneity-ism fall into this error: by posing the false dilemma "terrorism or opportunism," they turn out, in the last analysis, to be caught in the bourgeois dilemma of "voluntarism or fatalism."[118]

Sectarianism tends, through overestimating the role of organization in the revolutionary process, to put the Party *in place of* the masses, acting *for* the proletariat (like the Blanquists), and to congeal into a permanent split the historically necessary separation between the Party and the masses. In this way, the "correct" class consciousness is artificially dissociated from the life and evolution of the class. On the other hand, spontaneity-ism, by underestimating the importance of organizational factors, puts on the same plane the proletariat's class consciousness and the momentary sentiments of the masses, leveling-down to the lowest degree the actual stratifications of consciousness – or, at best, to their average level. In this way, one abandons the task of pushing forward the process of unifying these stratifications at the highest attainable level.[119]

The dialectical solution of the organization problem, transcending the choice between Jacobinism of the Party and "autonomy" of the masses, is to be found, according to Lukács, in the living interaction between the Party and the unorganized masses. The structure of this interaction is to be shaped by the process of evolution of class consciousness. In other words, the organizational separation between the Communist Party and the class is held to result from the heterogeneity of the proletariat in the matter of consciousness, but this is only a moment in the dialectical process of unification of the consciousness of the class as a whole. The autonomy of the vanguard organization is to serve as a means to adjust the tension between the highest objec-

---

[116] *Ibid.*, pp. 73, 51.
[117] *Ibid.*, pp. 299–300, 317–318, 327–328.
[118] *Ibid.*, pp. 326, 332.
[119] *Ibid.*, pp. 322–323, 326.

tive possibility and the actual level of consciousness of the average, in a way that can advance the process of coming to revolutionary consciousness.[120]

Looking at the problem from the angle of the internal structure of the Communist Party, Lukács tries, once more, to avoid the reified schemas of bureaucratic centralism and of ultra-"autonomism." While emphasizing that the capacity for revolutionary initiative presupposes strong centralization and thorough division of labor, he nevertheless points out the dangers of bureaucratization which are inherent in the contrast between a closed hierarchy of functionaries and a passive mass of adherents who follow in a sort of indifference that mingles blind trust with apathy. In conclusion, Lukács insists on the need for concrete interaction between the will of the members and that of the Party's central leadership. Through this relation it may be possible to do away with the harsh contrast, inherited from the bourgeois parties, between active leaders and passive masses, between leaders who act in place of the masses and masses who remain in a state of contemplative fatalism.[121]

e) *Trotsky and Bolshevism*

Trotsky saw his mistrust of Lenin's Bolshevism before 1917 as one of the major mistakes in his political life.[122] This mistrust, which was first expressed during the historic Congress of 1903, when the Party split, was justified by him, in terms very similar to Rosa Luxemburg's, in the pamphlet *Our Political Tasks* (1904). Like Rosa Luxemburg, the young Trotsky pointed out that one had to choose between Jacobinism and Marxism because the revolutionary Social-Democrat and the Jacobin represented "two worlds, two doctrines, two tactics and two mentalities that are opposed to each other." The leitmotiv of the pamphlet was the danger of "substitutism," represented by the methods Lenin advocated, methods which tend to make the Party substitute itself for the working class and which, inside the Party itself, have the result that "the party organization [the caucus] at first substitutes itself for the Party as a whole; then the Central Committee substitutes itself for the organization; and finally a single 'dictator' substitutes himself for the Central Committee." Against this danger, Trotsky proudly proclaims his hope that "a proletariat capable of exercising its dictatorship over society will not tolerate any dictatorship over itself."[123]

While criticizing the Bolsheviks, Trotsky did not concur with the purely "spontaneity-ist" theses of the "economists," but tended to reject both alike. Neither

---

[120] *Ibid.*, pp. 326–329, 338–339.
[121] *Ibid.*, pp. 336–338.
[122] In his "Testament" of December 1922, Lenin, however, urged that Trotsky ought not to be blamed for his past "non-Bolshevism."
[123] I. Deutscher, *The Prophet Armed* (1954), pp. 90, 93, 95. In Deutscher's view, the pamphlet was unfair to Lenin, but constituted, on the other hand a "faithful mirror" of the Stalinist future of the USSR. *Op. cit.*, p. 95.

could lead the proletariat: the former (whom he called "the politicals") because they wanted to substitute themselves for it, the latter because they trailed behind it. Whereas the "economists" were "marching at the tail-end of history," the "politicals" were "trying to transform history into their own tail."[124] This twofold repudiation appeared again in his writings on the revolution of 1905, in which he contrasted the Marxist Social-Democrat, for whom the taking of power is "the conscious action of a revolutionary class," both with Blanquism, which relies only on the initiative of conspiratorial organizations formed independently of the masses, and anarchism, which relies on the spontaneous and elemental eruption of the masses. In reality, behind this apparent "symmetry" lies a tendency on his part to drown the role of the Party in the revolutionary process, a tendency clearly expressed in passages such as this: "The subjective will of a party ... is only one of the factors involved, and not by any means the most important one."[125]

Another theme common to Trotsky and Rosa Luxemburg, which emerges after 1905, and which would not be abandoned by Trotsky during his Bolshevik phase (quite the contrary), was that of the conservatism or organizational inertia of the big socialist parties, something which he nevertheless thought the European proletariat would be able to shake off thanks to the influence of the future Russian revolution.[126]

The process of Trotsky's "conversion" to Bolshevism began mainly during the world war. The principal waymarks of this "long march" to Lenin were:

(a) his break in February 1915 with the "August bloc," in which Trotsky had participated since 1912 along with the Mensheviks and some dissident Bolsheviks;
(b) The pro-Bolshevik line of Trotsky's paper *Nashe Slovo* from 1916;
(c) Trotsky's collaboration when in exile in America with the Bolshevik group who puslished *Novyi Mir* (1917).

His final adhesion took place in the fire of revolution, in July 1917. One cannot understand the "Bolshevization" of Trotsky except in the light of the overwhelming events of 1917, which demonstrated to him (1) the limitations of the spontaneous mass movement which, left to itself, gives opportunites for maneuvers by bourgeois "moderates" (February) or else leads to terrible

---

[124] Trotsky, *Our Political Tasks* (London: n.d.), p. 77.
[125] *Results and Prospects* (London: 1962), p. 229; *1905* (London: 1972), p. 264.
[126] "The European Socialist Parties, particularly the largest of them, the German Social-Democratic Party, have developed their conservatism in proportion as the great masses have embraced socialism and the more these masses have become organized and disciplined ... The tremendous influence of the Russian revolution indicates that it will destroy party routine and conservatism and place the question of an open trial of strength between the proletariat and capitalist reaction on the order of the day." *Results and Prospects*, p. 246. We shall see later that Trotsky was to quote the beginning of the same passage in 1917, but this time with a different conclusion.

defeats (July); (2) the pressing need for a vanguard *organization* solidly rooted in the proletariat and capable of *directing* the insurrection for taking power.

Two other considerations enable us to appreciate Trotsky's decision:

> (1) Since his "conciliationism" of 1912–1914 was based above all on the hypothesis that a revolutionary crisis would bring about the fusion of the two factions of Russian Social-Democracy, the actual crisis of 1917, by digging an abyss between Menshevik reformism and the revolutionary radicalism of Lenin's party, forced him to abandon this mistaken assumption and to choose one of the two trends. It was for this reason that Lenin declared, on November 14, 1917, that since Trotsky had realized that unity with the Mensheviks was impossible, "there has been no better Bolshevik than Trotsky."
>
> (2) The Bolshevik Party that he joined was not the same as that of 1904. Not only had it become a party embedded in the mass movement, it had made, impelled by Lenin's *April Theses*, a turn to the left which incorporated the essentials of Trotsky's strategy of permanent revolution. (Some "Old Bolsheviks" even accused Lenin of having gone "Trotskyist.")

This adhesion to Bolshevism would not take place without Trotsky having to make a "heart-rending revision" of his earlier notions about organization – a revision not only in relation to Bolshevism but, in general, concerning the role of the vanguard organization in the proletarian revolution. A "symptom-seeking" study of Trotsky's first "Bolshevik" articles of 1917 enables one to perceive the beginning of the turn in his thinking. Particularly revealing is an essay on "International Tactics," in September 1917, in which he quotes his 1906 remarks (in *Results and Prospects*) on the conservatism of the European socialist parties. But, whereas in 1906, this analysis ended with a vague proclamation of the proletariat's capacity to break through conservative bureaucratic routine, Trotsky now draws a quite different conclusion: "New times demand new organizations. In the baptism of fire, *the revolutionary parties are now being everywhere created.*"[127]

The defeat of the German Spartacists in 1919 probably provided Trotsky with the final confirmation of the correctness of the organizational principles of Bolshevism. He saw the chief cause of the difficulties experienced by the German revolution precisely in "the absence of a centralized revolutionary

---

[127] "International Tactics," in Lenin and Trotsky, *The Proletarian Revolution* (1918), p. 277. (My italics – M. L.) In another article of the same period, Trotsky declares, writing as a Bolshevik: "It is now incumbent on our party, on its energy, its solicitude, its insistence, to draw all the inexorable conclusions from the present situation, and at the head of the disinherited and exhausted masses to wage a determined battle for their revolutionary dictatorship." "What Next?" in Lenin and Trotsky, *The Proletarian Revolution* (1918), p. 267.

party with a combat leadership whose authority is universally accepted by the working masses."[128]

From that time (1917–1918) until his death, Trotsky's conviction of the crucial importance of the Party, as revolutionary leader of the masses, as an absolutely indispensable condition for the taking of power by the proletariat, was to be one of the central axes of the theoretical system that he developed.

During a short period (1920–1921), this conviction of his assumed an extreme form, marked by an authoritarian ultra-centralism (which was condemned by Lenin and the majority of the Bolshevik Party): militarization of labor and statization of the trade unions.

In that brief interlude, Trotsky's "administrative-centralist" conceptions in the social and economic sphere found expression also at the level of his political views, affecting particularly the problematic of relations between Party and masses. For example, in his speeches at the Tenth Congress of the Bolshevik Party, in March 1921, Trotsky openly put forward the thesis that the Party must maintain its dictatorship "regardless of temporary wavering in the spontaneous moods of the masses, regardless of the temporary vacillations even in the working class." And, in an intervention at the Second World Congress of the Comintern, in July 1920, he expounded this splendid example of "substitutionist" ideology:

> Today we have received a proposal from the Polish government to conclude peace. Who decides such questions? We have the Council of People's Commissars but it too must be subject to certain control. Whose control? The control of the working class as a formless, chaotic mass? No. The Central Committee of the Party is convened in order to discuss the proposal and to decide whether it ought to be answered. And when we have to conduct war, organize new divisions and find the best elements for them – where do we turn? We turn to the Party. To the Central Committee.[129]

It is noteworthy that, even in this period, Trotsky had a much less simple attitude to the problems presented by the International. His view of the relation between Party and masses in Europe was very different from, if not contradictory to, the view he expressed for the USSR. In a speech in this period he took care to stress, with reference to Italy, that "the idea of replacing the

---

[128] Trotsky, *The First Five Years of the Communist International*, Vol. I (1973), p. 70.

[129] Deutscher, *The Prophet Armed*, p. 509; Trotsky, *The First Five Years*, I, pp. 127–128. Nevertheless, he tried from time to time to provide a democratic justification for his theses on the militarization of labor: "The militarization of labor, when the workers are opposed to it, is the state slavery of Arakcheyev. The militarization of labor by the will of the workers themselves is the socialist dictatorship." *Terrorism and Communism*, University of Michigan Press (1961), p. 147; see also P. Broué, *Le Parti bolchevique*, Ed. de Minuit (Paris: 1963), p. 140.

will of the masses by the resoluteness of the so-called vanguard is absolutely impermissible and non-Marxist." And in November 1920, in a speech about Germany in the Executive Committee of the Comintern, he defended the principle of dialectical reciprocity between leaders and masses:

> The education of the masses and the selection of the leaders, the development of the self-action of the masses and *the establishment of a corresponding control over the leaders* – all these are mutually corrected and mutually conditioned phenomena and processes.[130]

After this "authoritarian-militarist" episode, Trotsky began to develop a new conception of the Party, which he would always regard as the authentic continuation of Bolshevism (his opposition movement, first inside the USSR, then in exile, was to be called "Bolshevik-Leninist"). This conception united unshakeable confidence in the revolutionary potentiality of the masses with attribution of absolutely decisive importance to the vanguard party. The theme which welded together these apparently contradictory theses was that of the conservative role of the bureaucratic leaderships in the working-class movement.

This theme was the first to appear in his writings after the 1920–1921 interlude. It emerged already in 1922, almost unnoticeably,[131] and become central to his preoccupations in 1923, when, in *The New Course*, he denounced the growing tendency of the apparatus "to counterpose ... the leading cadres to the rest of the mass, whom they look upon only as an object of action," as well as the danger of "substitutism," which arises when the methods of the apparatus suppress living and active democracy in the Party, that is to say, when "the leadership of the Party gives way to administration by its executive organs (committee, bureau, secretary, etc.)."[132]

The first articulate and developed formulation of Trotsky's theory of the party appeared in his *History of the Russian Revolution* (1932), where he studied the role of the leadership and the masses in a revolutionary crisis, in the light of the experience of 1917 (but also in that of the defeats of 1919 and 1923 in Germany, of 1925–1927 in China, and of 1931 in Spain). This theory was built on two dialectically complementary axes: (a) the most indisputable feature of every revolution is the direct intervention of the masses in history; (b) "Just

---

[130] Trotsky, *The First Five Years*, I, pp. 353, 186. (My italics – M. L.)
[131] Deutscher, *The Prophet Unarmed*, 1959, p. 54.
[132] Trotsky, *The New Course*, pp. 18, 24. We hear an echo of Trotsky's pamphlet of 1904, with this difference that now, in 1922–1923, he counted on having Lenin as his chief ally against the bureaucratic apparatus represented by Stalin. See also the Left Opposition's 1927 platform: "If we really acknowledged that our party 'must be looked at from the top down,' that would mean that the Leninist party, the party of the mass of the workers, no longer exists." *The Challenge of the Left Opposition, 1926–1927* (New York: 1980), p. 352.

as a blacksmith cannot seize the red-hot iron in his naked hand, so the proletariat cannot directly seize the power: it has to have an organization accommodated to this task." This is the Party, the necessary and irreplaceable *instrument* of the revolutionary worker masses.

At the beginning of the revolution, the masses are set in motion mainly by "a sharp feeling that they cannot endure the old regime." It is only the leadership of the class, the party, that has a clear political program. But this program, in its turn, becomes effective only when it is approved by the masses, when the masses become conscious of the problems involved *through their concrete experience* during the revolutionary process. It is in the light of this complex dialectic of party and class that we have to understand the role played by the Bolsheviks in 1917. On the one hand, Bolshevism had absolutely no taint of any aristocratic scorn for the independent experience of the masses. On the contrary, the Bolsheviks took this for their point of departure and built upon it. That was one of their great points of superiority. On the other hand, in October, the Party was able to combine *conspiracy* with mass insurrection, conspiracy not in the Blanquist style, *instead of*, insurrection, but, on the contrary, *within it*, subjected to the mood of the masses.[133]

In 1933, after the disastrous defeat of the German CP (or, more exactly, of the Comintern's "line on Germany"), Trotsky decided to undertake the building of a new world party, the Fourth International. Implacable criticism of the bureaucratic leadership (both Social-Democratic and Stalinist) would be one of the political themes characteristic of the Trotskyist movement being formed.

---

[133] Trotsky, *History of the Russian Revolution*, one-vol. edition (1934), pp. 17, 1017–1018, 18, 809–810, 1019. Krasso claims, in his essay on "Trotsky's Marxism," that, in the *History*, "Trotsky's sociologism ... finds its most authentic and powerful expression," which "produces a view of the revolution which explicitly rejects political or economic variables as of permanent importance." *New Left Review*, No. 44, July–August 1967, p. 85. Yet one of the leitmotivs of the *History* is, *explicitly*, the capital and decisive role of the "political variables" – in particular, of the Bolshevik Party and Lenin, without whose "courageous determination" the October victory would have been impossible. *History, op. cit.*, p. 1016.

Krasso's fundamental mistake is to overlook the "theoretical break" in Trotsky's thinking in 1917, by constructing "a consistent ... unity, from his early youth to his old age," a unity made possible by "underestimation of the specific efficacy of political institutions" (pp. 85–86). He tries to attribute to this "sociologism" even those views of Trotsky's which he regards as correct: for example, on Nazism and the Comintern's line in 1929–1933 ("the third period"). Yet what is characteristic of Trotsky's writings on Germany in that period is precisely the close analysis of *political* problems (why Social-Democracy is not "social-fascism," etc.) and the dominant importance he ascribes to "the specific efficacy of political institutions," in this case the German CP, which he believes to be still capable, with a correct *political* line (united front of the workers' *parties* against fascism) of breaking the wave of Nazi onslaught. See E. Mandel, "Trotsky's Marxism: an Anti-Critique," in *New Left Review* No. 47, January–February 1968.

In this criticism he called to his aid the spiritual heritage of Rosa Luxemburg, who "passionately counterposed the spontaneity of mass actions to the ... conservative policy of the German Social-Democracy, especially after the revolution of 1905," an opposition which bore "a thoroughly revolutionary and progressive character."[134]

While he willingly pays homage to Rosa Luxemburg, Trotsky sees his movement above all as the legitimate heir of Bolshevism, which he defends in a polemic against Boris Souvarine and others, categorically rejecting the thesis which makes the Bolsheviks responsible for Stalinism, and again stressing the role of a party of the Bolshevik type as *indispensable instrument for self-emancipation by the masses*.[135] This problematic reappears in a famous pamphlet of the same period, *Their Morals and Ours* (1938), in which he defends the Bolshevik tradition against accusations of "Machiavellian immoralism." His methodological starting point is the dialectical interdependence of ends and means. So, since "the emancipation of the workers can only be the task of the workers themselves," a truly revolutionary party cannot employ means, procedures, or methods which "attempt to make the masses happy without their participation or lower the faith of the masses in themselves and their organization, replacing it by worship for the 'leaders.'"

When he emphasized like this the crucial bond between the vanguard and the masses, Trotsky was painfully aware of the isolated position of his own organization. From his striving to break out of this isolation was born in 1934 the tactic known as "entryism," the insertion of the vanguard into a mass workers' party – a tactic which bears a remarkable resemblance to that which Marx advocated in the *Communist Manifesto*. Trotsky himself was aware of this analogy and acknowledged it explicitly in a polemical passage of 1935 defending "entry-ism":

> The *Communist Manifesto* of Marx and Engels, directly aimed against all types of utopian-sectarian socialism, forcefully points out that Communists do *not* oppose themselves to the actual workers' movements but participate

---

[134] Trotsky, *Writings 1935–1936*, p. 30. In this article, Trotsky tries to draw an historically just balance-sheet of the thought of Rosa Luxemburg, one of "the three Ls" (the others being Lenin and Liebknecht) honored by the Fourth International. He acknowledges that "At a much earlier date than Lenin, Rosa Luxemburg grasped the retarding character of the ossified party and trade union apparatus and began a struggle against it." On the other hand, however, he says that "the whole of Germany's subsequent history amply showed that spontaneity alone is far from enough for success: Hitler's regime is a weighty argument against the panacea of spontaneity."

[135] "In the revolutionary vanguard, organized in a party, is crystallized the aspiration of the masses to obtain their freedom. Without the class's confidence in the vanguard, without the class's support of the vanguard, there can be no talk of the conquest of power." *Writings 1936–37*, p. 426.

in them as a vanguard. At the same time the *Manifesto* was the program of a *new party*, national and international.[136]

Another strategy of *mediation* between the revolutionaries and the masses which was inspired by the *Manifesto* was the "Transitional Program" presented by Trotsky to the founding congress of the Fourth International in 1938. This consisted of a system of ("transitional") demands which, starting from the present level of consciousness of the broadest sections of the working class, was meant to bring them more and more openly up against the very foundations of the bourgeois regime.

Trotsky's last retrospective on Bolshevism is to be found in his writings of 1939–1940, in which he studied the past with the hindsight stimulated by Stalin's large-scale purges in 1936–1938.

It must be said, first and foremost, that, right down to the eve of his assassination, Trotsky affirmed, more categorically than ever, his identification with the Leninist theory of the vanguard party. In an article of January 1940, he analyzed his attitude in 1912, admitting that "I was against the Leninist 'regime' because I had not yet learned to understand that in order to realize the revolutionary goal a firmly-welded centralized party is indispensable." He added that "Upon joining the Bolshevik Party Trotsky recognized completely and wholeheartedly the correctness of the Leninist methods of building the Party."[137] Nevertheless, Trotsky did not identify "the Leninist methods of building the Party" with certain theses of *What Is To Be Done?*, of which "the author . . . himself subsequently acknowledged the biased nature, and therewith the erroneousness, of his theory."[138] He even considered that his critique of Bolshevik centralism in 1904 (*Our Political Tasks*) was not wholly mistaken. While the pamphlet was certainly unfair to Lenin, it nevertheless contained a correct appreciation of the attitudes of the "committee-men" of the Bolshevik apparatus.

Trotsky therefore highlights "the negative aspect of Bolshevism's centripetal tendencies" which were manifest at the Third Congress of the Russian Social-Democrats (1905), and he criticizes the procrastinating role played by the Party in 1917, when "the masses . . . were more revolutionary than the Party and the Party more revolutionary than its machine."[139]

---

[136] *Writings 1935–1936*, p. 159. It must, however, be mentioned that a few years later (1938–1939) the "entry-ist" tactic was abandoned by Trotsky.
[137] Trotsky, *In Defense of Marxism* (New York: 1965), pp. 141, 139.
[138] Trotsky, *Stalin* (London: 1947), p. 58.
[139] *Ibid.*, pp. 61, 204. As for Lenin, "he represented not so much the Party machine as the vanguard of the proletariat." He wielded decisive influence because "he embodied the influence of the class on the Party and of the Party on its machine." *Ibid.*, p. 204.

All the same, Trotsky repudiated once more as empty and lacking in historical foundation the thesis according to which "the future Stalinism was already rooted in Bolshevik centralism." The roots of Stalinism were to be sought neither in the abstract "principle" of centralism nor in the "underground hierarchy" of the professional revolutionaries, but in the concrete conditions of Russia before and after 1917.[140] The purges themselves seemed to him to provide, paradoxically, the most crushing reply to critics of Bolshevism, in that Stalin had been able to establish his power definitively only through massacring the entire Bolshevik Old Guard.

f) *The people-guerrilla dialectic in Che Guevara*

Guevara's theory of guerrilla warfare, along with Castro-ism as a whole, brought in, as Régis Debray has rightly observed,[141] a new *problematic*, "a change of terrain in every sense of the word." It meant, in fact, a radical break with the "ideological field" of the traditional Left in Latin America, a break at both the theoretical level and that of political practice. The driving principle in it has to be sought in Latin America's recent history.

Guevara did not confine himself to giving new replies to the questions that the continent's Left had been asking for twenty years. He raised *new questions*, one of which, though not strictly "new," had more or less vanished from that Left's ideological universe: *how to break the military machine of the existing state?* This problematic, which had been formulated by Marx and Lenin in the light of the historical experience of the Paris Commune and the Russian Revolution, was "rediscovered," renewed, and adapted to the specific conditions of Latin America by Che, in the light of his concrete personal experience in Guatemala, where the left-wing Arbenz government had been betrayed by its army in 1954, and in Cuba, where, on the contrary, the revolution triumphed after breaking the army of Batista's regime and dissolving it completely.

Che's ironical scepticism towards "electoral and peaceful paths" was based on a realistic and clear-cut axiom: a genuine popular movement, even if it conquers power through an electoral process (a highly unlikely proposition, given the way this process was rigged in most of the countries concerned) will be overthrown very soon by a more or less bloody *coup d'état*, since the army is, as always, an instrument of the ruling oligarchy. From a politico-social analysis of the role played by the army in the modern history of Latin America, a history dominated by the endemic, continuous, and brutal recurrence of military *coups dêtat*, Guevara arrives at the same conclusion as Marx and Lenin: the revolution of the working people cannot be accomplished without destroying the military-police-bureaucratic machine of the bourgeois

---

[140] *Ibid.*, p. 61.
[141] R. Debray, *Revolution in the Revolution* (1968), p. 122.

state, without systematically and totally breaking the structures of the former regime's professional army. The mass of the people (Indians, peasants, and illiterate workers, with no right to vote) are outside the *pays légal,* and this is subject to a mechanism of institutionalized violence (the military *putsch*). This is the thesis which lies at the source of Guevara's strict, stubborn, and uncompromising adherence to a strategy of armed struggle.

This *question*: "how to eliminate the machine of state repression" dictates the answers given by Che: it is the basis of his entire theory of revolution, his entire doctrine of guerrilla warfare.

One of the most important answers is to be found on the first page of *Guerrilla Warfare* (1960): in underdeveloped Latin America, the terrain of the armed struggle must be, basically, the countryside. This answer implies a radical change of terrain "in every sense of the word" – not only geographical (the countryside) but also *sociological* (the peasants). The peasantry as active subject were (with rare exceptions, such as Mariategui) *outside the field of vision* of Latin America's "old Left." The great armed movements of peasants which shook the continent were headed by leaders who were not part of that Left: Zapata in Mexico, Sandino in Nicaragua, Galán in Colombia, Castro in Cuba, etc. One of the reasons why the traditional left did not "see" the revolutionary peasant was that to do so would create a *problem* for which that Left had no room: the problem of the front with the progressive bourgeoisie for the (peaceful) national-democratic revolution.

Guevara, on the contrary, proclaimed already in 1961 that in Latin America the national bourgeoisie was an ally of the imperialists and latifundia-owners against the people's revolution, which it feared more than anything else. In his article *Guerrilla Warfare, A Method*, he emphasized the union between the local bourgeoisies and American imperialism, together with the general polarization of class antagonisms in his continent. Che's logical conclusion was fully coherent with his analysis of the social contradictions. The revolution is directed, simultaneously, against the foreign monopolies and the indigenous exploiters: it is a *socialist* revolution. The socialist character of the Latin-American revolution was reaffirmed by Guevara in his last public message, the letter to the Tricontinental: "There are no other alternatives: either a socialist revolution or a make-believe revolution."[142] This lapidary formulation broke with a thirty-year-old tradition during which the majority of the Latin American Left shut itself up in the narrow and paralyzing framework of a false problematic, that of "the revolution in stages."

---

[142] Guevara, "Cuba – exceptional case or vanguard in the struggle against colonialism?" in *Che: Selected Works of Ernest Guevara* (Cambridge, Mass.: 1969), p. 174; *Guerrilla Warfare, A Method* (1961); *Message to the Tricontinental*, in *Venceremos! The speeches and Writings of Ernesto Che Guevara* (London: 1968), p. 267.

Guevara's doctrine on the role of the peasants (in the broad sense of "workers on the land") in the Latin-American revolution was based on two theses, one socioeconomic and the other politico-military:

1. The peasants (in many of these countries the majority of the population) are the class which is poorest, most wretched, most exploited, and most oppressed in Latin-American society. Their inhuman situation under the existing regime (and the impossibility of a real solution to it within the limits of this regime) makes them an enormous potentially revolutionary force.
2. The best base for a protracted armed revolutionary struggle against the government's police and army is the countryside, the *maquis*, the mountains. Only there can the revolutionary vanguard find refuge and, with the peasants' support, wage a long-term people's war, on a terrain and under conditions that are least favorable to the regular army.[143]

However, in Guevara's opinion, the peasants' guerrilla struggle will not be victorious without *union with the working class*, which enriches and ideologically develops the revolutionary movement and enables it to attain its ultimate and supreme stage, the proletarian general strike.[144] Furthermore, Guevara takes over, and quotes in his articles, two important propositions in the Second Havana Declaration:

1. The peasant is part of a class which, owing to the state of ignorance in which it is kept and the isolation in which it lives, needs revolutionary and political leadership by the working class and the revolution's intellectuals.
2. Through its reinforcement by the guerrilla force, the mass movement takes off, the old order gradually cracks up, and then the moment comes when the working class and the urban masses decide the outcome of the battle.

This vision of the final blow dealt to the state power by the action of the proletariat, which completes the process of revolutionary war, appears in several of Guevara's writings. He suggests, in a speech of January 27, 1959, that he and his comrades in arms in the Sierra Maestra did not fully grasp the importance of the urban workers and the possibility of an insurrectionary workers' strike until the political general strike of August 1957, which was declared in response to the murder by the police of the young leader of the July 26 Movement, Frank Pais. This strike, which Guevara describes as *spontaneous*, without leadership, preparation or control, paralyzed Santiago and Oriente province, and found echoes in all of the country's towns (Camaguey,

---

[143] *Guerrilla Warfare* (London: 1969), p. 13; "Cuba – Exceptional," *passim*.
[144] *Guerrilla Warfare*, p. 22; "Cuba – Exceptional," in *Che: Selected Works*, p. 63; "The Social Ideals of the Rebel Army," in *ibid.*, p. 198.

Las Villas, Havana), proving to the fighters in the Sierra that "new forces were joining the struggle and the fighting spirit of the people was growing."[145]

Did Guevara ever envision the possibility of an *essentially working-class and urban revolution* in the more industrialized countries of Latin America? The question is raised in some of his writings, but he preferred to leave it open, without giving a "definitive" answer. In his article "Cuba: exceptional case or vanguard in the struggle against colonialism?" (1961), he tackles the question in very cautious terms. He frankly admits that in such countries it is much harder to form guerrilla groups, but nevertheless thinks that the political nucleus of the struggle *may*, even in urbanized countries, be situated in the countryside (for reasons of security). But he also asserts the *possibility* of success for a popular revolt with an urban guerrilla base. Let it be added that Debray, in his essay of 1965 on Castro-ism, mentions Argentina as an essentially urban country where "the importance of the rural proletariat is minimal, in terms of their numbers, dispersion or weight in the economic life of the country. A rural *foco* can have only a subordinate role in relation to urban struggle in Buenos Aires, where the industrial proletariat is the prime force." Debray points to the absence of political liaison with the working class as the reason for the defeat of the guerrilla struggle by the EGP (*Ejercito Guerrillero del Pueblo* – People's Guerrilla Army) in the North of Argentina.[146] This does not invalidate rural guerrilla warfare as the general rule for the continent, but does suggest that the precise "hierarchical" relation between the guerrilla forces and the workers' movement in the towns must be adjusted in accordance with the concrete conditions of each country.

The Cuban revolution showed that the popular forces can win a war against the army, and that it is not always necessary to wait for all the conditions for revolution to be present: the insurrectionary *foco* can create them. These theses, which appear at the beginning of Guevara's famous manual for guerrilla warfare, are aimed against "revolutionaries or pseudo-revolutionaries who remain inactive and take refuge in the pretext that against a professional army nothing can be done, who sit down to wait until in some mechanical way all necessary objective and subjective conditions are given without working to accelerate them."[147]

The target of Guevara's criticism is the "fatalistic" position, which could be called "Kautskian" or "Plekhanovite," that was held by many of the leading circles of the continent's traditional Left, circles whose determinist-mechanistic materialism he rejects. In his remarkable "Notes for studying the

---

[145] *Reminiscences of the Cuban Revolutionary War* (1968), p. 146; "Social Ideals of the Rebel Army," in *Che: Selected Works*, p. 198.
[146] Régis Debray, "Castroism: the Long March in Latin America," in *Strategy for Revolution: Essays on Latin America* (New York: 1970), p. 44.
[147] *Guerrilla Warfare, A Method* (New York: 1961), p. 15; also in *Guerrilla Warfare* (1969), p. 13.

ideology of the Cuban revolution," published in October 1960 in the Cuban Army's review *Verde Olivo* – perhaps one of the first Marxist writings of the Cuban revolution – Guevara considers that Marx's most important contribution to social thought is his conception of man as not a slave and instrument of nature but "the architect of his own destiny."[148]

This does not mean that Guevara has fallen into a purely voluntarist notion of the revolution and guerrilla warfare: "Naturally, it is not to be thought that all conditions for revolution are going to be created through the impulse given to them by guerrilla activity. It must always be kept in mind that there is a necessary minimum without which the establishment and consolidation of the first center [*foco*] is not practicable."[149] The structure of Guevara's theory is that of Marx's dialectical thought, which rejects both metaphysical materialism ("conditions shape men") and utopian voluntarism. Like Marx, Che rejects the classical dilemma of fatalism or subjectivism, setting forward the principle of the dialectic of history: at the same time as conditions create man, man himself creates new conditions, through his *revolutionary praxis*. This principle inspires Che's doctrine on guerrilla warfare together with all his thinking on economic and social matters.[150]

Guevara's guerrilla theory has often been criticized as being contrary to Marxist tradition and a reversion to the Blanquist (or Bakuninist, or "adventurist," etc.) conception in which a band of determined revolutionaries can overthrow the existing state machine, seize power, and, after that, draw the people behind it.

In fact, Guevara never believed that the small nucleus which begins the guerrilla struggle could "make the revolution" or "take power." For him it was only the catalyst for beginning the people's war. It was for that reason that

---

[148] *Che: Selected Writings*, p. 50. It is in this sense that one must interpret Castro's famous slogan: "The duty of a revolutionary is to make revolution."

[149] *Guerrilla Warfare*, pp. 13–14.

[150] Guevara rejects the vulgar materialist ideology that regards full development of the socialist economy and the productive forces as "first condition" for the creation of a communist consciousness – an ideology according to which the new man will appear all by himself, automatically, at the moment when economic conditions will allow him to, like a fruit that becomes ripe when the season for ripeness arrives. For Che, it is only in the revolutionary praxis of building socialism *by socialist methods* and with active participation by the masses that men will change the economic structures and change themselves (in consciousness, character and morality). The changing of conditions and the changing of men must go together, linked one with the other, reinforcing each other in a process of dialectical reciprocity. The methods of the free market, of profit-calculation, and of general use of material incentives for individuals would hinder this process and interfere with the development of a new social consciousness among the people. "To construct communism simultaneously with the material base of our society, we must create a new man." *Socialism and man in Cuba*, 1965, in *Che: Selected Writings*, p. 159.

he rejected the etymological meaning of the word "guerrilla" (Spanish for "little war"). Far from being the little war of a small group against a vast army, guerrilla warfare is, for Guevara, *the war of the whole people against oppressive rule*. The people constitute the heart of the guerrilla army, it is behind every operation: its support is the *condition sine qua non* of the pursuit of guerrilla warfare and gives it the character of a *mass struggle*, a fight by the people for their liberation. The guerrilla army is only the armed vanguard of the fighting population, which gives that army its strength and *gradually transforms it into a powerful people's army*.[151]

What, then, is the relation between this vanguard and the masses, especially the peasant masses? Guevara does not treat this relation as one-sided, "from above to below," or as static, congealed in some rigid form. On the contrary, he conceives it as a dialectical process, contradictory and changing, of interpenetration between the armed nucleus and the people. In the first place, the guerrilla struggle must reflect the people's radical protest against the state and the ruling classes. It must be the faithful and consistent interpreter of the desires, aspiration, dreams, needs, and demands of the popular masses in general and the peasant masses in particular. On the other hand, it brings among the rural population the revolutionary ideology of the towns and performs the function of a *catalyst* which crystallizes the "subjective conditions" by arousing revolutionary consciousness and fighting enthusiasm. This role as *catalyst*, which reveals the *political* character of the guerrilla struggle (without neglecting its military dimension), is played at two levels: not only at that of the immediate surroundings (the peasants) of the armed nucleus – by awakening awareness of the *possibility* of victory, by force of arms, over the established power – but also in the social and political arena on the national, and sometimes international, scale. On June 13, 1967, after some striking victories in the guerrilla struggle, Che noted in his Bolivian diary "The interesting thing is the political convulsion the country is in and the fabulous number of pacts and counter-pacts there are. Rarely is the possibility of the guerrillas becoming a catalyst seen so clearly."[152]

What happens, according to Che, is that "a genuine interaction is produced between these leaders [of the guerrilla force], who with their acts teach the people the fundamental importance of the armed fight, and the people themselves who rise in rebellion and teach the leaders these practical necessities [of the revolution] of which we speak. Thus, as a product of this interaction between the guerrilla fighter and his people, a progressive radicalization

---

[151] "It is imperative to point out that one cannot hope for victory without the formation of a popular army." *Che: Selected Works*, pp. 100–101; "Qu'est-ce qu'un guerilléro?", in Guevara, *Souvenirs de la guerre révolutionaire* (Paris: 1967), pp. 200, 211.
[152] *The Complete Bolivian Diaries of Che Guevara* (London: 1968), p. 168.

appears which further accentuates the revolutionary characteristics of the movement and gives it a national scope."[153]

In his *Reminiscences of the Revolutionary War* Guevara describes how, during the armed struggle in Cuba, this reciprocal process developed so as to result, little by little, in the fusion of the guerrilla force with the peasant masses in a relatively homogeneous politico-military whole. It was thanks to this process that not only the revolutionary consciousness of the illiterate peasants but also that of the guerrilla force's urban cadres was strengthened and developed. This close and indissoluble unity between the guerrilla force and the people was not something immediately "given": it was the product of the *revolutionary praxis* during which the guerrilla force became popular and the people became revolutionary. The revolutionizing (*umwälzende*) praxis of the guerrilla force led to the destruction not only of the power of the ruling classes (the police, the army, the state machine) but of the foundations of that power in the people's consciousness (fear, passivity, apathetic fatalism, servile obedience).

In conclusion, we can put up the hypothesis that Guevara's thought contains, in an original synthesis, adapted to the specific historical conditions of the Latin-American revolution, two *apparently contradictory* tendencies:

1. Lenin's 1902 thesis of the nucleus of professional revolutionaries, strongly structured, disciplined, and hierarchized, which here becomes the guerrilla *foco*;
2. Rosa Luxemburg's thesis on the coming to consciousness of the broad masses of the people through their concrete revolutionary practice. For Guevara, the violent clash with the established authorities is "the people's school," and he adds this phrase, which resembles something found in the writings of both Lenin and Rosa Luxemburg: "One day of armed struggle in defense of its conquests or for realizing its social aspirations teaches a people much more than anything else can."[154]

Guevara resolved this contradiction dialectically by treating these two conceptions as *two moments in a process*, that process which leads from the clandestine preparation of the guerrilla nucleus to the taking of power through the mass strike.

The first moment is the stage in which the guerrilla force is organized, a conspiratorial task *par excellence*, remote from popular action and confined to a small group of initiates, a party operating in clandestinity. This conspiratorial character also marks, to some extent, the beginning of guerrilla operations, still separated from the peasant masses by mutual distrust and fear. Gradually, the guerrilla force takes root among the peasants, develops and

---

[153] *Guerrilla Warfare*, p. 47.
[154] Guevara, speech for January 6, 1961, in *Pensamiento Critico*, No. 9, 1967, p. 101.

grows stronger through their support: the war begun by a small armed nucleus becomes a revolutionary struggle of the rural masses.

Finally, the last stage is that in which the working class and other working people in the towns launch the general strike which crowns and completes the revolution. I have already mentioned how the spontaneous character of the political strike in Santiago in August 1957 struck Guevara. This did not lead him into a "cult of spontaneity" (since he stresses the need for careful preparation of the insurrectionary workers' strike through underground work) but rather an understanding of the general strike as a popular movement based on the initiative and activity of the popular masses themselves. This conviction of his was especially strengthened after the defeat of the revolutionary strike proclaimed by the July 26 Movement on April 9, 1958. Che subjected that unfortunate attempt to a radical critique. The cause of the defeat, in his view, lay in the fact that the strike's organizers failed to grasp the significance and tactics of mass struggle. They took it upon themselves to effect a clandestine putsch by calling the strike over the radio, as though by surprise, without retaining their links with the workers at the base, and, above all, they did not observe the rule "that the workers, in the exercise of their revolutionary activity, should choose the appropriate time."[155] One cannot refrain from comparing this analysis of Che's with Rosa Luxemburg's writings on the general strike, where she criticizes the conception of the mass strike held by the Social-Democratic leaders in Germany – "the fixed and hollow schema of a sober political 'action' executed with a prudent plan decided by the highest committees." The experience of the revolutionary strikes of 1905 showed, according to Rosa Luxemburg, that "the mass strike cannot be called at will, even if the decision to call it comes from the highest committee of the strongest Social-Democratic Party."[156]

For Guevara, rural and urban guerrilla warfare, underground work and mass struggle, armed combat and political action, guerrilla *foco* and general strike are all only different features and complementary moments in one and the same historic movement – the revolutionary war which, under the leadership of a vanguard organization,[157] gradually integrates in its ranks small peasant proprietors and factory workers, revolutionary intellectuals and illiterate proletarians, radical students and agricultural workers, and which has

---

[155] *Reminiscences*, pp. 242–243; "Social Ideals of the Rebel Army," in *Che: Selected Works*, p. 198: "Notes for the Study of the Ideology of the Cuban Revolution," in *Selected Works*, p. 53.
[156] Rosa Luxemburg, *Selected Political Writings*, pp. 236, 244.
[157] Guevara does not always mention the role of the revolutionary party, but in a text of 1963 (his introduction to the book *El partido marxista-leninista*) he points out the role of the Marxist-Leninist party as leader and catalyst – "vanguard of the working class that guides the workers to the path to victory . . . for its mission is to find the shortest route to achieve the dictatorship of the proletariat." *Che: Selected Works*, p. 104.

for its immediate aim the defeat of the military-and-police state machine, the first, fundamental, necessary and indispensable condition for the socialist revolution.

What is characteristic of Guevara's method is just this way of perceiving each aspect, each stage, each factor in the struggle not as an isolated, absolute, congealed, reified metaphysical entity ("*the* party," "*the* guerrilla *foco*," etc.) but as part of an historico-social totality. The role, status, significance, and meaning of each element can be understood only in its relation to the whole: the total process, the revolutionary movement.

Index

"Address of the Central Council to the League" (Marx)   149–152
alienation of labor   86, 88
Allgemeine Literatur-Zeitung   38
American National Reformers' movement   123n6
anarchism   185
Argentina   195
Association of the Patriotic Press   73n32
atheism   88–89
Augsberger Allgemeine Zeitung   31, 33n43

Babouvism   70–71, 87, 103
Bauer, Bruno   24, 25, 34, 40, 52, 97, 131
Belleville Banquet   65n5, 68n13, 72
Bentham, Jeremy   99n127
Bernstein, Eduard   162, 163
Blanc, Louis   50, 81n66
Blanquism   185, 196
"Blanquist" coup (May 12, 1839)   74n34
Bolshevism   168, 184–192
Bonapartism   15
bourgeois messianism   13–15
bourgeoisie
   and Communist Party   141n59
   German *vs.* French   55–56
   "The Jewish Question" as criticism of   52–53
   liberal, and Young Hegelians   23–27, 35–38
   Marx's evolving thinking on   40
   myth of savior from on high and   13–15, 72
Buonarroti, Philippe   69–71, 76

Cabet, Etienne   76
Camphausen, L.   37
Chartism   77–81, 116, 117, 127–130, 127n21, 128n22, 131, 145
   see also Fraternal Democrats
Chartism (Carlyle)   78
civil society   106–107
The Civil War in France (Marx)   158, 159n37
class   6–9, 43
The Class Struggles in France 1848–1850 (Engels)   19
class-consciousness
   change of, as neo-Hegelian postulate   110–111
   communist consciousness in other than proletariat   116, 140–141
   and English workers' movement   138
   evolution of, towards clarity   102–103
   imputed and psychological   9–10, 182–183
   and industrialization   77–78
   Lenin's theory of   166–167
communism
   criticism of crude, utopian, or idealist forms by Marx   87–88
   development, in France   64–69
   Icarian   76
   limitations and transcendence of   90
   Marx's attitude toward, in 1843   45–47
   and Marx's break with Hegel   40–42
   Marx's definition in *Manuscripts of 1844*   88–89
   Marx's early encounters with   30–34
   of the masses   19–21, 101–103
   materialist   69, 71–73
   philosophical   51–54, 88, 95
   as practical movement   111
   social character of   40–41, 93
   workers' groups as point of departure of   63–64
Communist Correspondence Committee (Brussels)
   break with Weitling   121–122
   circular against Kriege   122–123
   circular to Köttgen   126
   and League of Just   123–125
   link with Chartists   127–128
   members   121
   origins   120–121
Communist League
   distinctive features of   133–134
   occupational composition of   134–136
   origins   130–132
   rules of, contrasted with League of Just   132–133
communist literature   68
communist parties, theories of
   Bolshevism   168, 184–192
   centralism   187, 191
   danger of substitutism   184
   Hungary   182–184
   Italian Communist Party   178–181

and Jacobinism   150, 184
and Lassalle   152–155
and masses   175, 178–179, 185–191
and messianism   153, 155
as revolutionary leader of masses   185–191
Russian Revolution of 1905–1906   168, 173
Russian Social-Democratic Party   165–171
sectarianism of   155, 156–157, 182, 183
and self-emancipation of proletariat   163, 170–171
spontaneity-ism of   181–182
and Stalinism   180, 192
substitutism   184, 187, 188
communist party, Marx's theory of
Communist Correspondence Committee   120–130
Communist League   130–136
construction of, from below to above   126, 180
early incarnation of   125
The Manifesto of the Communist Party   139–147
Marx's first use of term   116–117
The Poverty of Philosophy   137–139
and Proletarian Movement   136–147
as vanguard of and within working-class parties   143–147
communist revolution, Marx's theory of
development in writings
Economic and Philosophic Manuscripts of 1844   85–91
The German Ideology   109–116
The Holy Family   96–103
"The King of Prussia and Social Reform"   91–96
Theses on Feuerbach   103–109
facts and values related in   10–13
myth of savior from on high   13–15
origins of revolution   114–116
scientific nature of   3
settings for and conditioning of   4–10
Silesian weavers' revolt as catalyst for   84, 91–94
two key ideas of   112–113
and workers' struggles in Paris   49
communists, role of, in revolution   21, 136–137, 143–147
The Condition of the Working Class in England (Engels)   77
conditioning, of doctrines   4–10
The Conspiracy of Babeuf (Buonarroti)   70
"Critical Marginal Notes." See "The King of Prussia and Social Reform" (Marx)
Critique of the Gotha Programme (Marx)   154
Cromwell, Oliver   17
Cuba   192–200
cult of personality   19
Darmès, communist worker   67–68
De la Misère des classes laborieuses en Angleterre et en France (Buret)   77
democracy   41–42, 43, 129
Der Socialismus und Communismus des heutigen Frankreichs (Stein)   66
Deutsch-Französische Jahrbücher   35, 36, 38, 47, 51–52
Dézamy, Théodore   31–32, 68n13, 71–73
doctors, and communist beliefs   135n43
"Doctor's Club"   24
domestic industry   81–84

Economic and Philosophic Manuscripts of 1844 (Marx)   47, 85–91
education   105
egalitarian revolution   71
egoism   53
emancipation
political only   53
self-emancipation of proletariat   15–21, 81, 94, 101, 106, 149, 150, 158–159, 163
universal, human   53–54, 56n119, 57n122
Engels, Friedrich
on Chartist socialism   79
on consciousness of masses   19
on English workers' movement   77–78
and *The German Ideology*   109–110
and German Social-Democracy   159–164
and *The Holy Family*   96
and Paris section of League of Just   124–125
on socialism as bourgeois movement   63–64
England. See Chartism; workers' movement, English
entryism   190–191
The Essence of Christianity (Feuerbach)   58–59, 85, 104
European Socialist Parties   185n126, 186
Ewerbeck, August H.   124

Fascism   180
Feuerbach, Ludwig   57–58, 89, 100
First International   136, 155–157
Fourier, Charles   99n127
Fourth International   189–190, 191
France
communists in, and Marx   50
example of proletariat as formative   57
newspapers' views of Germany   44
Paris Commune   19, 157–159, 159n37
secret societies, generally   15–16, 64–73, 69n15
Third Estate   55
see also workers' movement, French
Fraternal Democrats   128n22, 129–130, 143–144
La Fraternité   31, 65n3
Friedrich Wilhelm IV   24, 36
Froebel, Julius   37–38, 38

General Association of German Workers 152–153
General Strike, Party and Trade Unions (Luxemburg) 171, 176
German communist party 116, 117
The German Ideology (Marx) 34n48, 52, 57, 66, 109–116
German People's Society (Deutscher Volksverein) 73n32
German Social-Democratic Party 159–164, 171–178, 185n126
Germany
  bourgeoisie in 23–27, 35–38, 55–56
  economic underdevelopment 6
  French newspapers' views of 44
Gotha program 154, 160
Gramsci, Antonio, Marxist theory of 178–181
Guarantees of Harmony and Freedom (Weitling) 75–76
guerilla warfare, Che's doctrine of 192–200
Guerilla Warfare (Guevara) 193
Guevara, Ernesto "Che," Marxist theory of 192–200

Hallischen Jahrbücher 24
Harvey, George Julian 127, 127n21, 128n22, 144
Heilberg, Louis 121
Heine, Heinrich 66, 68n12, 82n69, 83
Herr Vogt (Marx) 123n7
Hess, Moses 31, 34, 37, 40, 49, 51–52
Histoire de dix ans (Blanc) 50
History and Class Consciousness (Lukács) 2n2, 182
History of the Russian Revolution (Trotsky) 188
Hobbes, Thomas 18
Höchberg, Dr. 160
Hoffken 37
The Holy Family (Marx) 66, 70, 71–72, 96–103
humanism, positive 89–90, 95
Hungary 182–184

ideas
  origin of revolutionary 114–116
  partial autonomy of sphere of 5–6
  power of 33–34, 33n43, 34nn46–47
ideological unmasking 1
Ideology and Utopia (Mannheim) 1n1
imputation 6–7, 8
individualism 98
industrial revolution, impact on social relations 77–78
"International Tactics" (Trotsky) 186
International Workingmen's Association (First International) 136, 155–157
Introduction to the Contribution to the Critique of Hegel's Philosophy of Law (Marx) 26–27, 33, 40, 42, 50, 54–61, 91–92
Italian Communist Party 178–181

Jacobinism 15, 17, 71, 72, 76, 150, 184
"The Jewish Question" 51–54
Jones, Ernest 128, 144
"Junius Pamphlet" (Luxemburg) 177n94

Kautsky, Karl 63–64, 167n54, 174n80
Kayser affair 161, 163
"The King of Prussia and Social Reform" (Marx) 91–96
Kommunistische Zeitschrift 131
Kriege, Hermann 121, 122–123

labor movement
  militarization of labor 187n129
  reinforcement and reorientation of 20
  see also workers' movement, English; workers' movement, French
Lassalle, Ferdinand 152–155
Latin America 192–200
League of the Just 73–76, 117n185, 121, 123–124, 123n8, 130–133
League of the Proscribed 73n32
leiden 44
Lenin, Vladimir Ilich Ulyanov, Marxist theory of 60, 165–171, 191
Leveller movement 17
liberalism 23–27, 38
List, F. 37
London Democratic Association 128
London League of Communists 18
London Workingmen's Association 78
Lukács, Georg, Marxist theory of 181–184
Luxemburg, Rosa, Marxist theory of 171–178, 190n134

Machiavelli 178, 181
Manchester, Eng. 78n54
The Manifesto of the Communist Party (Marx and Engels) 139–147
Mankind as it is and as it ought to be (Weitling) 74
Mannheim, K. 1n1
Manuscripts of 1844. See Economic and Philosophic Manuscripts of 1844 (Marx)
Marxism, Marxist study of 1–3
Marx's writings. See writings, Marx's
Mass Strike, Party and Trade Unions (Luxemburg) 171, 176
masses
  communism of 19–21, 101–103
  and parties 136–147, 175, 178–179, 185–191
  and spirit 96–98
materialism 98–101, 103, 105
Maurer, Dr. G. 73

messianism 15–16, 75, 76, 153, 155
Middle Ages 41, 56n119
militarization of labor 187n129
Mosel peasantry 25
Münzer, Thomas 17

Narodnaya Volya 165
National Reform Association 116, 117n185, 122n6, 145
Nazism 189n133
neo-Babouvism 69–71, 74
neo-Christianity 32
neo-Hegelianism
  criticism of, in *The German Ideology* 110–111
  Friedrich Wilhelm IV's anti-Hegelianism 24
  Hegelian Left and liberal bourgeoisie 23–25, 35–38
  influence of, on Marx 6, 27–29, 34–35
  Marx's break with 40, 49
  and Silesian revolt 5
The New Course (Trotsky) 188
Note sul Machiavelli (Gramsci) 181

objectivism 11
One Step Forward, Two Steps Back (Lenin) 165
Our Political Tasks (Trotsky) 184, 191
Overton, Richard 17
Owen, Robert 99n127, 103, 105n146, 117

Paris Commune 19, 157–159, 159n37
Paris insurrection of 1839 130
parties, literary and philosophical 116–117
passivity of matter 44–45
peasants, in revolution 192–199
permanent revolution, theory of 55–56, 149–152
petty-bourgeoise 6
philanthropy of communism 89
philosophy and the world, theory of relations between 34–35
Philosophy of Law (Hegel) 35, 53
philosophy/philosophers
  as authority of proletariat 60, 94–95
  class origins and 6–9
  Marx's conception of role of 139
  and origins of revolutionary ideas 114–116
Pillot, Jean-Jacques 68n13
political revolution, social aspects of 93–94
"The Poor Weavers" (Heine) 82n69, 83
poverty 29–30, 139
The Poverty of Philosophy (Marx) 137–139
Preliminary Theses for the Reform of Philosophy (Feuerbach) 58
press-freedom 26
Pressverein 73n32

Principles of the Philosophy of the Future (Feuerbach) 89
private interest/property 26–27, 28n23
  as consequence of alienation 86–87
proletariat
  arming of 151
  characteristics of 56–57, 94
  class-consciousness of 19, 77–78, 102–103, 137–138, 166–167, 182–183
  and Communist Party 136–147
  first appears in Marx's writings 55
  as fundamental setting for scientific socialism 5
  historical interests of 2
  imputed consciousness of 9–10
  introduction to socialism from without 60, 94–95
  in *Introduction to the Contribution to the Critique of Hegel's Philosophy of Law* 42, 51, 91–92
  not used by Marx in *Rheinische Zeitung* 30
  revolutionary character of 113–116
  self-emancipation of 15–21, 81, 94, 101, 106, 149, 150, 158–159, 163, 170–171
  self-organization of 139–140, 139n56, 142
  social structure of 4–5
  as suffering and passive 44–45, 58, 59
  unity of 72, 80
  see also poverty
Promenades dans Londres (Tristan) 79–80
property 28n23, 31
Proudhon, Pierre-Joseph 31, 32, 47n95, 126–127
Prussia
  Friedrich Wilhelm IV's anti-Hegelianism 24
  Hegelian Left, and state 23–25, 35–36
  suppression of *Rheinische Zeitung* 37–40

reason 47
Reformation 17
La Réforme 65n3
representation, theoretical 7–9
Republic of Workers' Councils 182–184
Revolutionary Communist Society 68n13
revolutionary praxis 94, 104–109, 113–114, 173–174, 196
Rheinische Zeitung
  banned 37–40
  communism 30–34
  Marx leaves 39
  Marx's loyalist declarations 36
  origins of 23–25
  philosophy and the world 34–35
  poverty 29–30
  state and private interest 26–29
Ruge, Arnold
  correspondence with 32, 33n42, 37–38, 42–49

and German liberation   40
and "King of Prussia" article   96
Marx's break with   59
and Silesian revolt   92–93
Russian Revolution of 1905–1906   168, 173
Russian Social-Democratic Party   165–171

sans-culottes   17
Schapper, Karl   124n8, 131
science, revolutionary nature of   3, 10–13
Second Havana Declaration   194
secret societies, generally   15–16, 64–73, 69n15
  see also specific societies and organizations
sectarianism, of Party   155, 156–157, 182, 183
Seiler, Sebastien   121
settings, socio-historical   3–10
Silesian weavers, revolt   5, 81–84, 91–94, 130
Sinnlichkeit   107–108
situational determinism   2
social determination   1
socialism
  as bourgeois movement in 1847   63–64
  and Chartism   79
  criticisms of   46–49
  introduction to proletariat from without   60, 94–95, 167n54
  Lassalle's "state socialism"   152–155
  scientific *vs.* utopian   48
  utopian   15–16, 19, 32, 46, 48–49, 75, 81, 141–142
Society of Egalitarian Workers   66n5, 67–68, 69n14
Society of "The Families"   68n14, 74n32
Society of the Rights of Man   69n14, 73n32
Society of the Seasons   67, 69n14, 74n32
socio-historical analysis   3–10
Sozialdemokrat   155, 164
Spartacists   186
spontaneity-ism   181, 182
Stalin, Josef   171
Stalinism, 180   192
state
  defeat of military-and-police machine   192–200
  Lassalle's "state socialism"   152–155
  nature of   26–29
Stein, Lorenz von   66–68, 79
substitutism   184, 187, 188

theft, of private property   31n35
Their Morals and Ours (Trotsky)   190
theoreticians
  as authority of proletariat   60, 94–95
  class origins and   6–9
  Marx's conception of role of   139

and origins of revolutionary ideas   114–116
role of in revolution   21, 136–137, 143–147
theory, and practice   34, 34nn46–47, 101, 108–109
Theses on Feuerbach (Marx)   35, 46, 59, 103–109
totality, methodological category of   3
trade unions. *See* labor movement
Tristan, Flora   65n3, 79–81
Trotsky, Leon, Marxist theory of   184–192

Union Ouvrière (Tristan)   80–81
unions. *See* labor movement

Weber, Kiel Georg   125n11
Weitling, Wilhelm   74–76, 94, 121–122, 131
What is Property? (Proudhon)   31
What is To Be Done? (Lenin)   60, 165, 168–169
workers' councils   151–152
workers' movement, English   77–81, 127–130, 137, 138
workers' movement, French
  communist secret societies of   15–16, 64–73, 69n15
  Marx gripped by   49–50
  occupational composition of secret societies   69n15
  as point of departure of communism   63–64
Working Men's Association   128
writings, Marx's
  "Address of the Central Council to the League"   149–152
  The Civil War in France   158, 159n37
  Critique of the Gotha Programme   154
  Economic and Philosophic Manuscripts of 1844   47, 85–91
  The German Ideology   34n48, 52, 57, 66, 109–116
  Herr Vogt   123n7
  The Holy Family   66, 70, 71–72, 96–103
  Introduction to the Contribution to the Critique of Hegel's Philosophy of Law   26–27, 33, 40, 42, 50, 54–61, 91–92
  "The King of Prussia and Social Reform"   91–96
  The Poverty of Philosophy   137–139
  Theses on Feuerbach   35, 46, 59, 103–109

Young America   117n185
Young Hegelians. *See under* neo-Hegelianism

About Haymarket Books

Haymarket Books is a non-profit, progressive book distributor and publisher, a project of the Center for Economic Research and Social Change.

We believe that activists need to take ideas, history and politics into the many struggles for social justice today. Learning the lessons of past victories, as well as defeats, can arm a new generation of fighters for a better world.

It was August Spies, one of the Martyrs who was targeted for being an immigrant and an anarchist, who predicted the battles being fought to this day. "If you think that by hanging us you can stamp out the labor movement," Spies told the judge, "then hang us. Here you will tread upon a spark, but here, and there, and behind you, and in front of you, and everywhere, the flames will blaze up. It is a subterranean fire. You cannot put it out. The ground is on fire upon which you stand."

Visit our online bookstore at www.haymarketbooks.org.

Also From Haymarket Books

WOMEN AND SOCIALISM
Sharon Smith   1 931859 11 6   May 2005
The fight for women's liberation is urgent—and must be linked to winning broader social change.

THE WORLD SOCIAL FORUM: STRATEGIES OF RESISTANCE
José Corrêa Leite   1 931859 15 9   April 2005
The inside story of how the worldwide movement against corporate globalization has become such a force.

YOUR MONEY OR YOUR LIFE (3rd edition)
Eric Toussaint   1 931859 18 3   June 2005
Globalization brings growth? Think again. Debt—engineered by the IMF and World Bank—sucks countries dry.

LITERATURE AND REVOLUTION
Leon Trotsky   1 931859 21 3   May 2005
A new, annotated edition of Leon Trotsky's classic study of the relationship of politics and art.

THE FORGING OF THE AMERICAN EMPIRE
Sidney Lens   0 745321 00 3   2002
This is the story of a nation—the United States—that has conducted more than 160 wars and other military ventures while insisting that it loves peace. In the process, the U.S. has forged a world empire while maintaining its innocence of imperialistic designs. Includes a new introduction by Howard Zinn.

www.ingramcontent.com/pod-product-compliance
Lightning Source LLC
Chambersburg PA
CBHW051543020426
42333CB00016B/2066